IMAGES
of America

OKTIBBEHA COUNTY

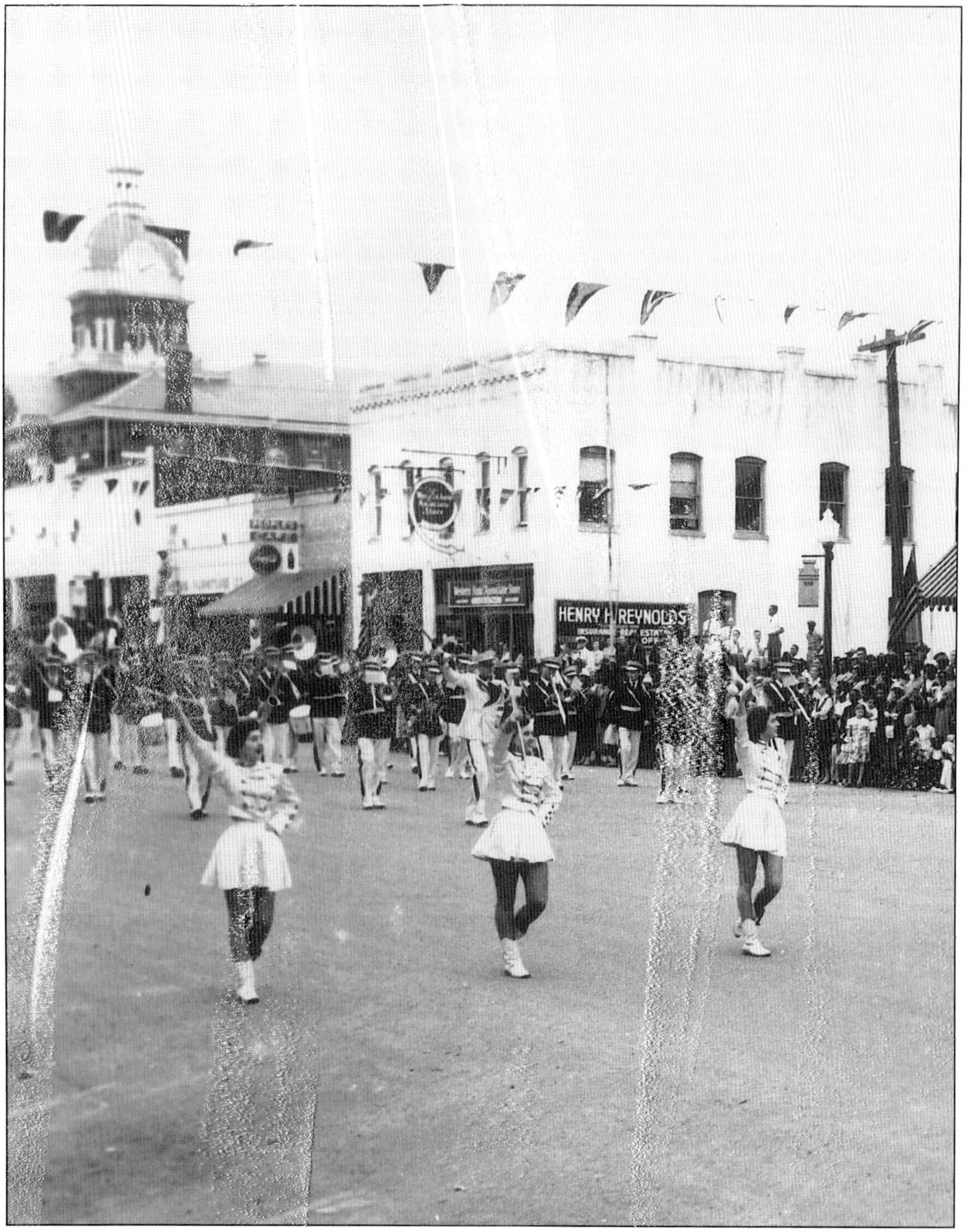

F.S. Cole opened Western Auto in 1939. It was originally located on the corner of Main and Lafayette Streets. In 1951, Mr. Cole moved the business two doors up the street—between Scales Department Store and Peoples Cafe. It remained at this location until 1965, when Mr. Cole sold the business to V.J. Robinson. (JSC.)

IMAGES
of America

OKTIBBEHA COUNTY

James S. Cole

ARCADIA
PUBLISHING

ISBN 978-0-7385-0566-4

Published by Arcadia Publishing
Charleston, South Carolina

Printed in the United States of America

Library of Congress Catalog Card Number: 00-101919

For all general information contact Arcadia Publishing at:
Telephone 843-853-2070
Fax 843-853-0044
E-Mail sales@arcadiapublishing.com
For customer service and orders:
Toll-Free 1-888-313-2665

Visit us on the Internet at www.arcadiapublishing.com

Contents

Acknowledgments

The images in *Oktibbeha County* are grouped by areas of interest, such as transportation, schools, and churches. The photographs are not in chronological order, but when available, the date the picture was taken is provided. Many of the pictures were taken from family albums and capture the "ordinary" ways of life. Most pictures in this volume are from Jimmy Cole's collection, Oktibbeha County Heritage Museum, and photographer Fred Blocker. Throughout the text, the images are followed by these photo credits:

Photo Credit	Donated by	Images found on page(s)
AS	Ann Sanders	31,122
BFH	Ben Hilbun	14,77
BG	Buddy Goodman	28,53,55,58,60,66,69,70,73,79,80,83,88, 90,94
BH	Billy Hunt	15,21,113
BK	Boswell Kennard	14
BS	Betsy Stark	16,17,21,48,52,82,96,100,101,102,104
CD	Carol Davis	98
CJ	Carroll Jones	33
CR	Clifford Richey	36,67,85,88,95,105,106,125
EB	Ed Blasingame	36,60,68,69,72,76,107
EBS	Ed Buckner Sr.	15,50
EM	Ed Montgomery	34
EO	E.O. Templeton	75,84,87,121
FB	Fred Blocker	10,12,17,18,24,25,26,27,28,29,30,31,38, 40,42,46,47,59,70,78,79,80,81,95,118, 119
FOB	Florence Oakley Box	23,29
HB	Mrs. Henry Beattie	32,76,96,110
HT	Harry Teasley	71,75
JB	James Bryant	128
JJ	Johnny Johnson	89
JK	James Kellum	45
JM	Jim McKee	39,86,122
JSC	Jimmy Cole	9,10,19,20,22,30,35,41,43,50,51,52,55, 57,59,61,62,66,71,73,81,86,89,90,91,92, 99,101,103,104,105,107,108,111,113, 115,116,117,119,120,121,124,126,127
JW	John Walker	11,20,33,39,74
MAP	Mary Anne Parrish	112
MB	Mary Bell	18,46,91,97,98,109,112,114,116
MG	Mark Guyton	74
MQ	Mildred Quinn	117
MS	Mark Smith	83
NM	Namie Mitchell	64
OHM	Oktibbeha County Heritage Museum	11,12,13,37,41,43,44,54,56,63,64,65,67, 72,77,96,103,118
PR	Peggy Raines	78
PS	Perry Sellars	44,56,93
RC	Ruth Camp	35,42,49,114,123,124,126,127
SC	Shannon Carter	87
SM	Sonny Mullins	45,49

TC	Tom Cook	40
TMW	T.M. Waller	109,110
WFM	W.F. Murphy	13,15,27,51
WM	William Miley	115

The assistance of Mary Bell, Fred Blocker, Nora Cole, Buddy Goodman, the Oktibbeha County Heritage Museum, Tricia Pace, and Mark Andre Singer were invaluable in producing this book.

Introduction

In 1820, the territory known as Oktibbeha County was part of the land held in common with the Choctaw Indians. In 1819, the American Board of Missions settled the county by sending missionaries to teach the Choctaws Presbyterian religion, agriculture, and industrial education.

The Choctaw Indians owned more than 11,000 square miles in Mississippi. By 1830, after the Treaties of Doak's Stand and Dancing Rabbit Creek were signed, the Choctaw ceded their lands—including Oktibbeha County—to the United States government.

With time, the county developed in all directions. The Indian Agency, which was located east of Noxubee River, became one of the first communities with a post office. There were three focal settlements that grew from Oktibbeha County including Mayhew, Folsom, and Boardtown.

Many of Oktibbeha County's communities had unique pasts of their own. A railroad station built in 1884 helped to establish 15 businesses, including a bank and a jail in Longview. The largest tannery in the state also was located in Longview. It was used to supply the Confederate government with boots, shoes, saddles, and bridles, but was destroyed by Colonel Grierson's battalion during the Civil War. In the early 1920s, Charles A. Lindberg spent time in Maben to repair his crashed plane. The first homicide was said to have taken place in the Bell Schoolhouse community. Some of the county's communities have all but dissipated, but some are still self-contained.

Oktibbeha County's roots were planted in agriculture. In the early times, eastern Oktibbeha County was occupied by the wealthy Presbyterians and Episcopalians, who owned slaves to work the land. The yeoman farmers were left with the wooded and hilly land in the western part of the county. The old saying "cotton was king" did not rein true for this county. Although cotton was the largest crop, the soil was not ideally suited for cotton. Later, the Civil War took most able-bodied men from their farms, making existence extremely difficult.

After the war, General Stephen D. Lee and Colonel John M. Stone became the most celebrated Confederate leaders residing in Oktibbeha County. Another prominent figure, Colonel W.B. Montgomery, changed life in this county by introducing a new industry spawned by the Jersey cow. Colonel Montgomery also helped start the first land-grant school. The first session of A&M College began in 1880 with General Lee as president.

Hard times were well known in Starkville. In 1875, a fire spread through Starkville destroying 50 businesses and the county courthouse. Between 1910 and 1920, many of the area's black residents moved to the north to seek better paying jobs. Again from 1914 to 1918, the county lost many residents who fought in World War I (WWI). Like the rest of the country, the 1930 Depression hit Oktibbeha County. One of the effects of the Depression was the removal of most telephones from the county's businesses and homes.

The downtown area has remained a thriving part of Starkville. In the early 1950s, the stores on Main Street stayed open until midnight on Saturday night, and on Sunday, the town closed. On Wednesday, when stores closed at noon, many of the businessmen went fishing together. By the 1960s, the stores began closing at 6 p.m. nightly. In 1878, the county was dry, but in 1887, whiskey was sold on Main Street. A 1939 photograph pictured a beer sign on Bell's Cafe. In the 1950s, the county became dry again.

Life during the 1950s was simple. Chief Josey's "police station" was considered the third table in People's Cafe. The police made calls from a phone on a light pole in the middle of town, and covered benches were located on the corner of Jackson and Main Streets, across the street from the YMCA building on campus and next to the laundry. Because there were few cars in the county, college students used the benches to wait for rides. Highway 12 ran through campus and down College Drive, Greensboro Street, and Whitfield Street. The mill area, which is known as the Cotton District today, was called the "Needmore Area." Most residents felt like there was an imaginary line drawn from the mill area to the rest of Starkville. Crossing this imaginary line was considered dangerous. Oktibbeha Gardens was the town's first subdivision. Many houses in the subdivision went all electric. In the winter of 1951, an ice storm caused a power outage for several days. The families in Oktibbeha Gardens were forced to move in with friends who had older homes with gas heat.

Many of the landmarks and family descendants pictured in this book still remain in the county today. Although Oktibbeha County has experienced tremendous growth, there are still glimpses of yesteryear all around. It is the photographed memories that help to keep us connected to our past.

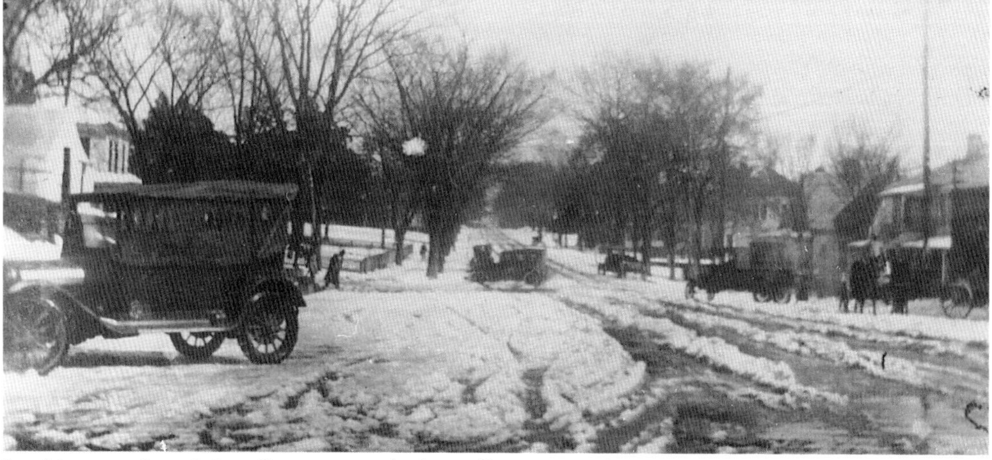

Looking east from Main Street towards the college, an early 1920s snow is pictured. (HT.)

One

SCHOOLS AND CHURCHES

Faith and education were important to the first residents of Oktibbeha County, as evidenced by the Presbyterians settling the county at Mayhew Mission, which was a school for Native Americans. This mission soon expanded to a second mission located on Robinson Road (see page 111). Adaton Methodist Church's first services were held in what was known as the "cook house" from 1856 until being officially organized in 1878. In 1880, a number of Jewish families moved to the county.

Starkville's first school was a one-room log cabin, which was also used as the county courthouse. The school's teacher, David Ames, was a highly educated lawyer and served as justice of the peace. In 1854, the Starkville Academy for Women opened. Starkville purchased the land in 1897 to build the Grade School, which was expanded in 1910. It is currently the location of Overstreet Elementary School. Starkville High School was built in 1925 in the current location of the Greensboro Center.

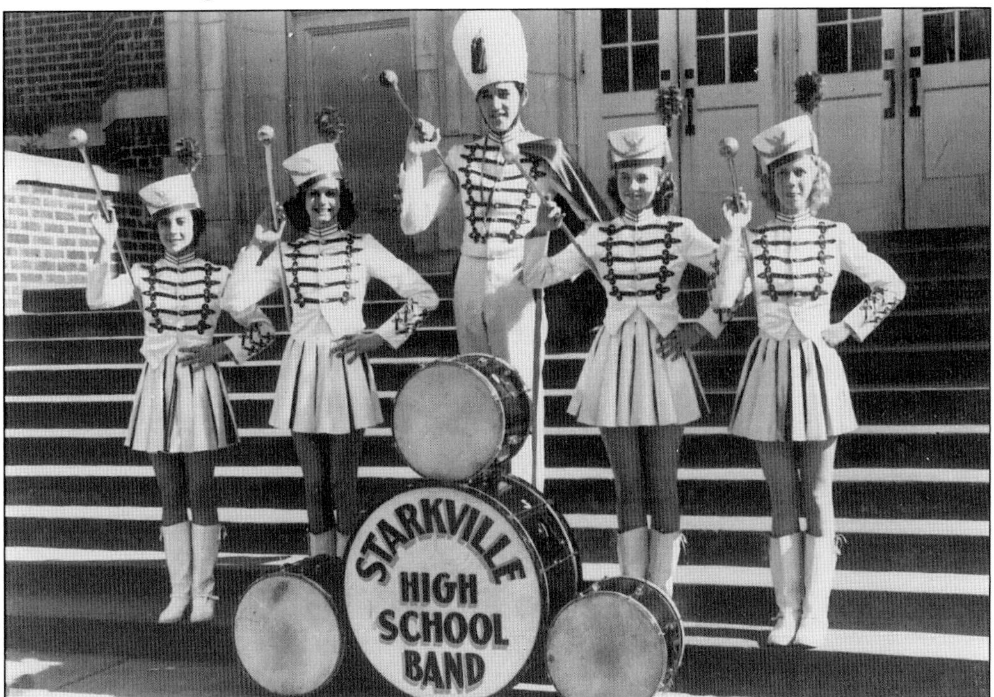

Pictured in 1940 are Starkville High School majorettes (left to right) Dot Bedenbaugh, Bernice Ballard, Pennix Barton, Grace Henry Goodman, and Betty Johnson Jones. (JSC.)

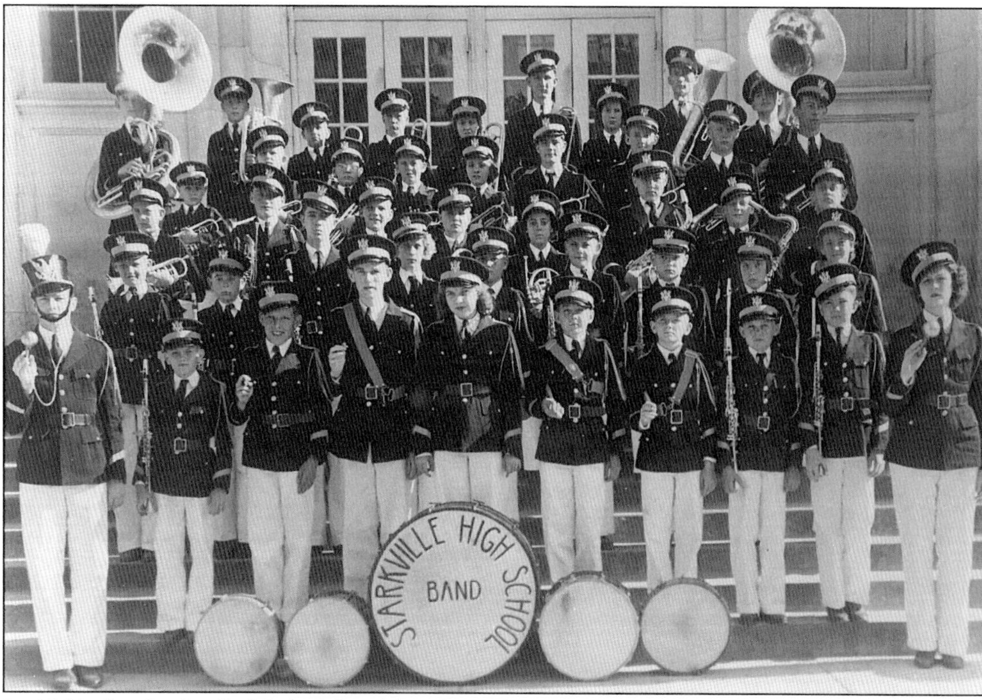

In 1941, the Starkville High School band stands at attention on the front steps of Starkville High School, the current location of the Greensboro Center. (JSC.)

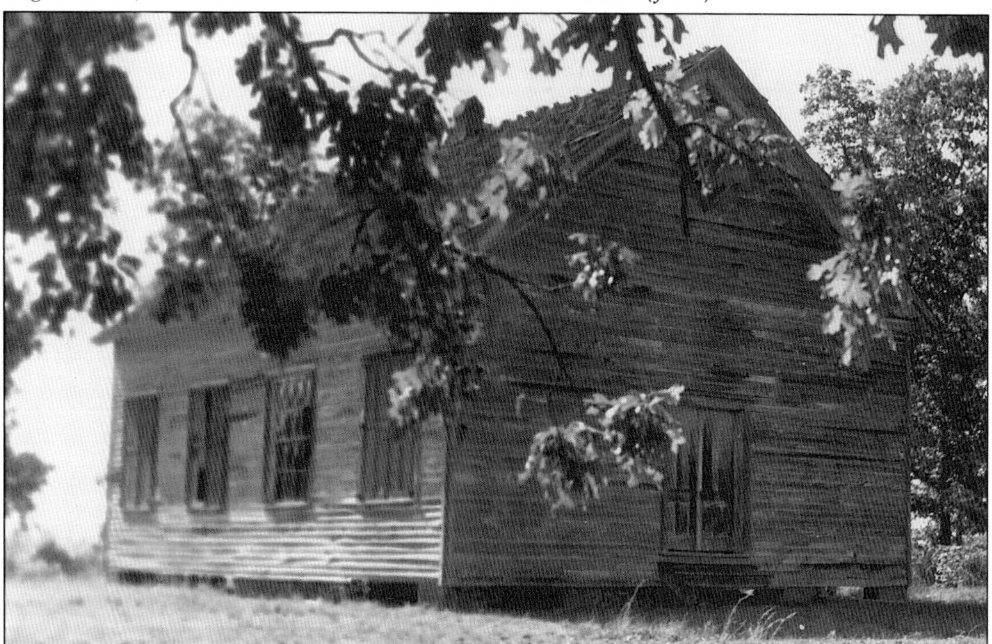

Salem Baptist Church was one of the first churches ever built in the county in 1835. It is located in the Oktoc community, which is in the southeast part of the county. At the time, most churches were held in members' homes. The union churches were interdenominational with Baptist, Presbyterian, and Methodist religions. (FB.)

First United Methodist Church was built in 1888 and had electric lights installed in 1903. (OHM.)

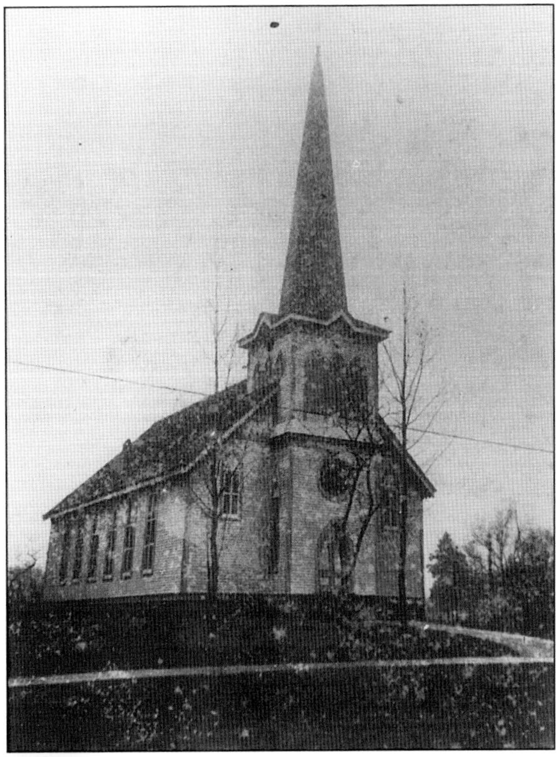

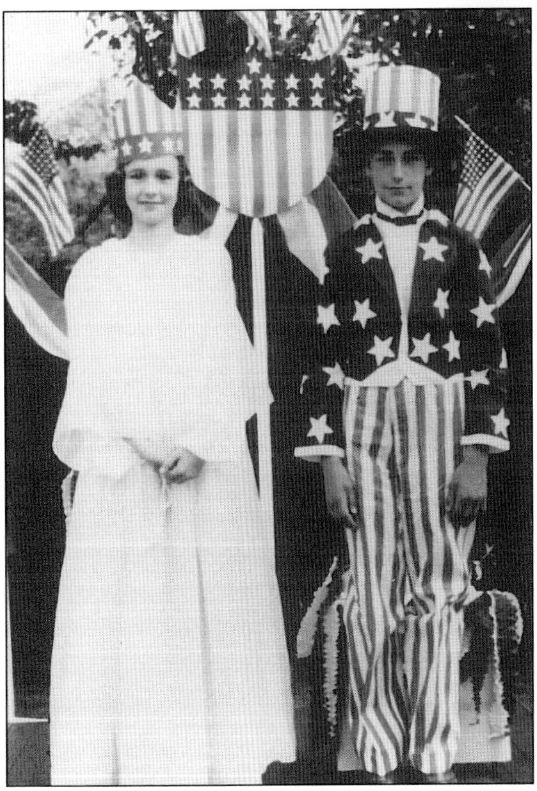

Dressed for their 1935 play are Jane Evans and John Walker, who played Uncle Sam in a costume his mother made. (JW.)

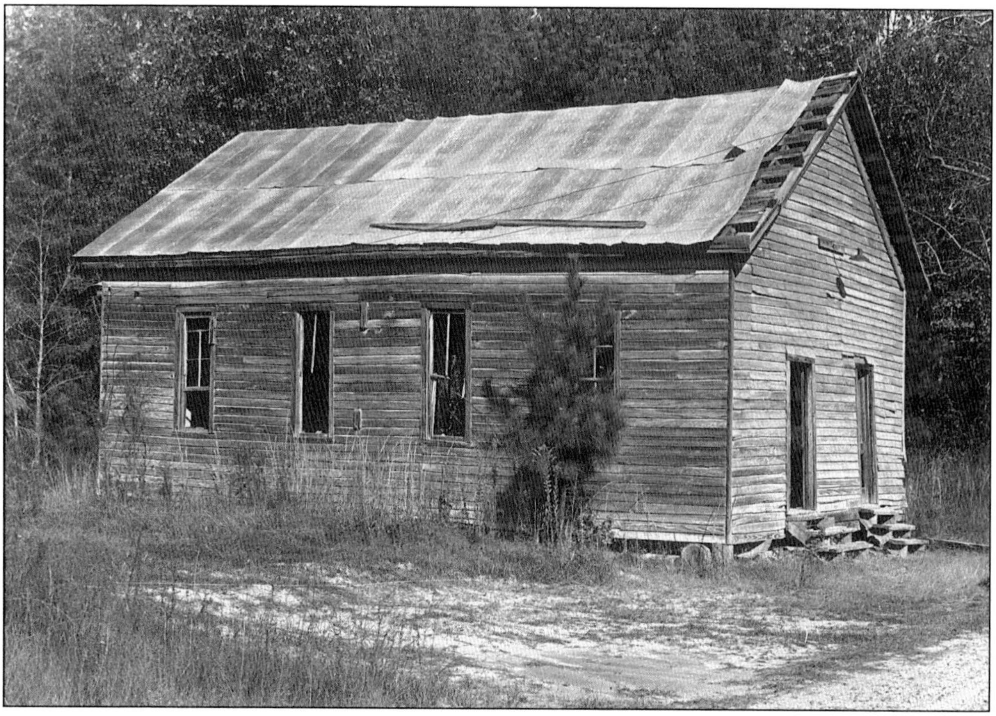

Pictured in 1960, Cedar Grove Baptist Church was located in the southern part of the county. (FB.)

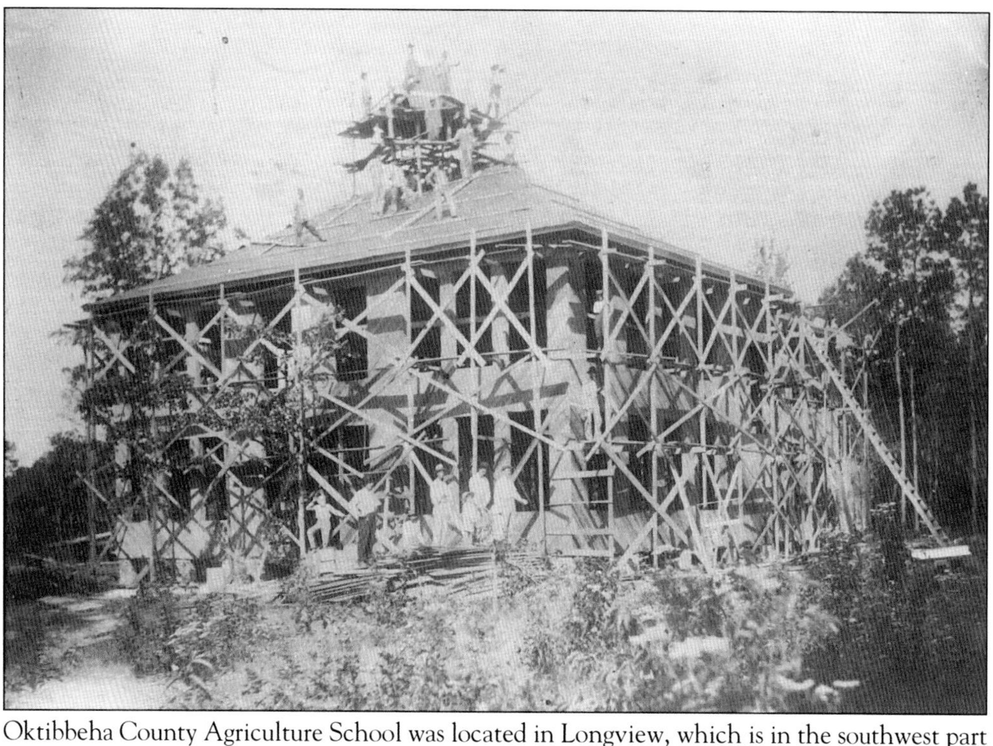

Oktibbeha County Agriculture School was located in Longview, which is in the southwest part of the county. The school was under construction in this 1911 picture. (OHM.)

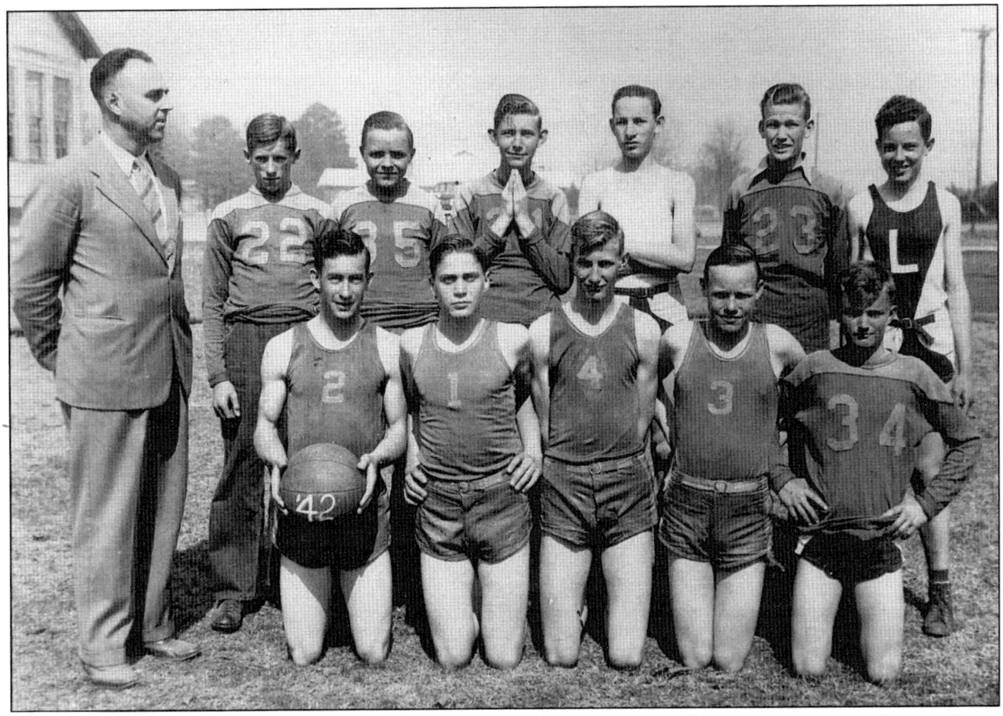

Members of the Oktibbeha County Agriculture School basketball team are pictured here, from left to right: (front row) Curtis Hamill, Tom Cook, Carrol Sanders, Lavern Wallace, and Gerald Jackson; (standing) Lem Stallings, Harold Daugherty, Layman Wallace, Harold Sanders, Eudell Hudspeth, Donald Dean Quinn, and James Oswalt. (WFM.)

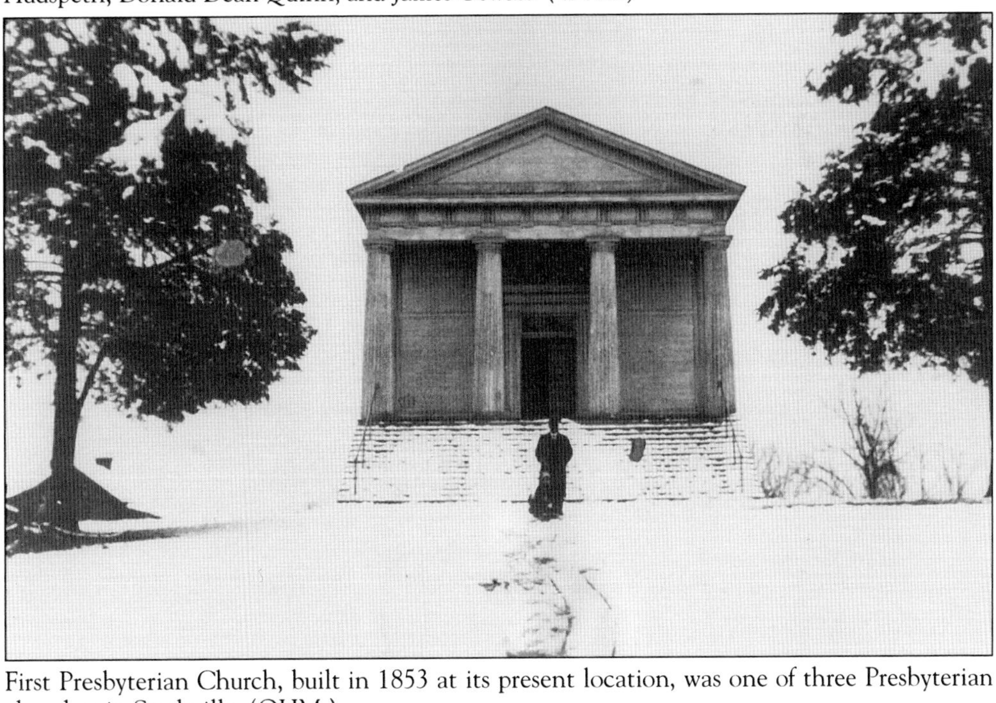

First Presbyterian Church, built in 1853 at its present location, was one of three Presbyterian churches in Starkville. (OHM.)

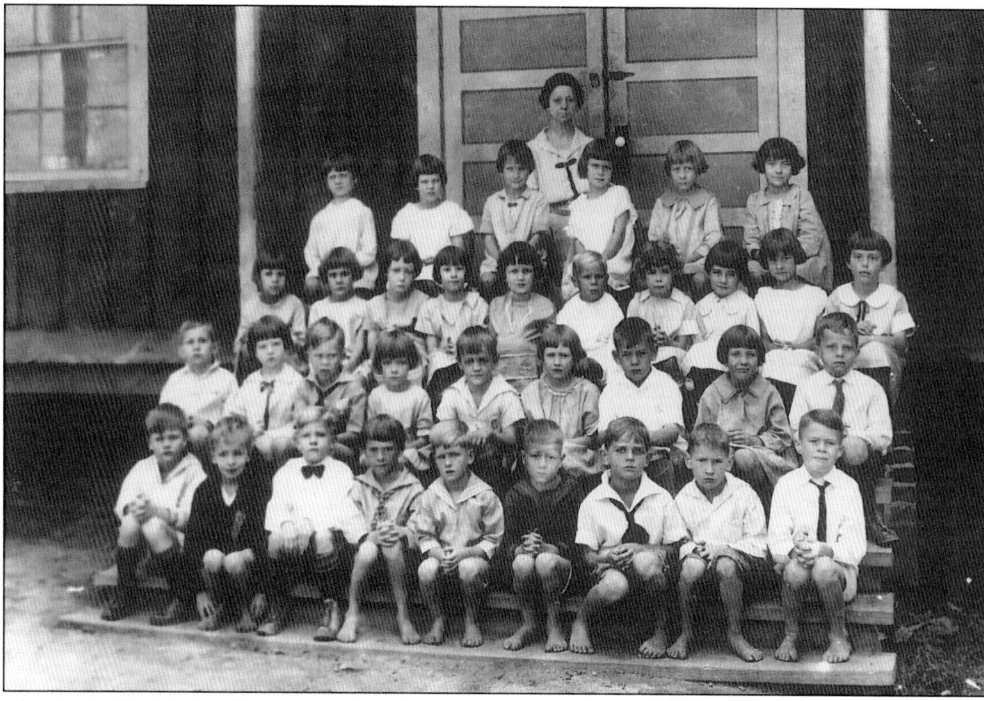

The Little Red Schoolhouse, used by first graders, was located behind Overstreet School. Ms. Annie Dell Perkins taught the class of 1924. (BK.)

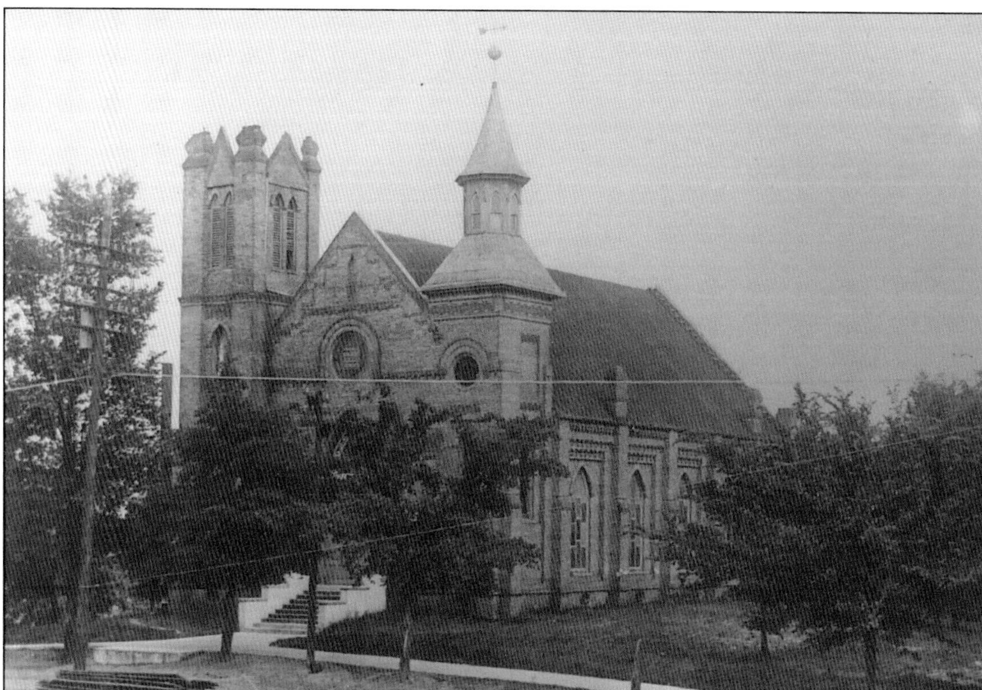

First Baptist Church's second building, which is still in use today, was built in 1889 at a cost of $12,000. The church started with 12 white people and one black slave. (BFH.)

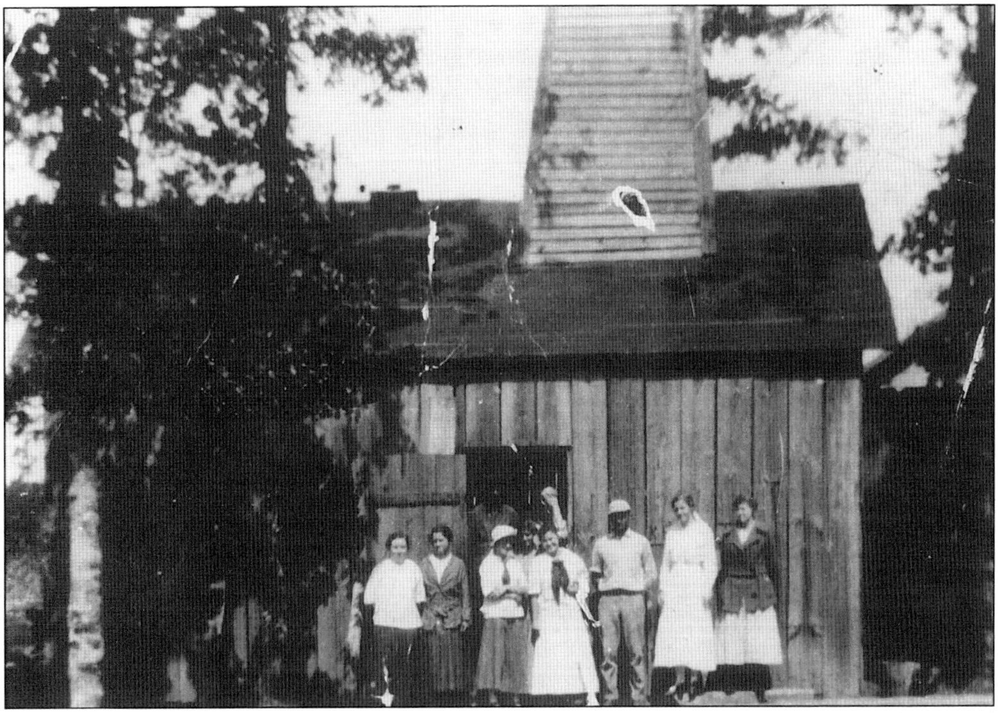

Seitz's Chapel, a school in Longview, had a chimney lined with mud and straw and covered with wood. (EBS, WFM.)

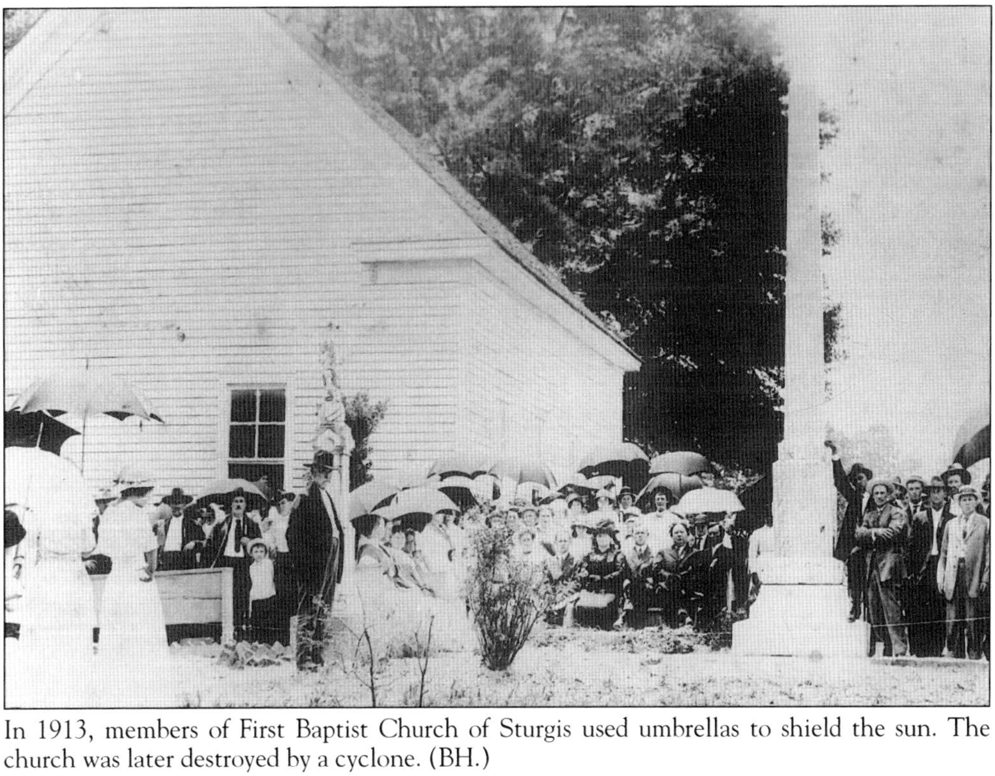

In 1913, members of First Baptist Church of Sturgis used umbrellas to shield the sun. The church was later destroyed by a cyclone. (BH.)

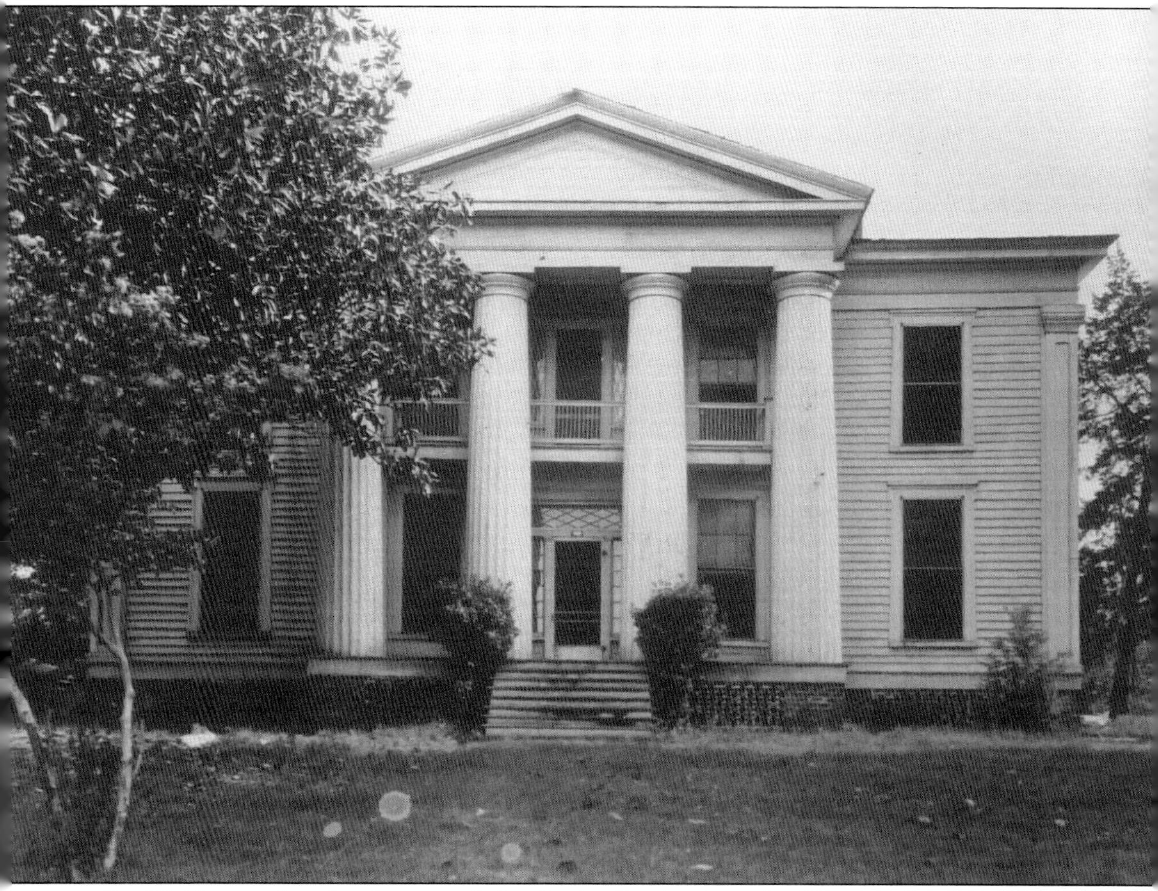

Dr. Webb served as headmaster of the Starkville Academy for Women. During the Civil War, the school was used as a temporary hospital. In 1879, it merged with Sellars Institute for Women. It was later owned by a member of the Montgomery family, Mrs. Edwards, who ran it as a boarding house, and the Maxwell family. In 1926, the home was torn down by Borden to construct a new home for the plant manager. The school is pictured here in 1854. (BS.)

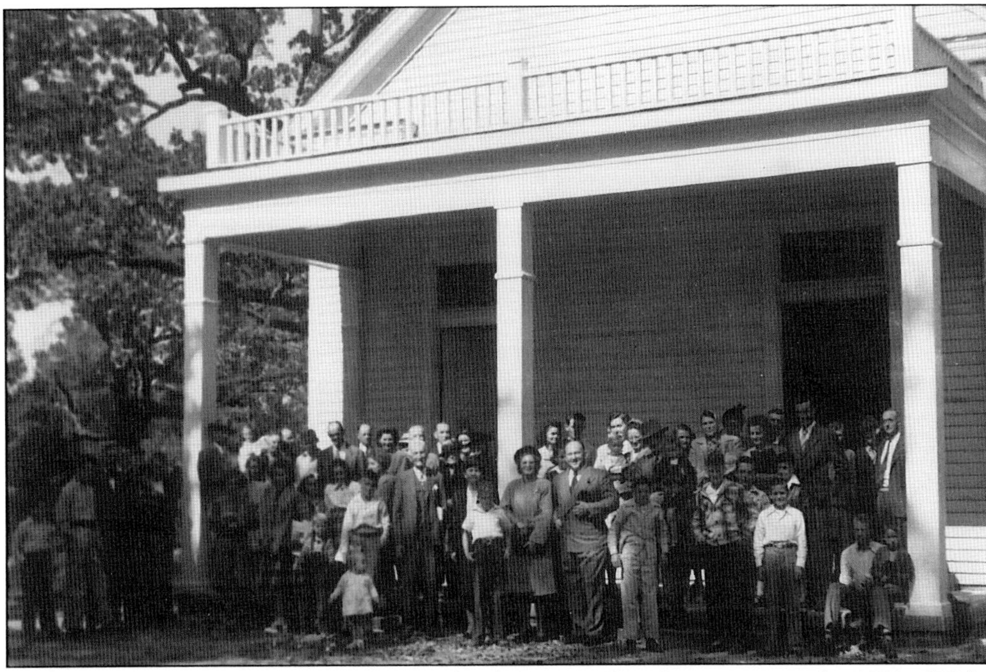

Members of Salem Baptist Church built Bethesda Baptist Church sometime in the 1840s. (FB.)

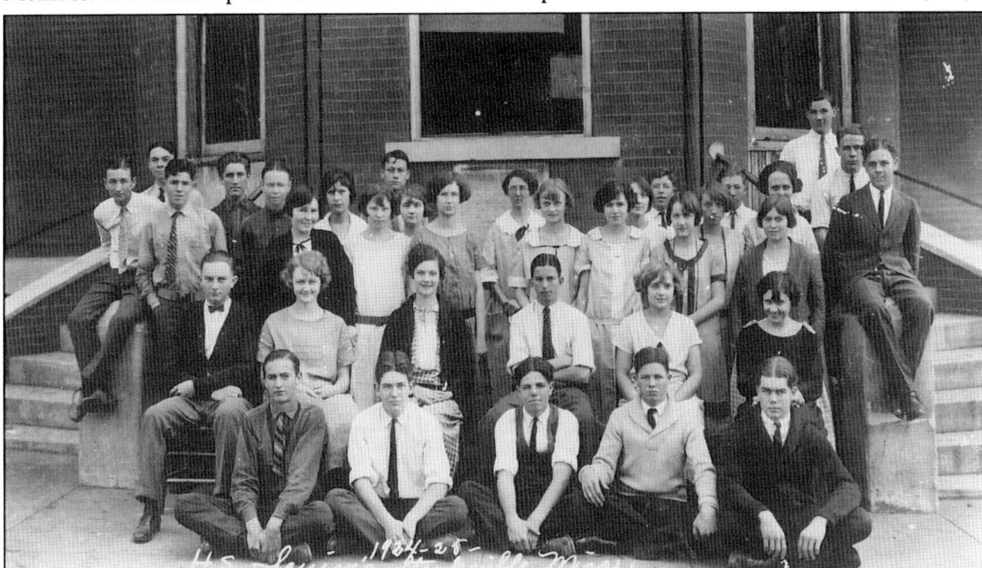

Pictured in this 1924–25 Grade School class are the following, from left to right: (front row) unidentified, John Herbert, John Eckford Hartness, Walker Duff, Sudduth, and unidentified; (second row) unidentified, Frances Ward, Carolyn Herbert, Albert Sidney Crigler, Elizabeth Gunn, and Almira Hogan; (third row) unidentified, Catherine Crumpton, unidentified, Frances Moore, Sarah Stiles, Eva Richey, Eloise Lanier, ? Willis, Emily Williams, and Theodore Stark; (fourth row) Chick Clayton, unidentified, Riley Patterson, Rose Weddle, James Dodd, Fanny Lampkin (teacher), Gertrude Carpenter, Rudolph Monosmith, Lavach McIlwain, Sammy Slaughter, and Randolph Stark. The Grade School is now known as Overstreet Elementary School. (BS.)

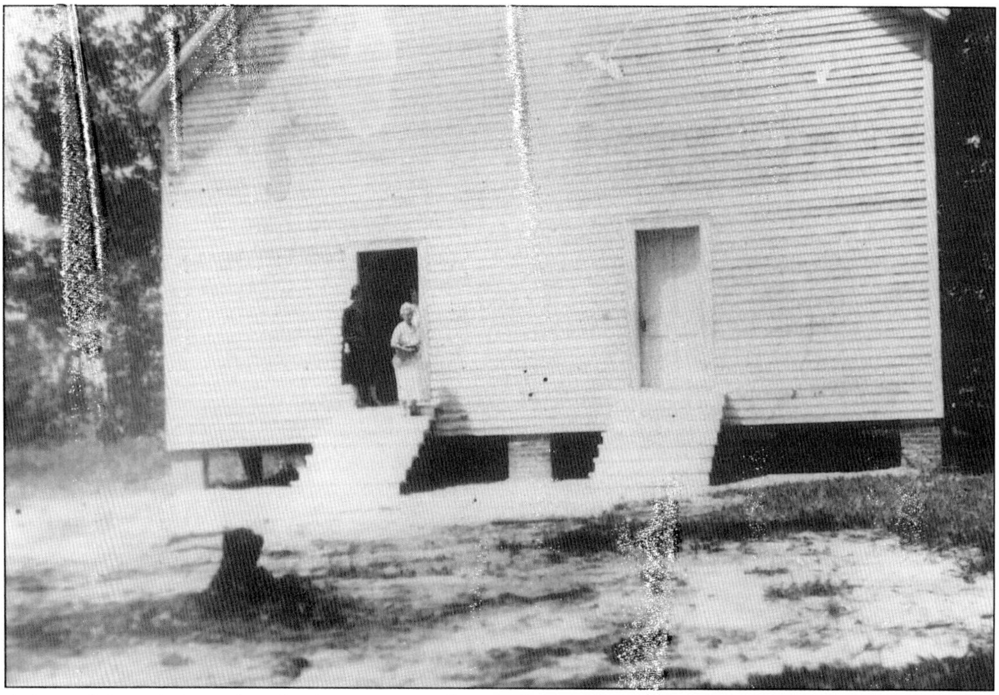

Adaton United Church, which was erected in 1880, was known as Steele's Chapel in honor of the two individuals who donated the land for the church. (MB.)

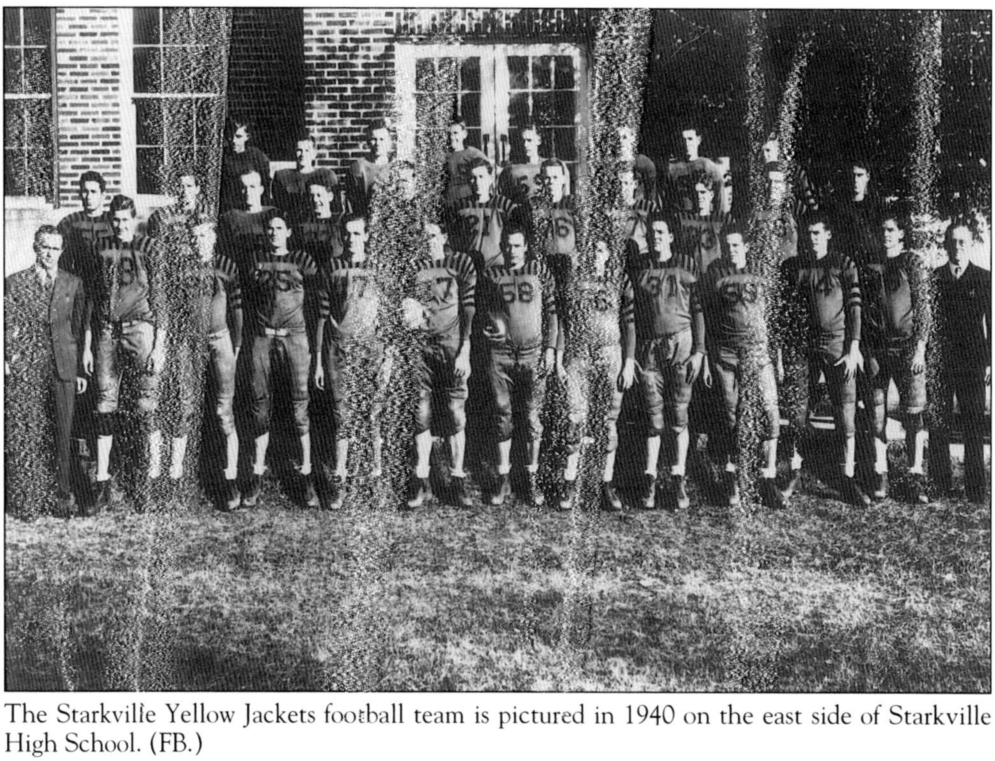

The Starkville Yellow Jackets football team is pictured in 1940 on the east side of Starkville High School. (FB.)

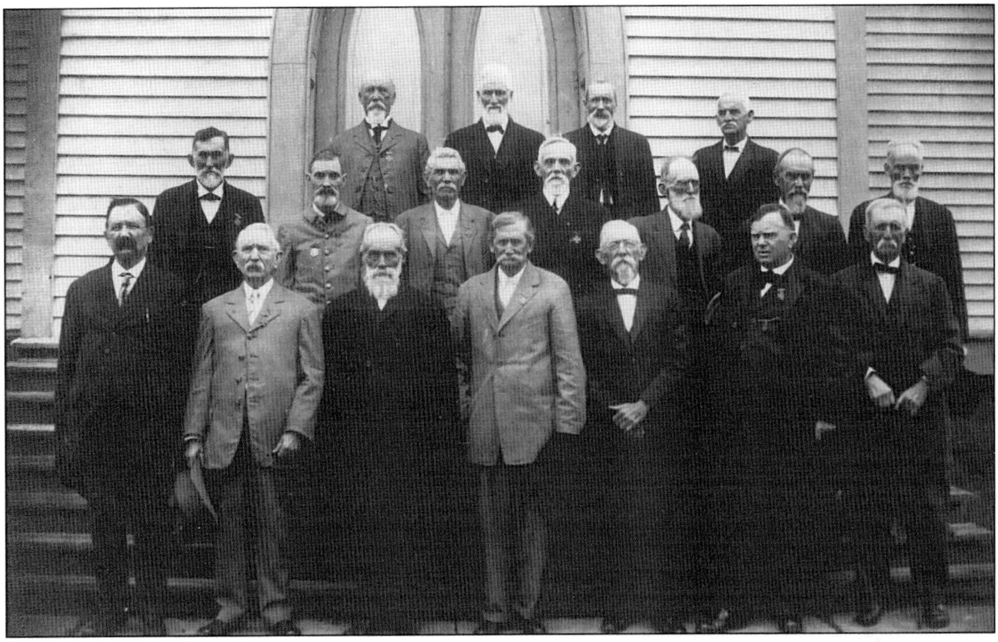

Civil War veterans are pictured in front of First United Methodist Church in 1910. They are as follows, from left to right: (front row) H.T. Saunders, T.W. Sheavers, Lanier, D.W. Outlaw, John Burgin, Wiley Nash, and unidentified; (second row) Hearon, F.C. Gregg, L.D. McDowell, W.H. Magruder, J.A. Rand, and unidentified; (third row) W.H. Reynolds, unidentified, J.T. Jones, and S. Critz. (JSC.)

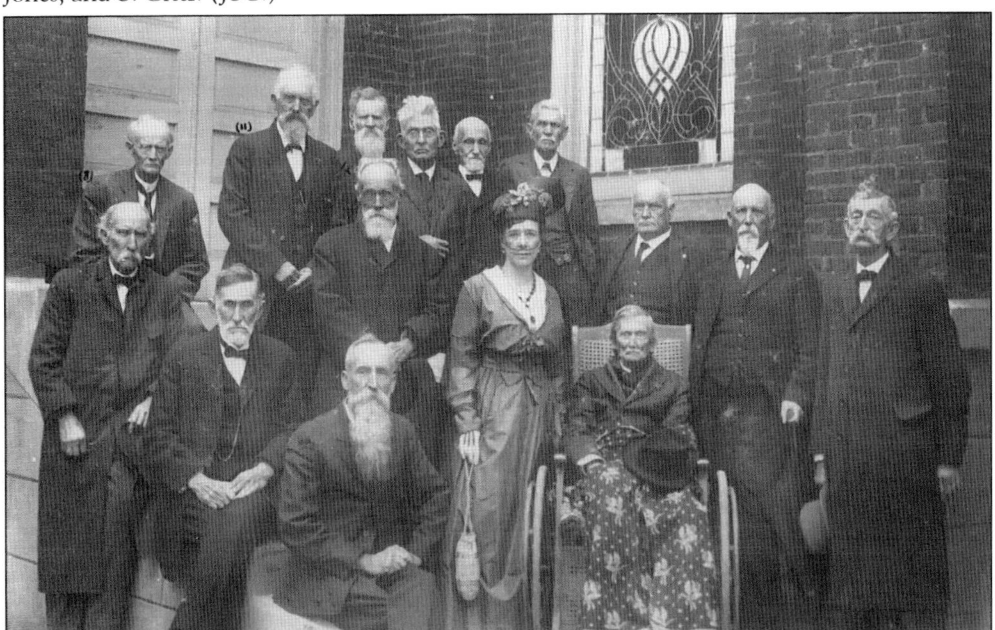

Civil War veterans are pictured on the east side of First Baptist Church in 1910. From left to right are G.M. Vaughn, F.E. Hearon, J.A. Glenn, Mrs. D.E. Slaughter, D.W. Outlaw, W.H. Reynolds, James Carpenter, C.E. Buntin, Lanier, A.H. Reynolds, James McCreight, G.C. Thompson, T.E. Marshall, Reverend T.C. Weir, L.D. McDowell, and B.P. Williams. (JSC.)

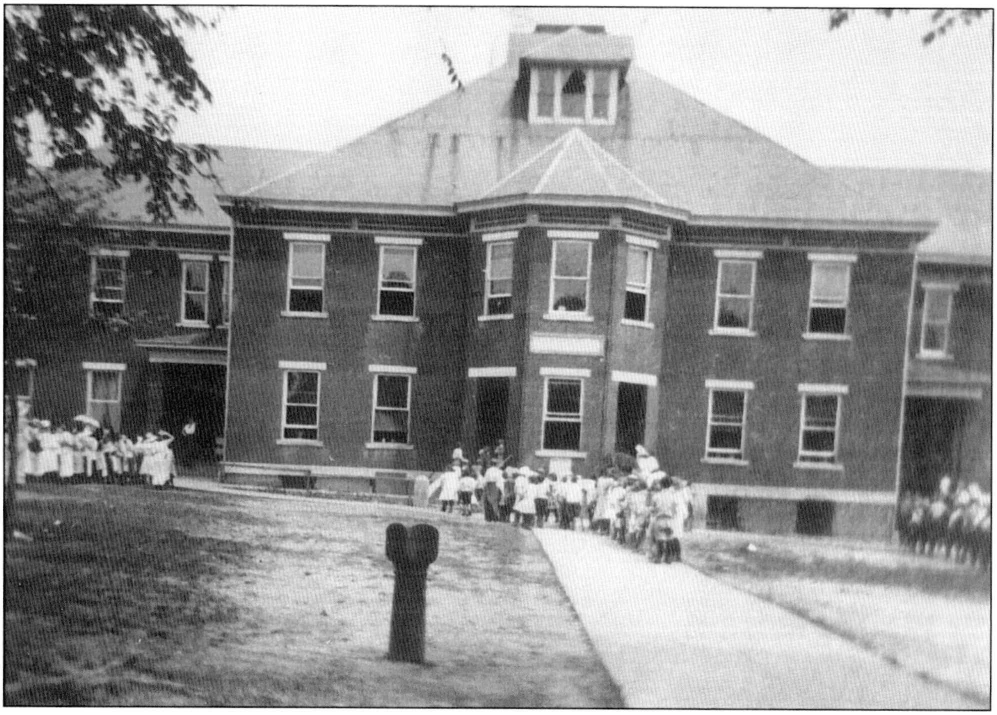

Construction on the Grade School, which was located on the site of the Sellars Institute for Women, started in 1897 and was completed in 1899. It is now known as Overstreet Elementary School. (JSC.)

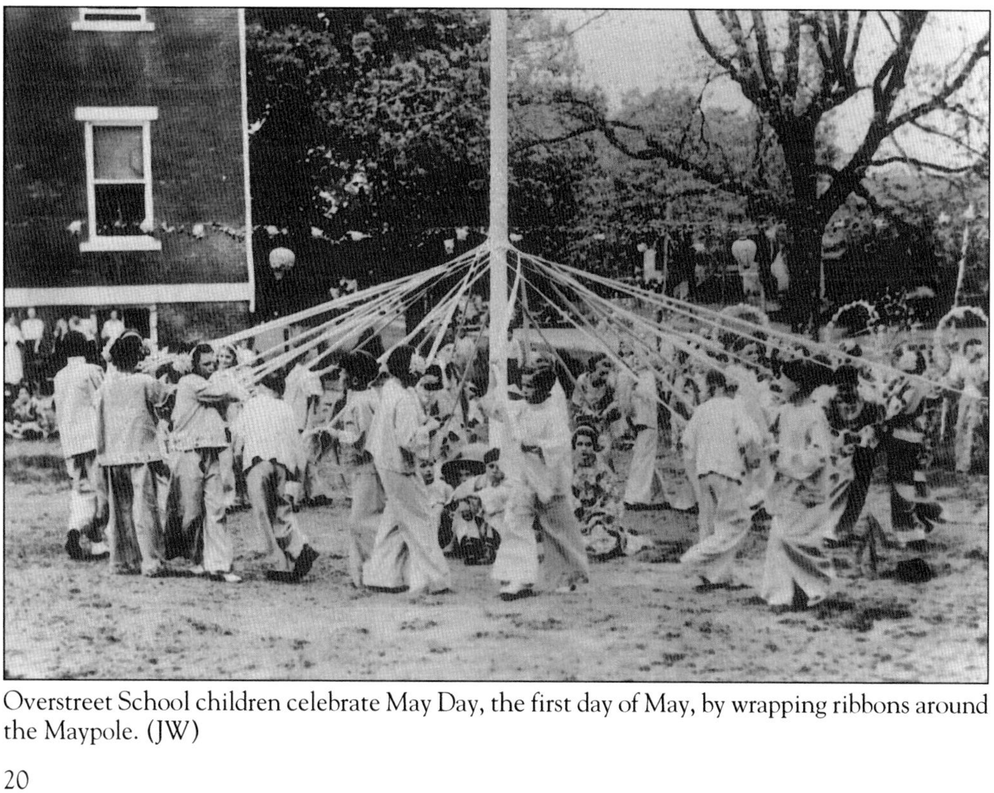

Overstreet School children celebrate May Day, the first day of May, by wrapping ribbons around the Maypole. (JW)

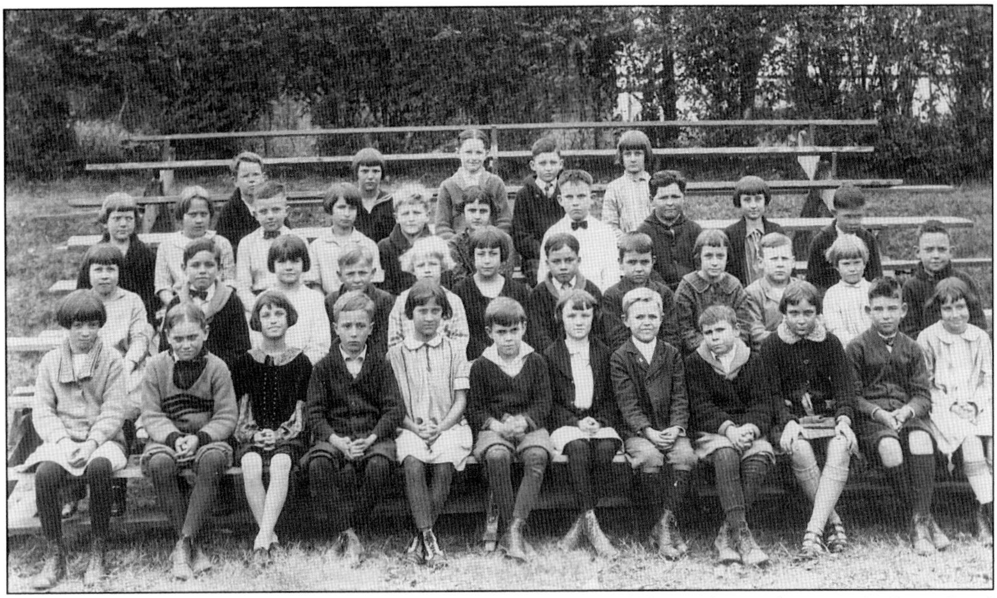

Prior to 1925, Overstreet School taught first through twelfth grades. After 1925, the school housed first through fourth grades. Pictured are students from an Overstreet School's fourth-grade class, from left to right: (first row) unidentified, Ellie Hogan, unidentified, Miles Patterson, Betsy Stark, Eddie Harned, Marie Swindle, Phillip Matthews, Matthew Mitchell, Missy Hogan, Henry Montague, and Maisie Elkin; (second row) unidentified, unidentified, Susie Moore, unidentified, Grosie Heath Saunders, Mary Alice White, James Seitz, unidentified, Francis Drane, unidentified, Dessie Whitehead, and unidentified; (third row) Bessie Alberta McIngvale, Mildred Willis, John Carpenter, Mary Grey Gieger, Frank Smith, Helen Navarro, D.W. McIlwain, unidentified, Beverly Didlake, and unidentified; (fourth row) John Kennard, unidentified, unidentified, unidentified, and Edna Josey. (BS.)

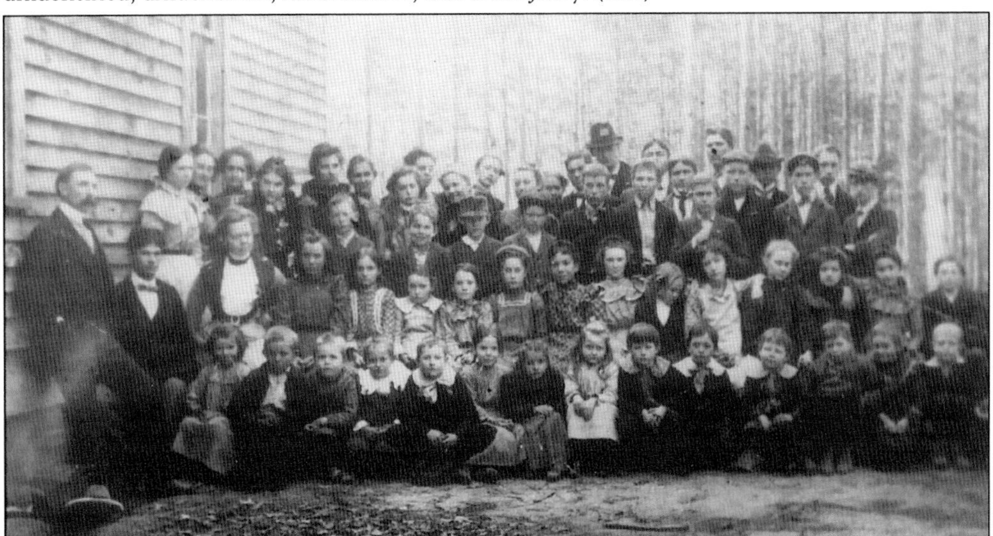

Sturgis School, which was replaced in 1915 with an eight-room school, boasted of having a three-teacher school when this picture was taken in 1900. Sturgis is located southwest of Starkville. (BH.)

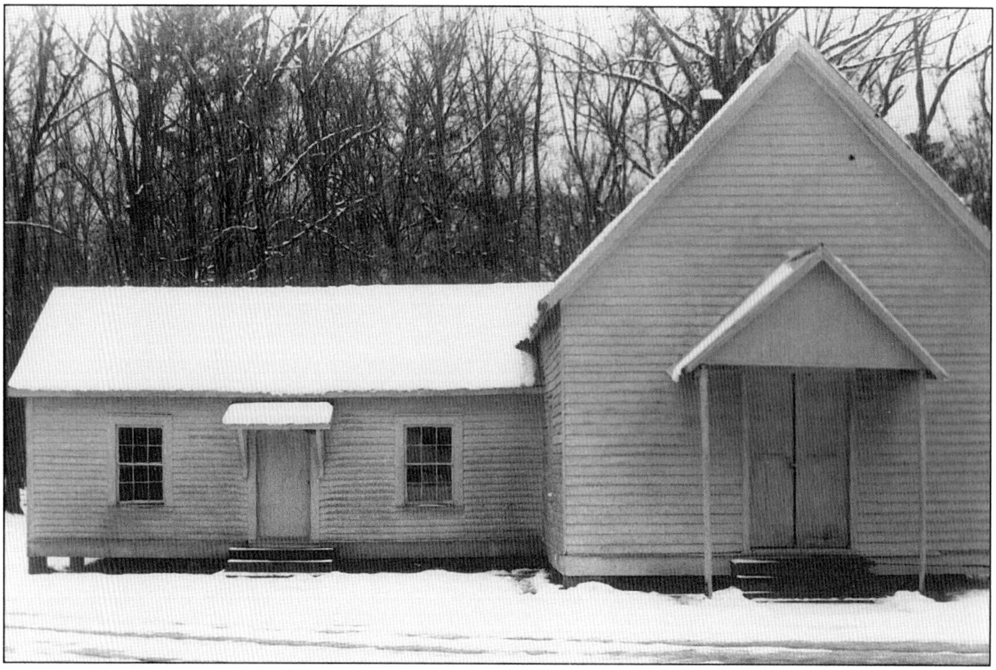

The Bell Schoolhouse, located on Highway 389 North, was a one-room school that was later attached to the church and used as a community center. Several doctors lived in the Bell Schoolhouse community. Across the road from the schoolhouse, the Wofford property had a lake that was used to run a steam boiler, which ran the steam engines to the gristmill, sawmill, and cotton gin. (JSC.)

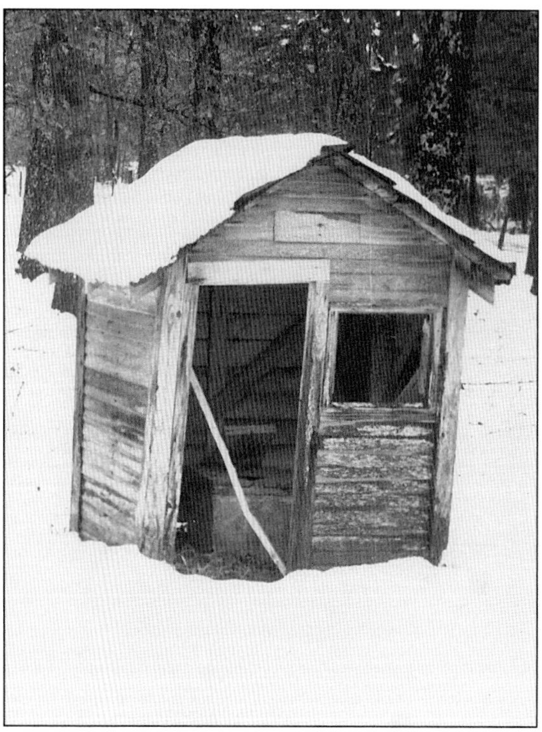

Bell Schoolhouse students took restroom breaks in this facility. By March 15, 1926, residents of Starkville were required to connect to the city sewer system.

Two

COMMUNITIES

Farming was the chief occupation for the county residents. Most young men established their farms before moving their family to the county. Some of the larger farms, which had 10,000-plus acres, were owned by the Outlaw and Montgomery families.

With the installation of the railroads in the 1870s, the demand for crossties rose. As this demand increased, the county's timber industry grew. Benefiting most from the crosstie business was Longview, which became known as the "crosstie capitol of the world."

The opening of the Borden plant in 1926 made Oktibbeha County the "dairy center of the south." Today, only six dairies remain in the county.

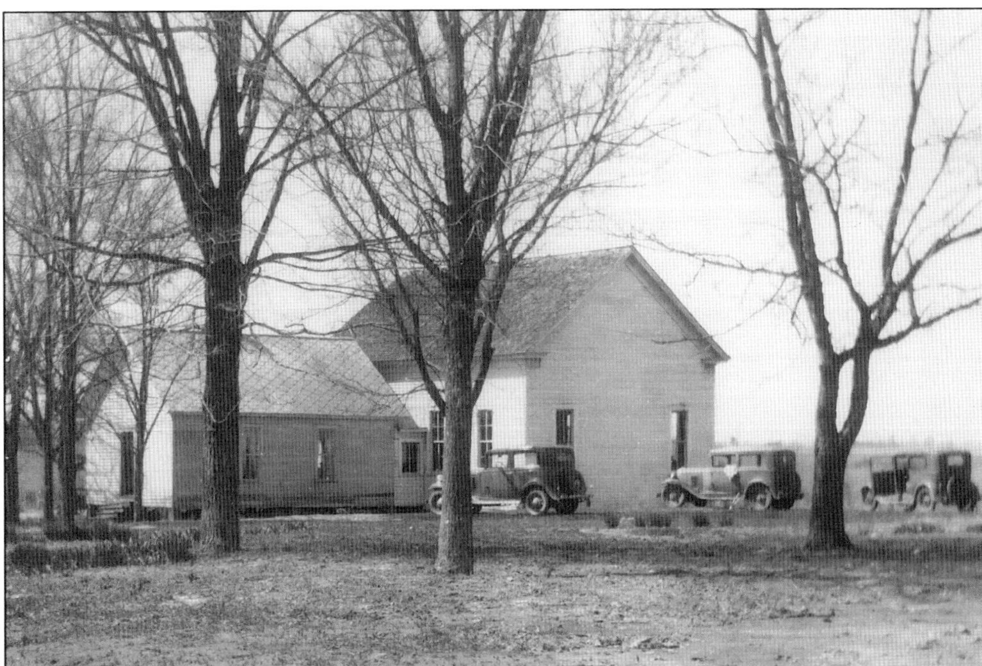

The Cumberland Presbyterian Church and old one-room schoolhouse were purchased and joined to use as a community center in 1932. The building is known today as the Oktoc Community Center. (FOB.)

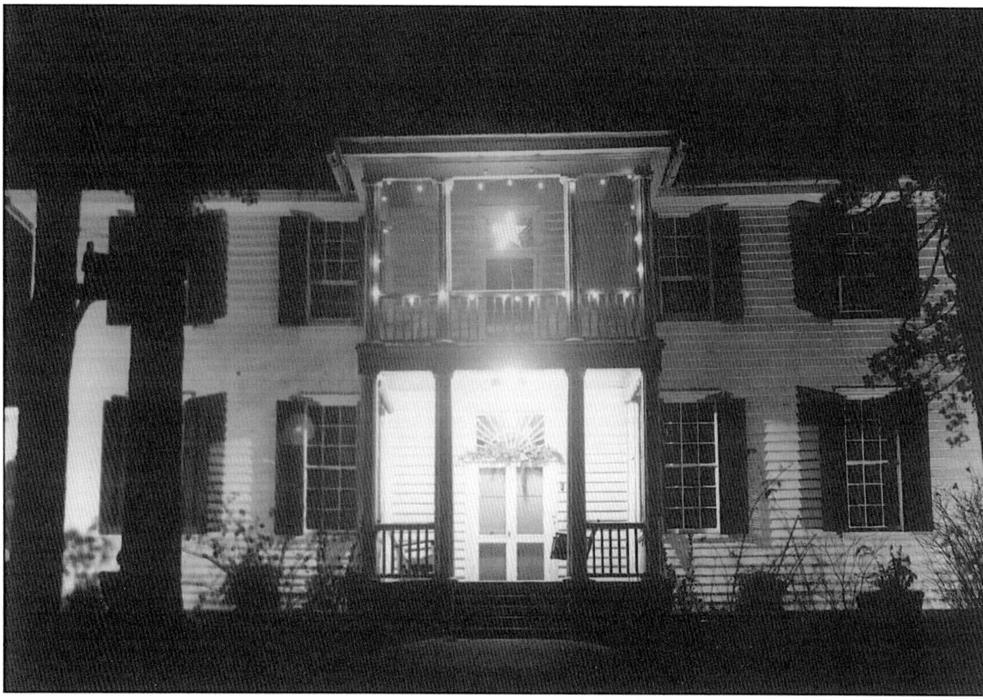

This home, built in 1836 on a large cotton plantation, was known as the Outlaw-Page Home, but it was called "the Cedars." (FB.)

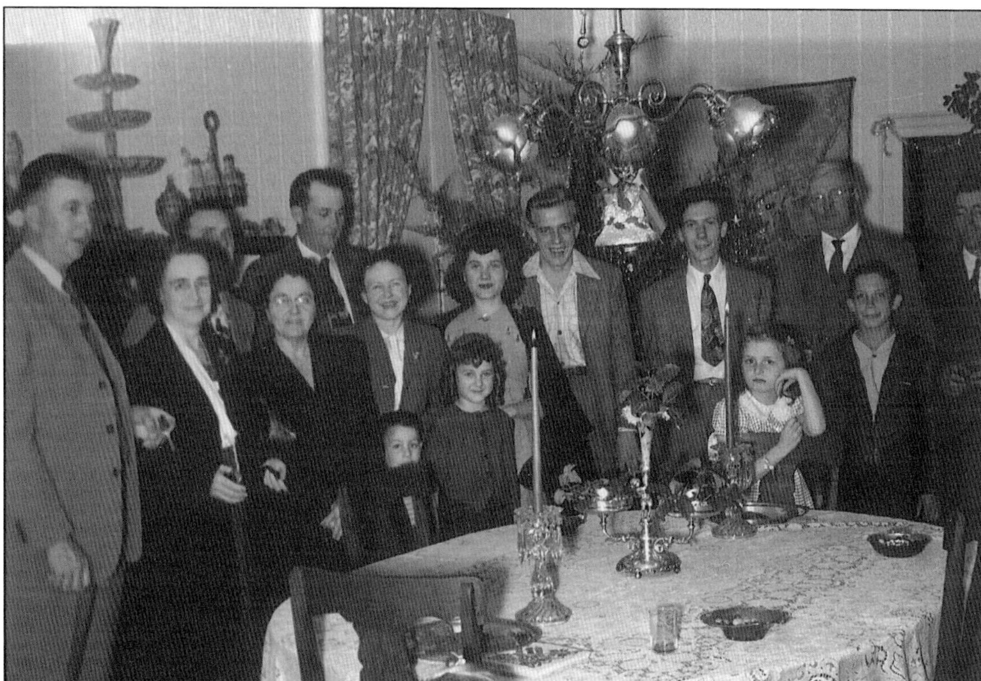

Folks gather around The Cedars dining room table. The Cedars housed some of the finest antiques in the county. When items in the house were being sold, antique dealers traveled from as far as 1,000 miles away to bid on the goods. (FB.)

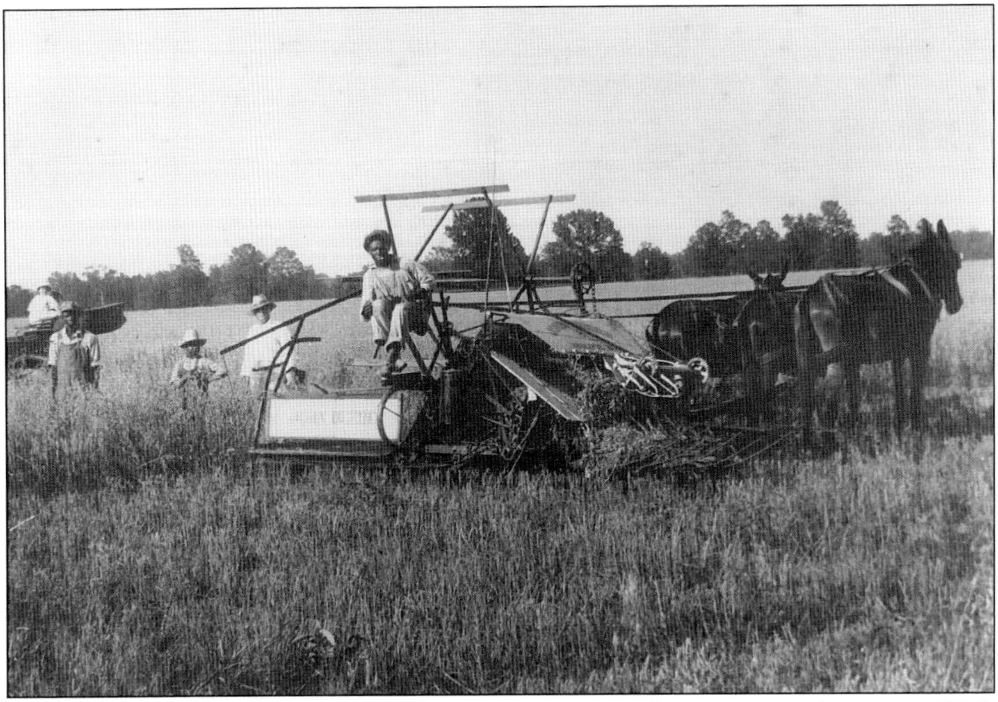

This reaper machine was one of the early John Deere pieces of equipment in the county. (FB.)

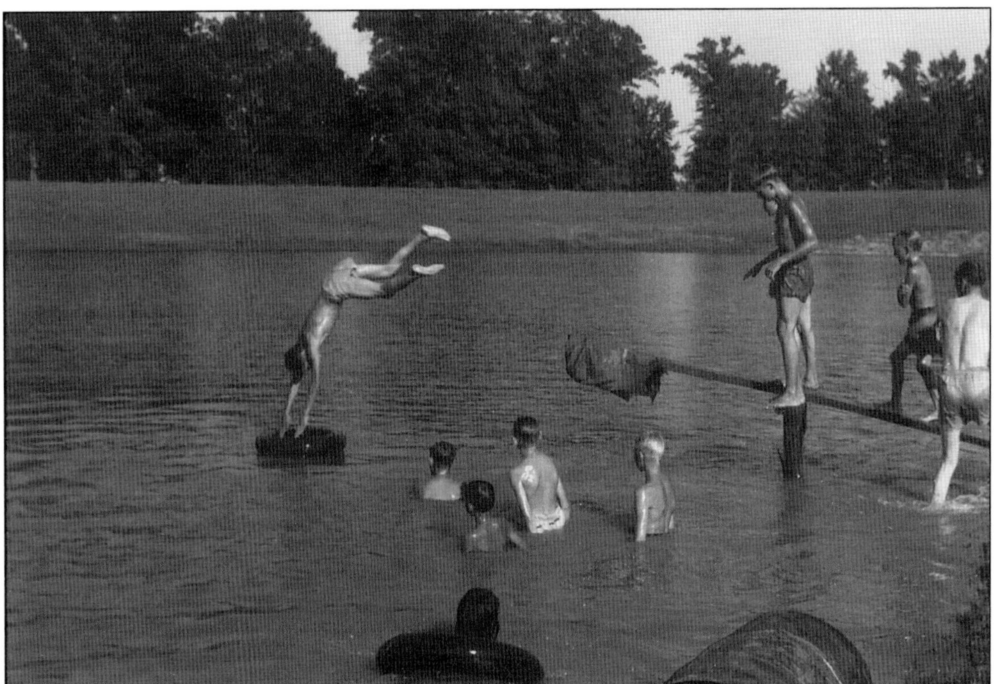

In this picture, kids enjoy taking a dip in this Oktoc farm pond. (FB.)

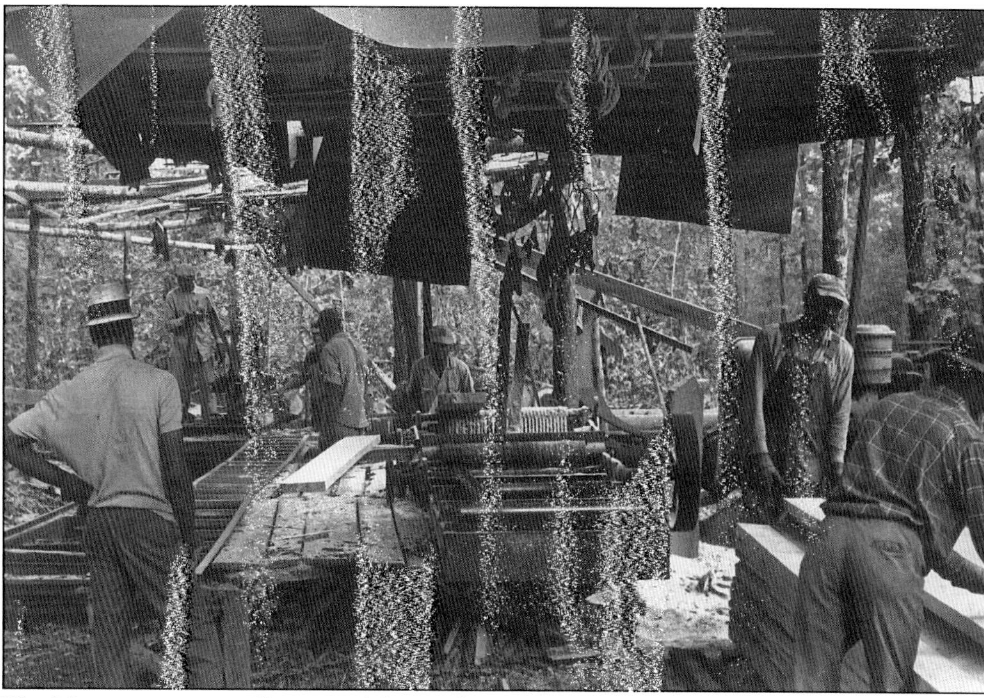

The Montgomery sawmill, pictured during the 1960s, was moved around the county. (FB.)

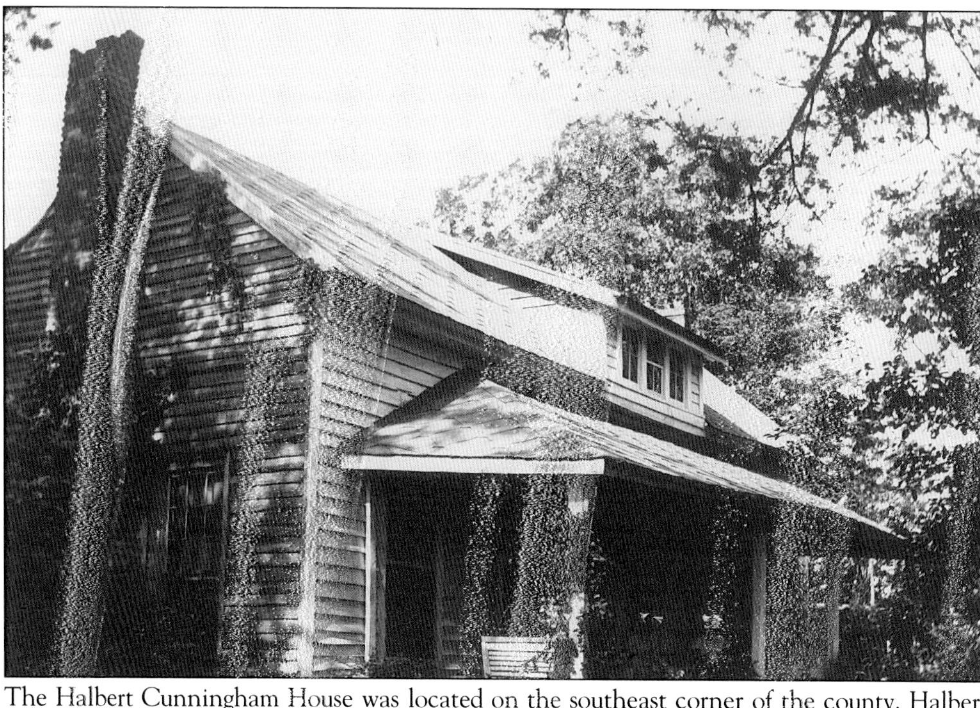

The Halbert Cunningham House was located on the southeast corner of the county. Halbert Cunningham was one of A&M College's first graduates and later became a professor for the college. (FB.)

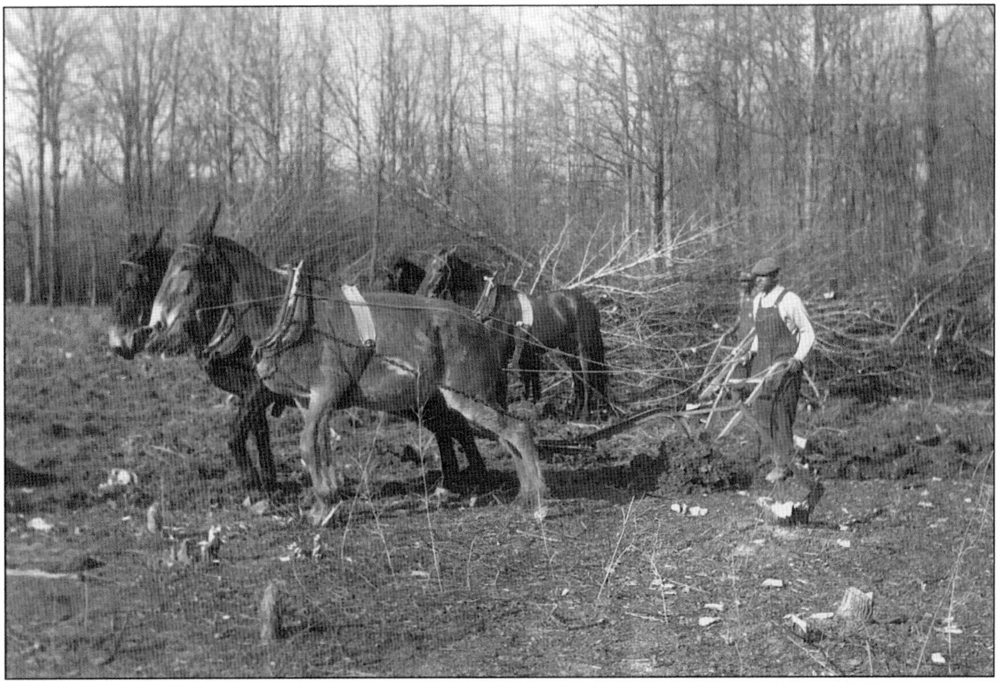

Clearing the land was a hard job. Col. Montgomery (see page 34) understood the negative effects of planting cotton year after year. He also discovered that Johnson grass grew well in lime soil. (FB.)

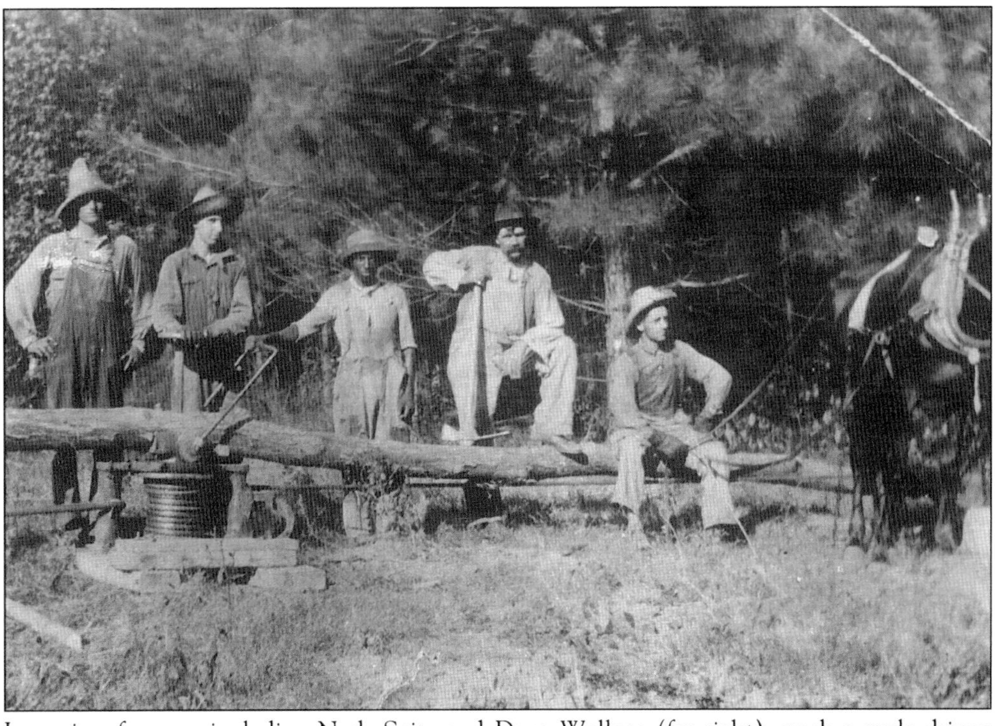

Longview farmers, including Nash Seitz and Dave Wallace (far right), work a mule-driven wench used to pull stumps. (WFM.)

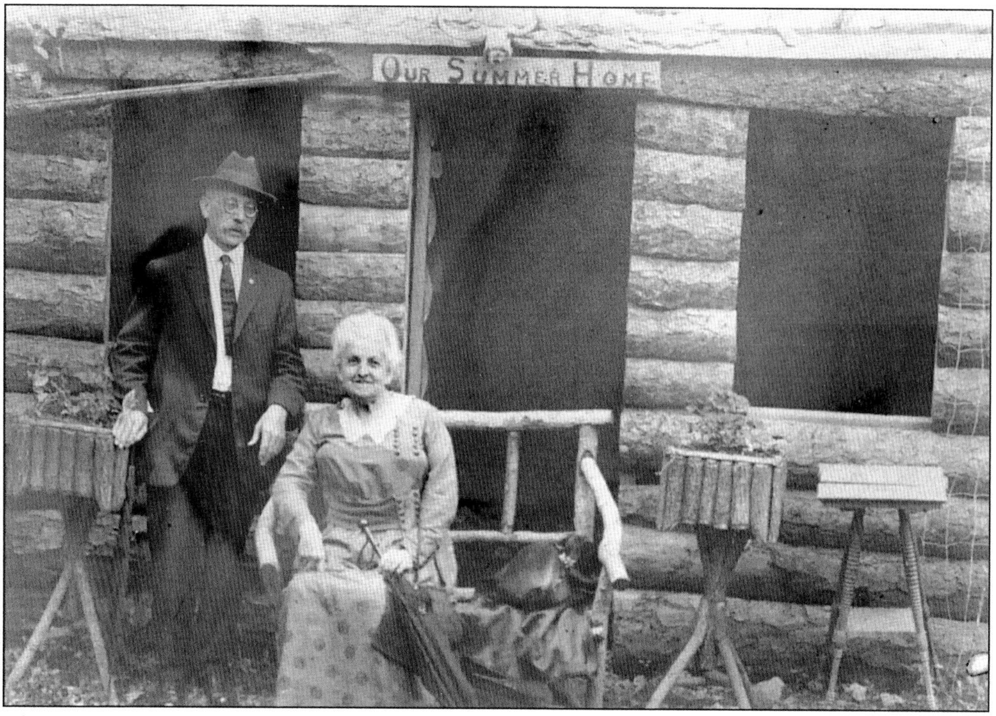

The Goodman Camphouse, affectionately known as "Our Summer Home," was located on Tibbee Creek Road, which later changed to Old West Point Road. Philip and Helen Goodman are also pictured on page 53. (BG.)

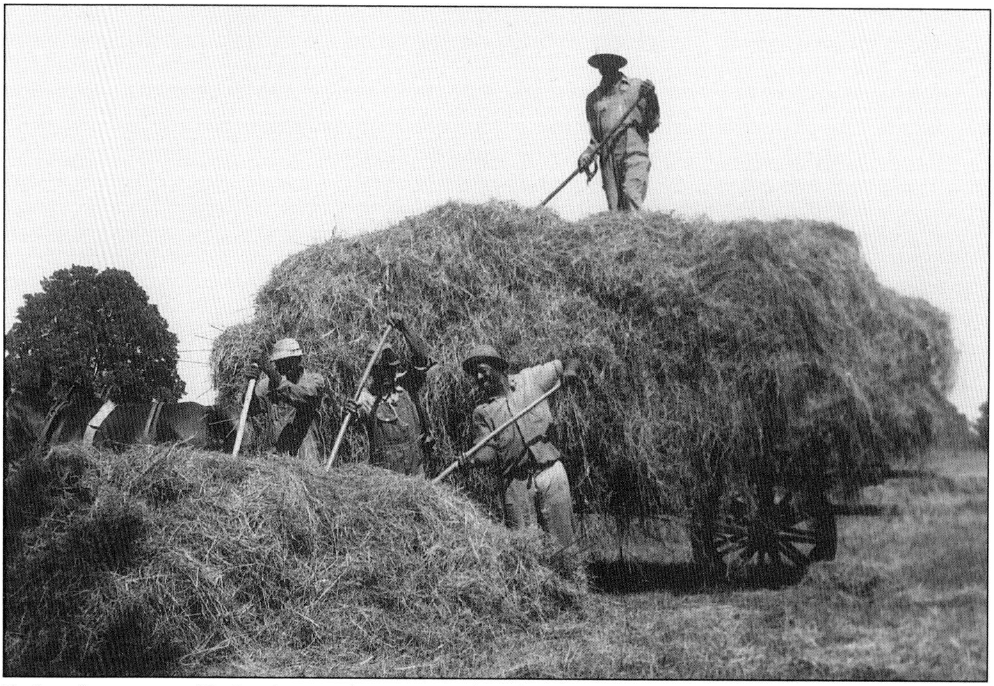

Before farmers used bales, haystacks were used to feed the 30,000 cows that lived in the county in 1929. (FB.)

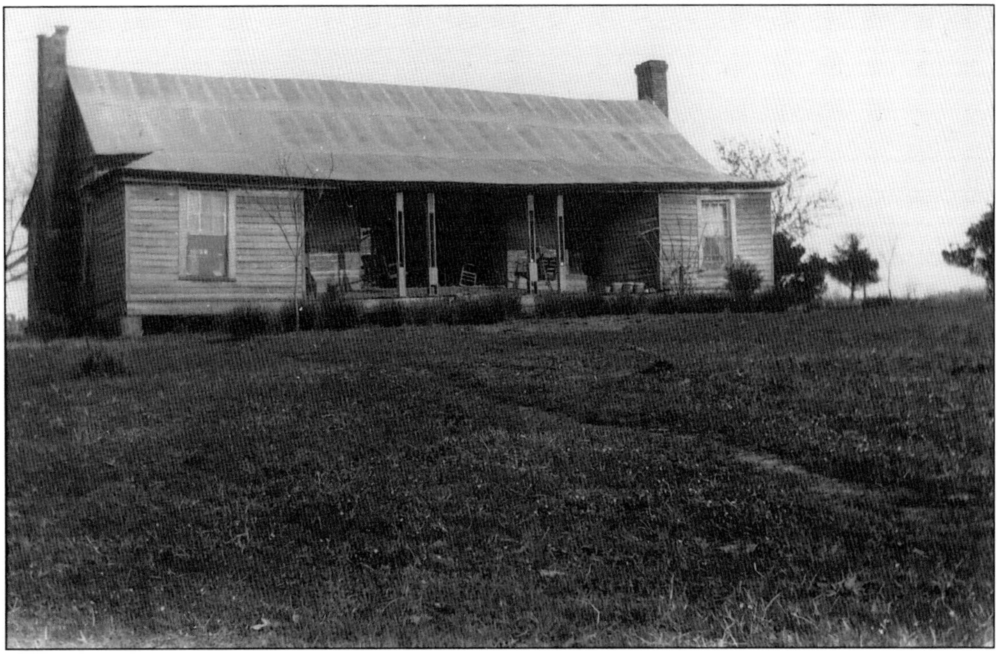

A traditional dogtrot home, like the Oakley farmhouse, has its kitchen and sleeping area separated by a breezeway. (FOB.)

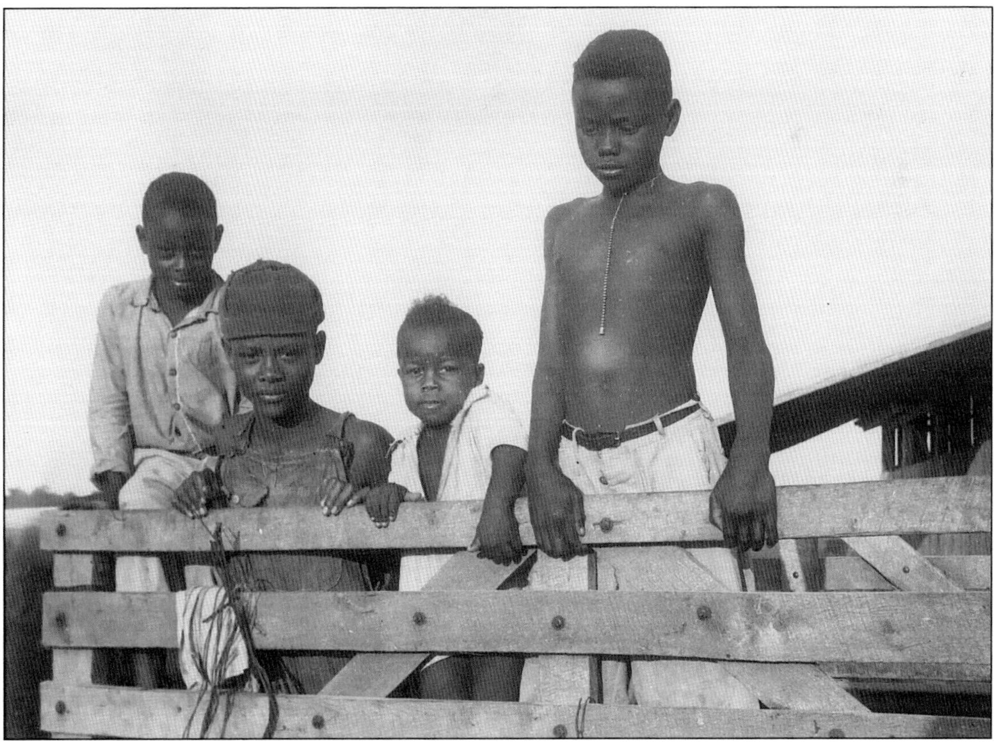

An Oktoc farm gate serves as the boys' prop. (FB.)

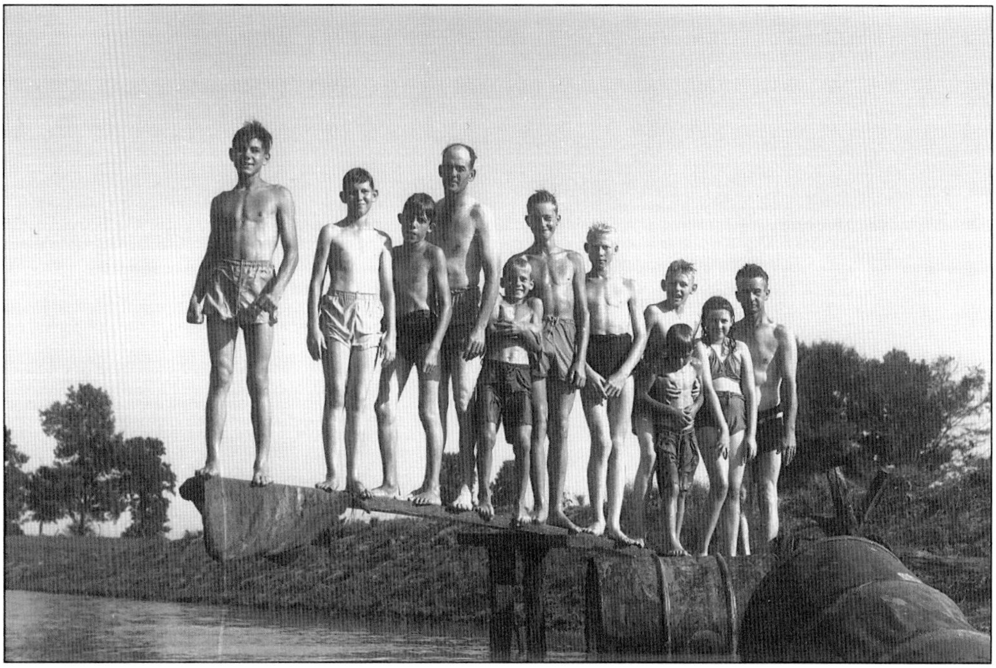

Ellis Self, Waverly Oakley, Joe Self, Hilman Gentry, ? Self, Stanley Gray, Howard Gray (small boy), Buddy Gentry, Wayne Gentry, Dee Gentry, and Ellis Self Sr. are pictured at E.M. Self's pond in the Oktoc community in 1947. (FB.)

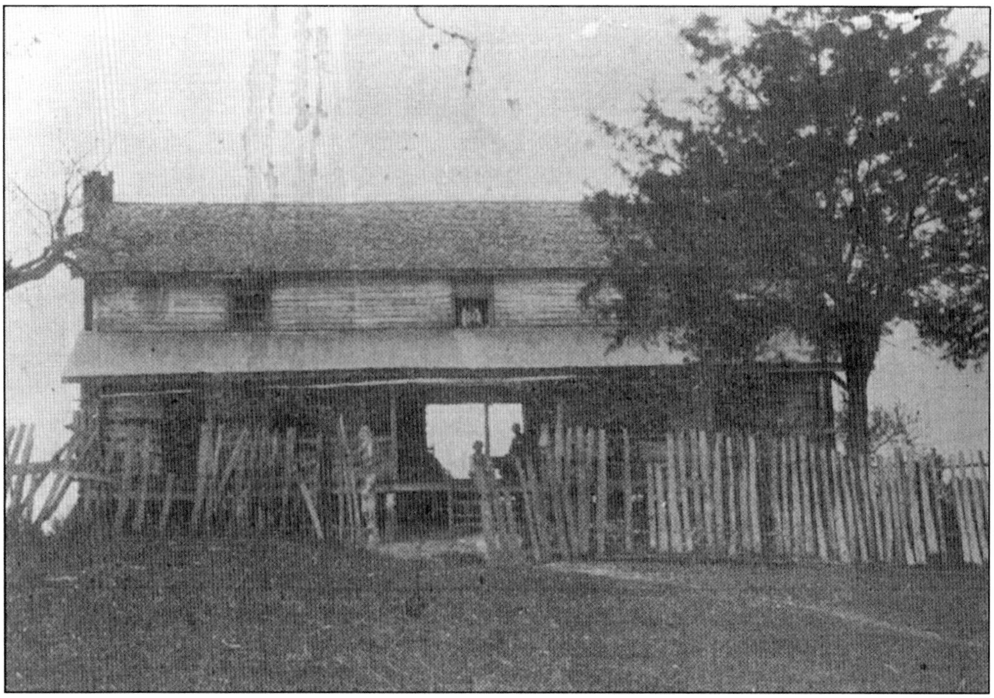

Folsom Inn, which was built on Robinson Road (see page 111) around 1820 by the half Choctaw Indian, David Folsom, was an inn and stagecoach stop. The inn was known for its heavy drinkers and nightly brawls. (JSC.)

Ed Buckner Sr. and the daughter of Mr. and Mrs. Tony snack on their Cracker Jacks while standing on crossties stacked in Longview. Crossties were stacked for more than a mile on both sides of the railroad tracks. Mr. and Mrs. Tony ran a dummy line, which was a scaled-down railroad used to haul crossties. Longview was considered the crosstie capital of the world. Crossties were, and continue to be today, the leading use of hardwood. (AS.)

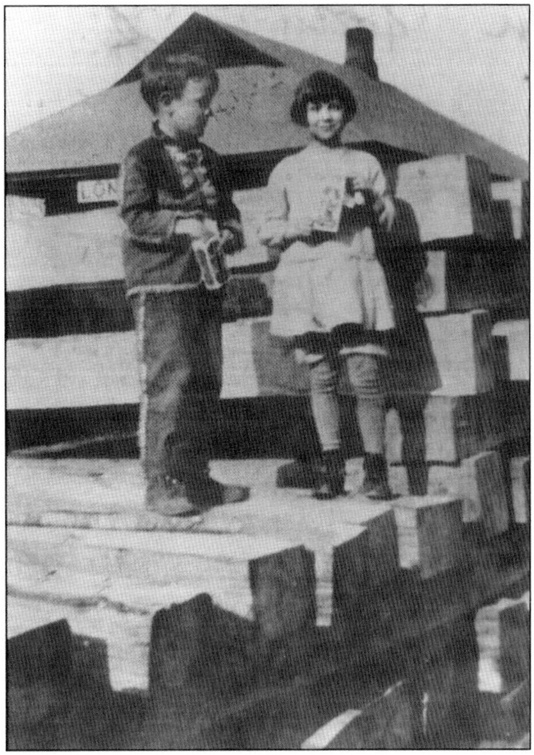

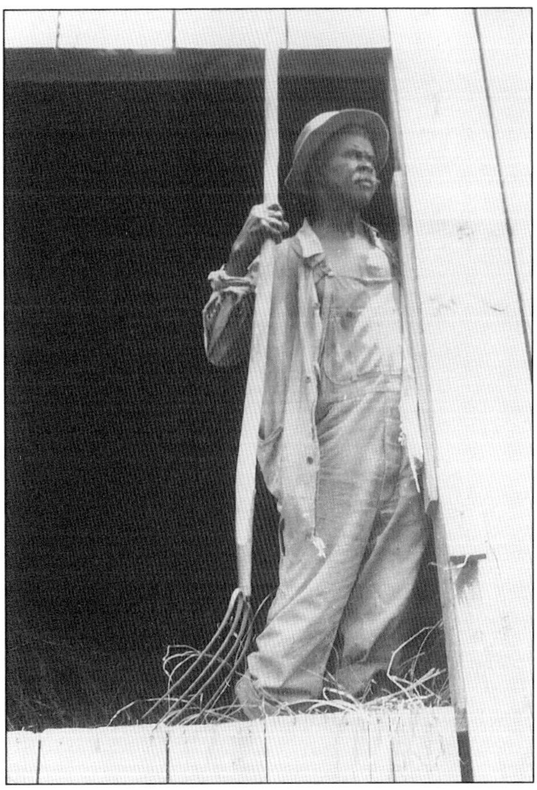

Jordan Carr waits to put hay in a barn located in the Oktoc community. (FB.)

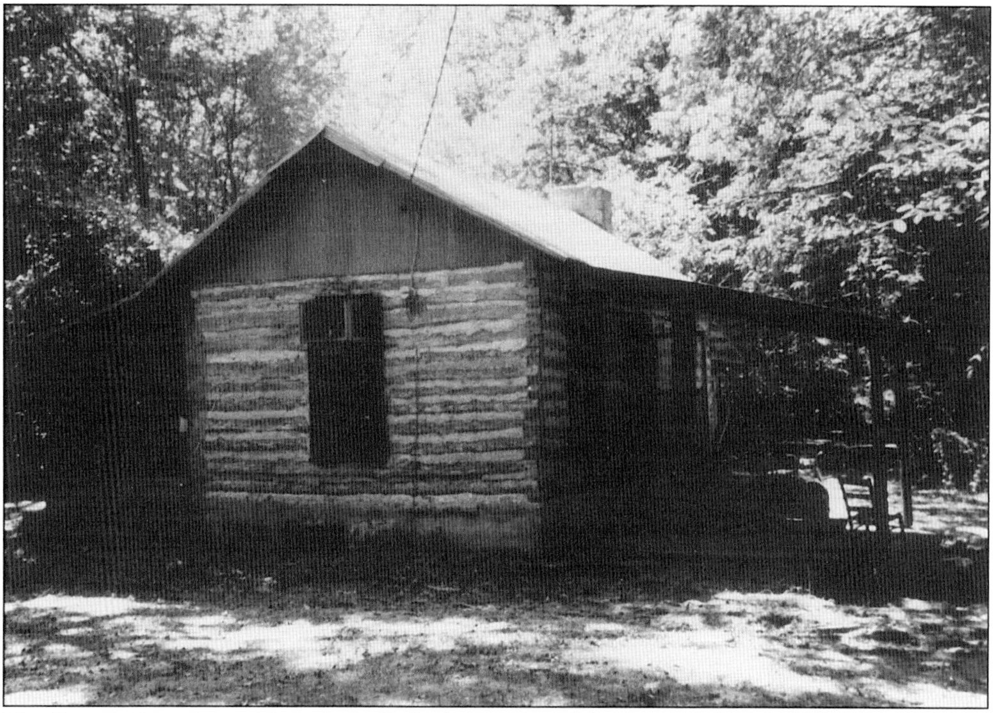

The Beattie Camphouse was originally built in town. When they disassembled the cabin, each log was numbered to help rebuild it in the southeast part of the county. (HB.)

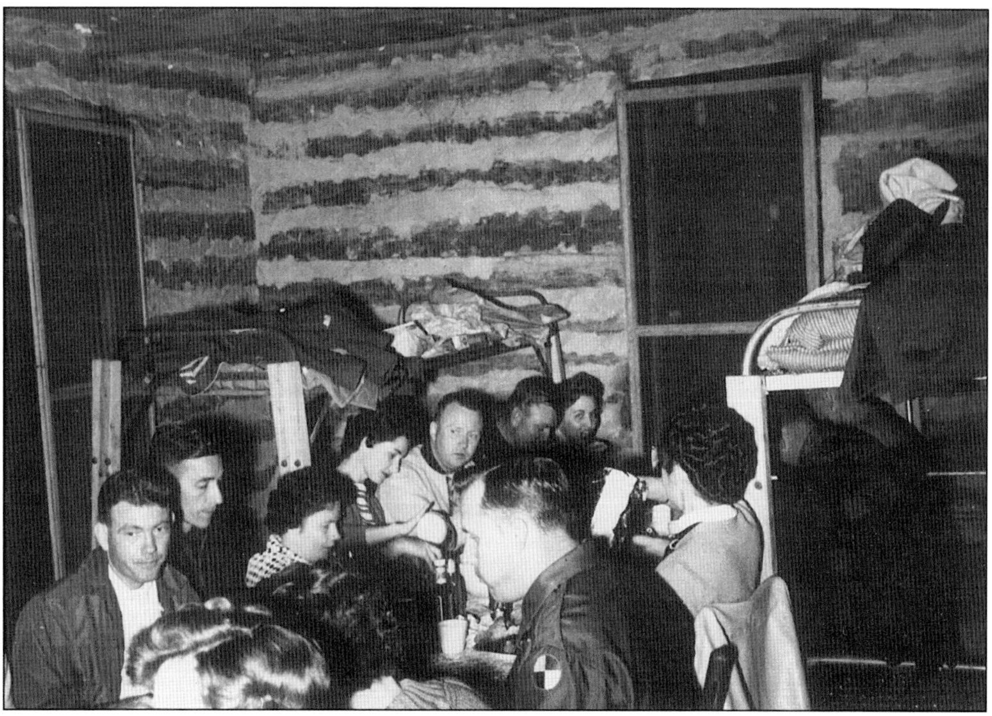

This supper club dines at the Beattie Camphouse, with E.O. Templeton facing front left. (HB.)

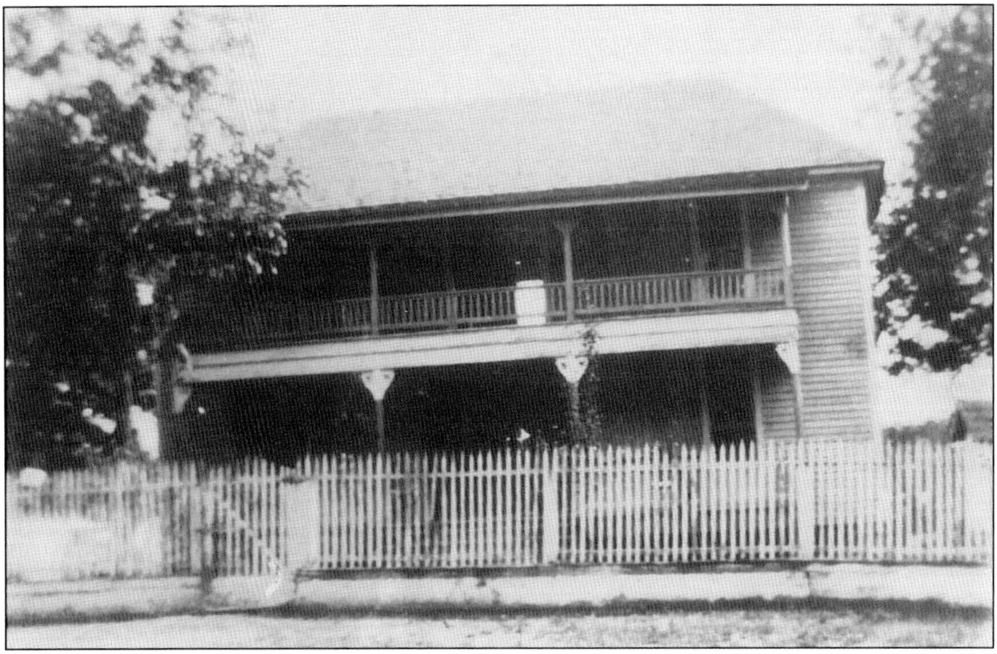

John Christopher, who had 12 children, built his home in the Adaton community, which is 10 miles west of Starkville. Most Adaton community farms were smaller than those in the eastern part of the county. (JW.)

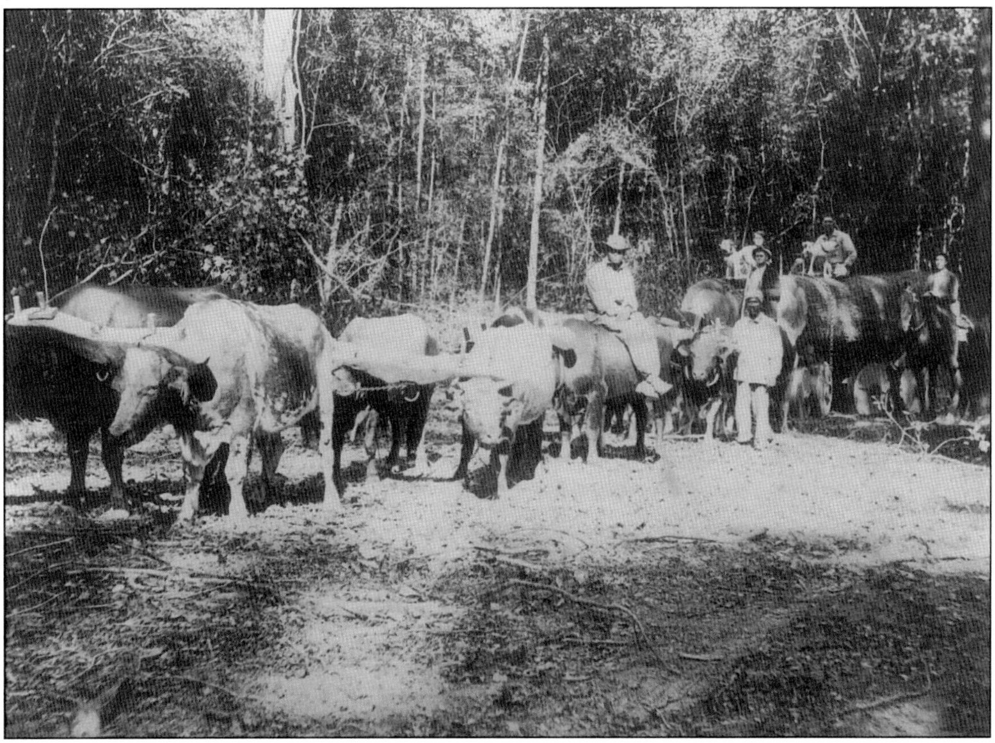

The oxen haul logs, on a wagon with wheels cut from logs, to the southern part of the county, while James M. Gray follows on Keaton Tower Road off of Highway 25. (CJ.)

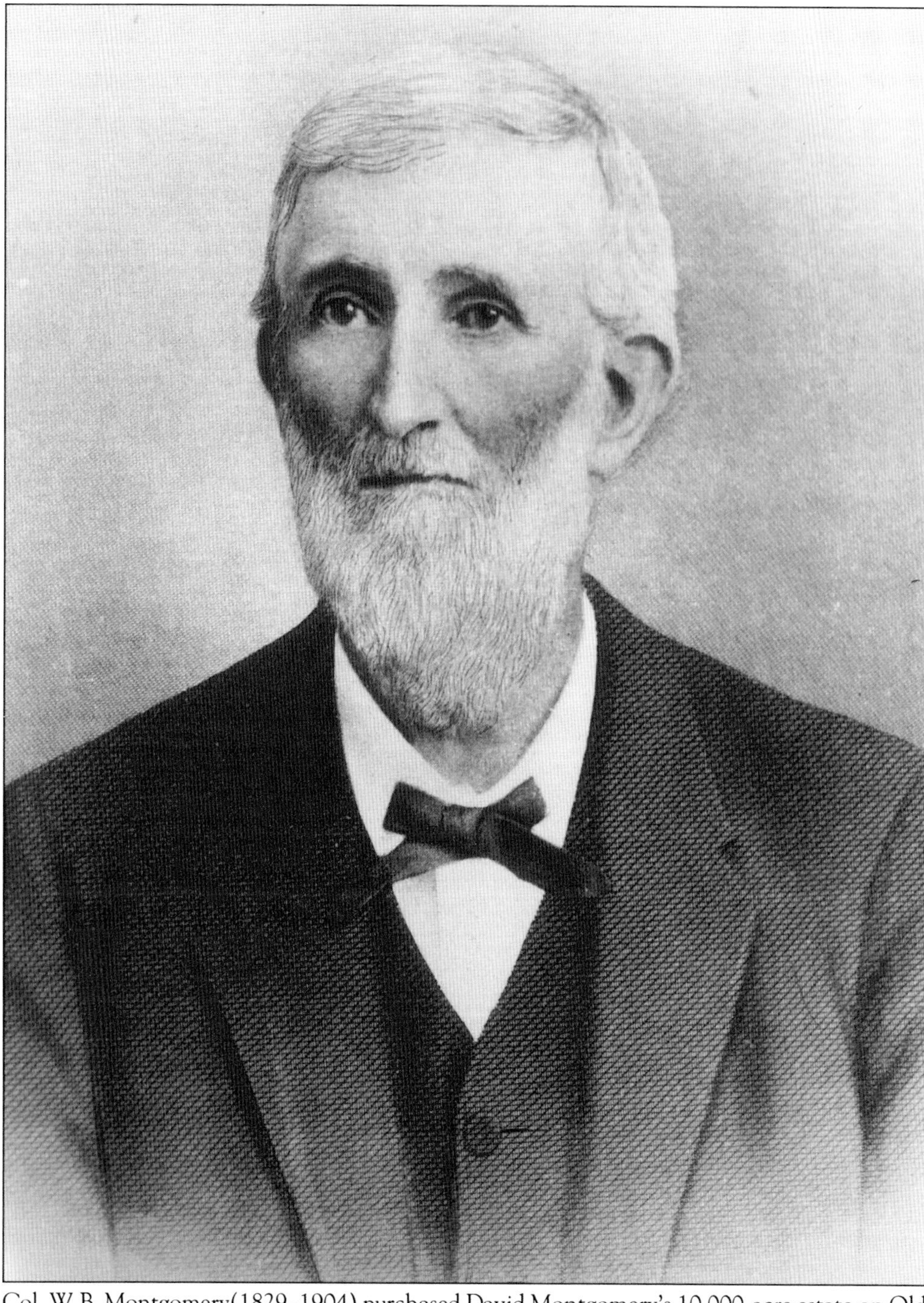

Col. W.B. Montgomery(1829–1904) purchased David Montgomery's 10,000-acre estate on Old West Point Road. Col. Montgomery's contributions to the county included importing the first Jersey cows to Mississippi; owning one of the two underground dairies in the United States; utilizing oxen to churn butter; publishing the *Southern Livestock Journal* in 1880, which was later bought by *Progressive Farmer*; and helping establish A&M College and the Starkville Institute for Women as cited in Judge Carroll's *Historical Sketches of Oktibbeha County*. (EM.)

The Montgomery Home, which was designed by a Dutch architect, was built from 1836 to 1840. The inside walls were 15 inches thick, and the outside walls were 16 inches thick. Upstairs, there were two large rooms divided by massive sliding doors that, when opened, created a spacious ballroom. (RC.)

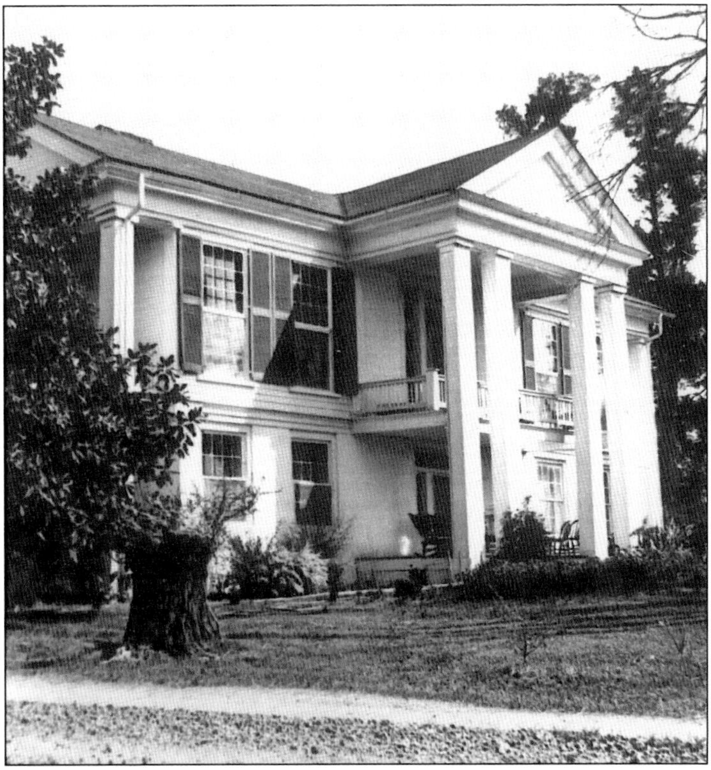

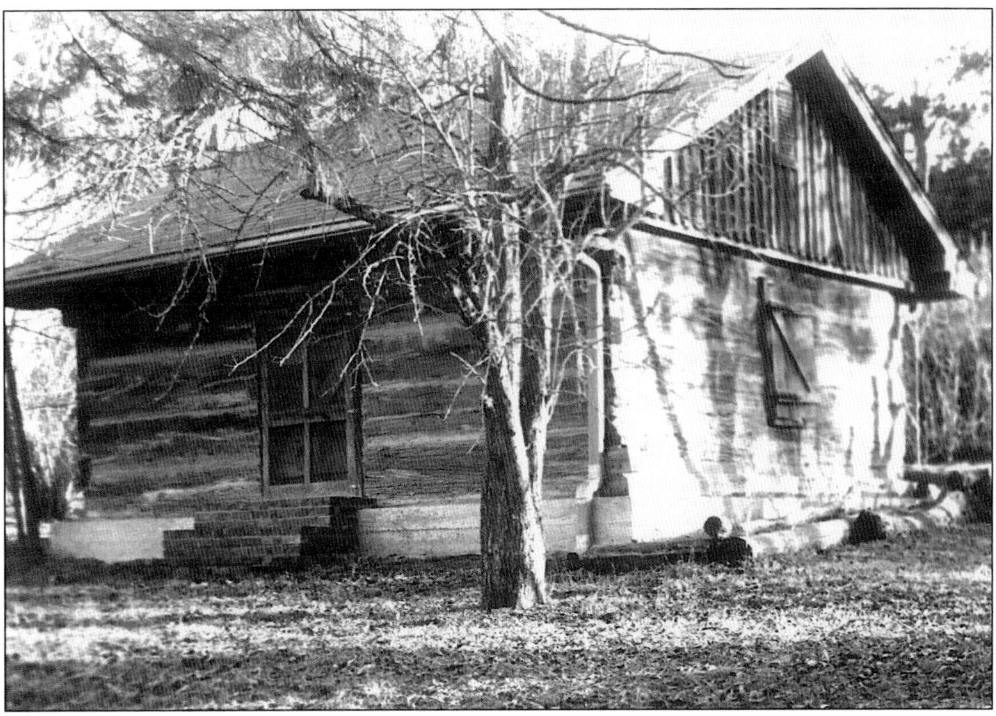

This log cabin housed the Montgomery family while the main house was being built. The cabin was rebuilt in the 1970s. (JSC.)

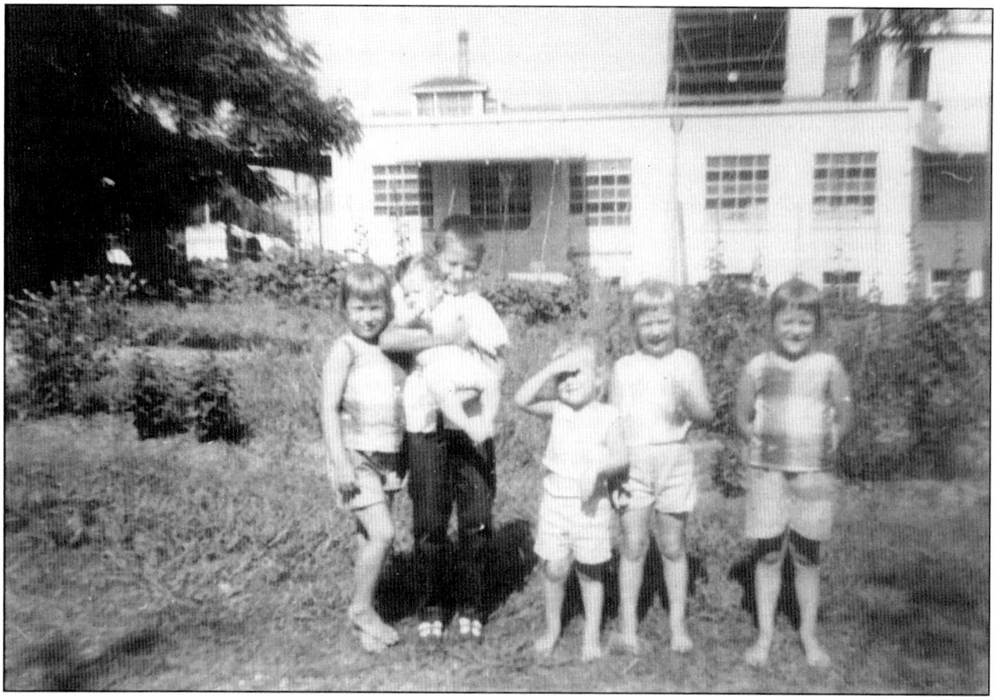

The Blasingame kids stand in front of the Cooperative Creamery, which was located on the east side of Starkville. When the creamery was opened in 1912 by 19 dairymen who owned 250 cows, it was the first of its kind in the nation. It closed in 1972. (EB.)

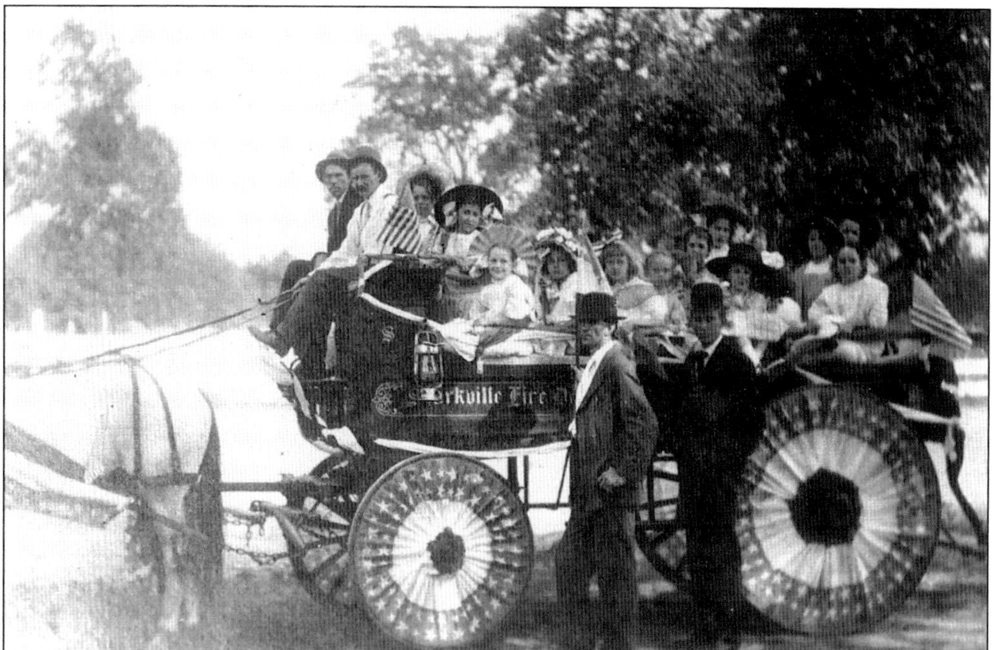

This float was used in a two-day celebration for the Borden plant's 1926 opening. The first day of the celebration on March 10th was for the white people, and the second day, March 11th, was for the black people, as cited in the February 12, 1926 edition of the *Starkville News.* (CR.)

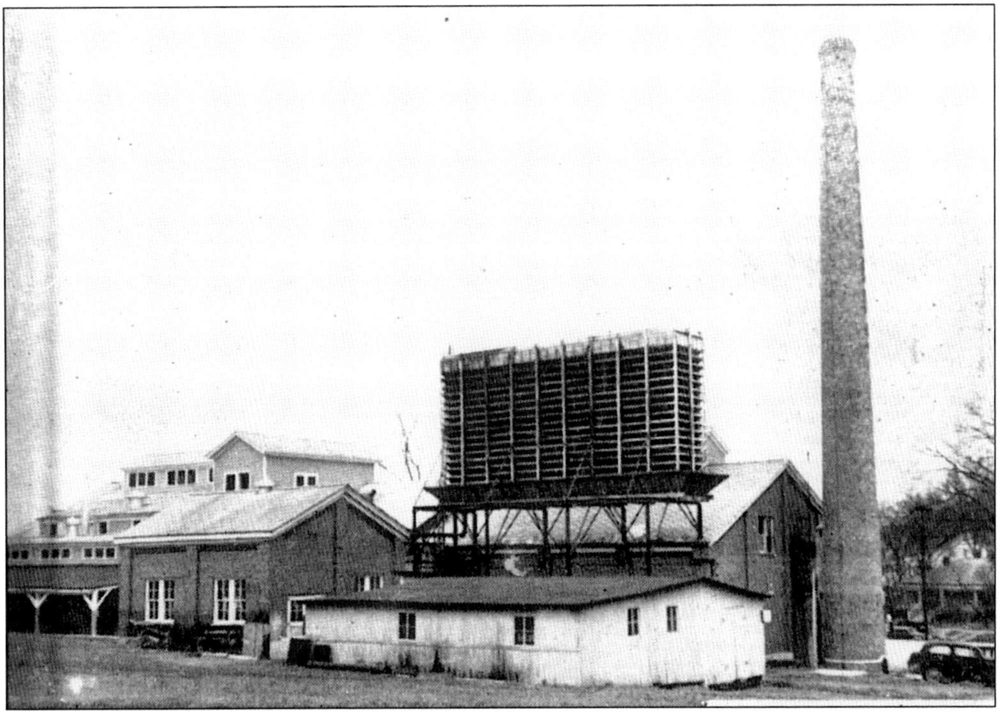

When it opened in 1926, Borden cost $300,000 to build and equip and was the first milk condenser plant south of the Mason-Dixon line. (OHM.)

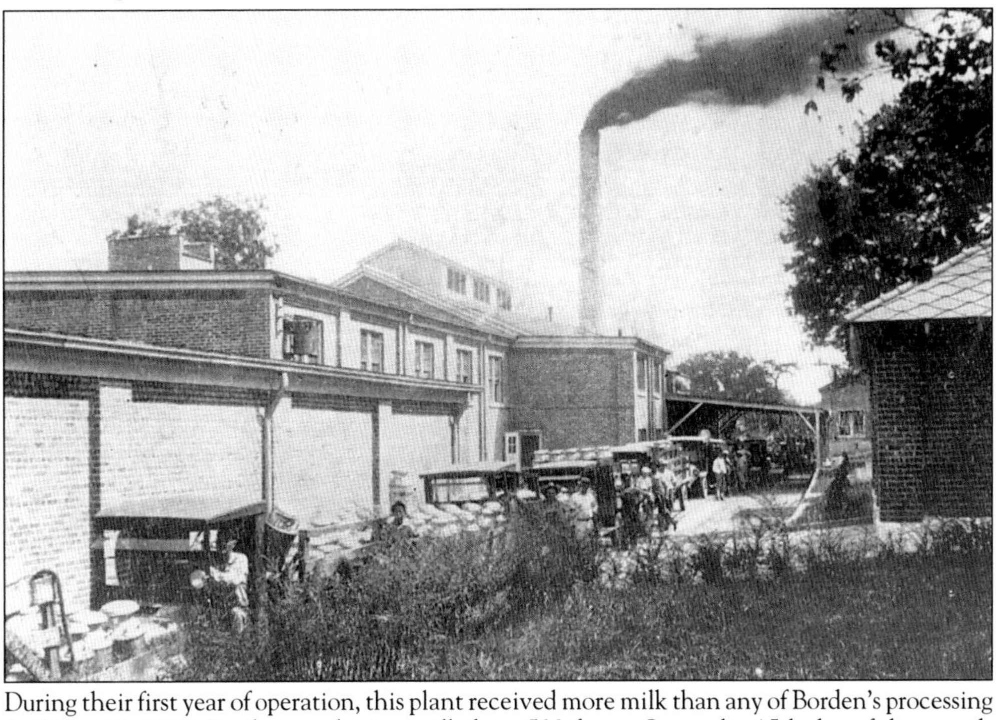

During their first year of operation, this plant received more milk than any of Borden's processing facilities. By 1929, Borden was buying milk from 500 farms. Soon, the 15th day of the month became known as milk payday. (OHM.)

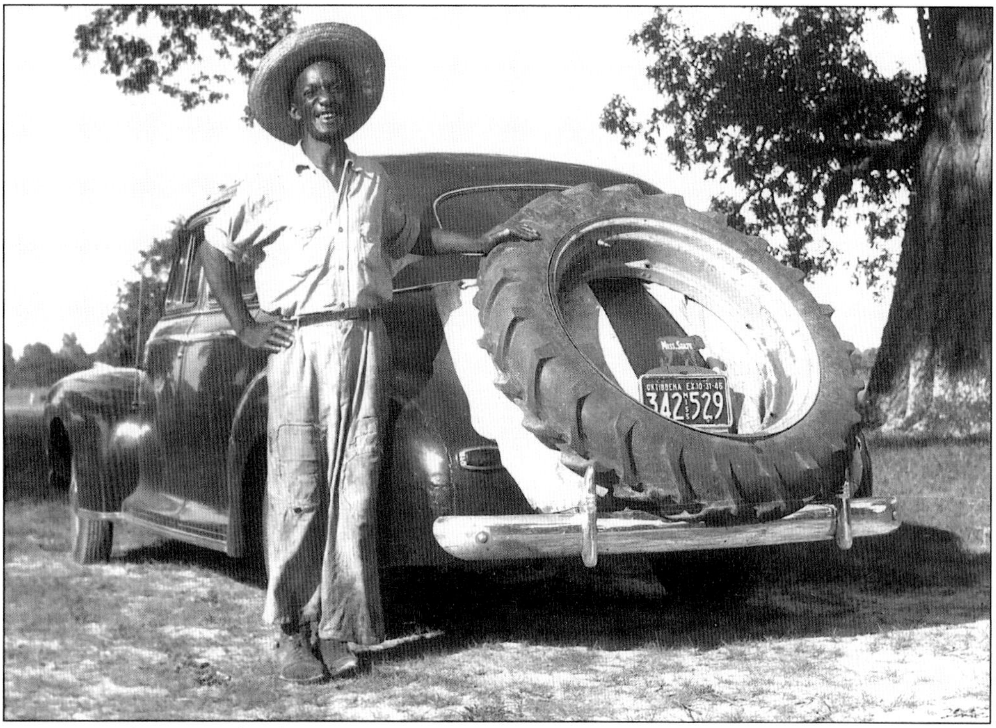

A man uses his car to haul a tractor tire. During the spring, many people converted their cars into trucks to haul cans of milk. Sometimes the cans were tied to the bumper of the car. (FB.)

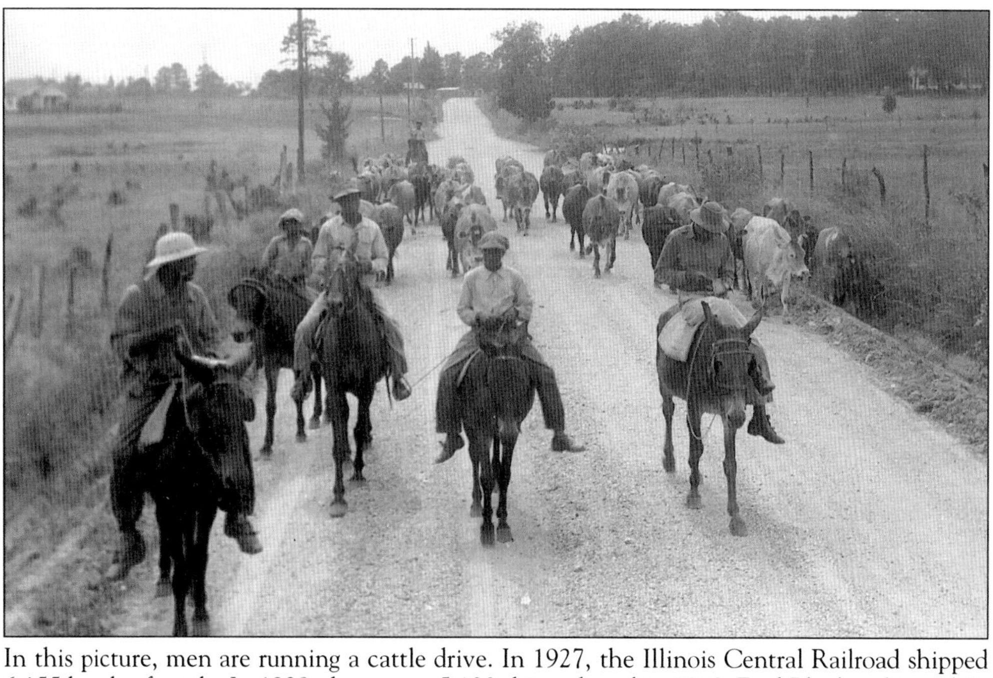

In this picture, men are running a cattle drive. In 1927, the Illinois Central Railroad shipped 6,155 heads of cattle. In 1928, there were 5,100 shipped, and in 1948, Fred Blocker shipped 15 train cars of cattle in one day. (FB.)

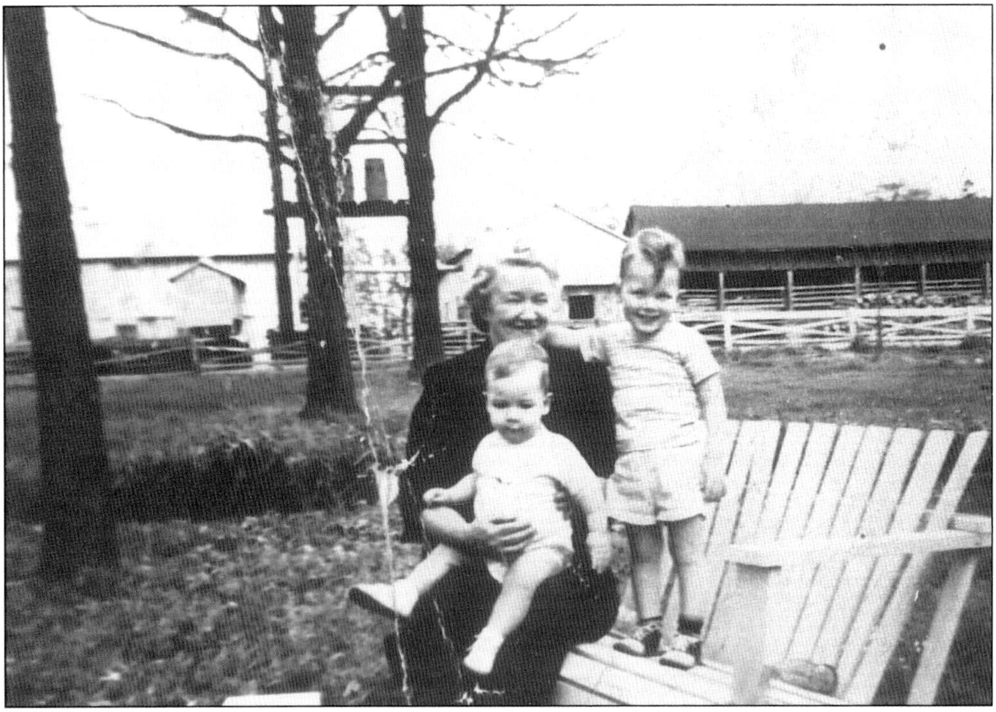

Bob and Jim McKee are pictured on Russell Street in front of the cattle pens, which sat next to the GM&O railroad station. (JM.)

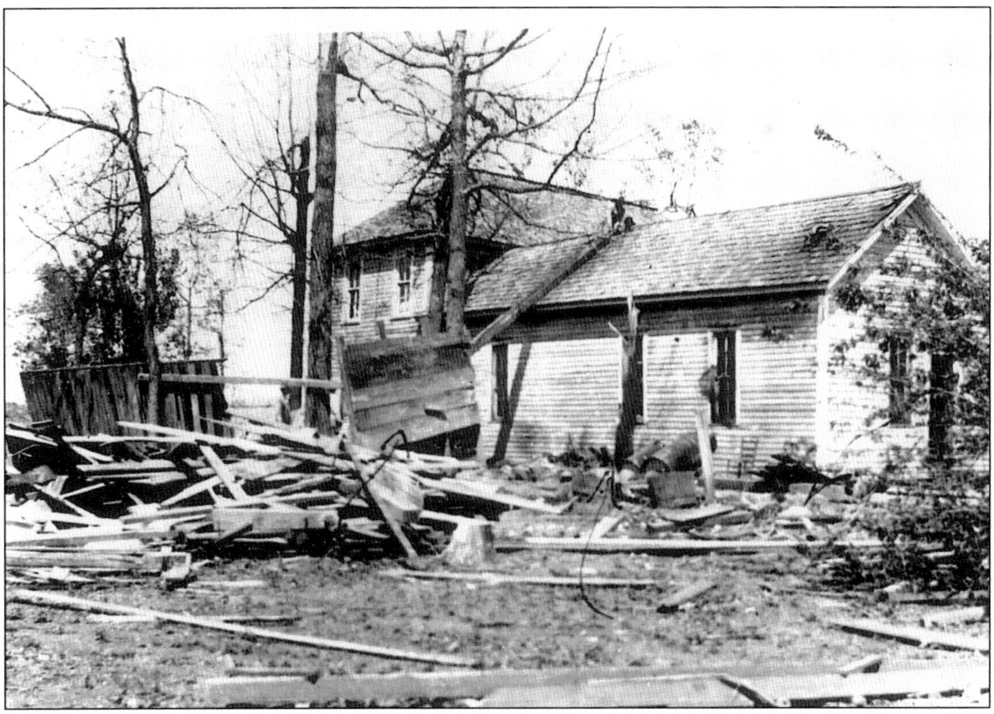

A 1921 cyclone hit the Christopher Home, located in the Adaton community (see page 33). This cyclone destroyed many houses and the school at Self Creek. (JW.)

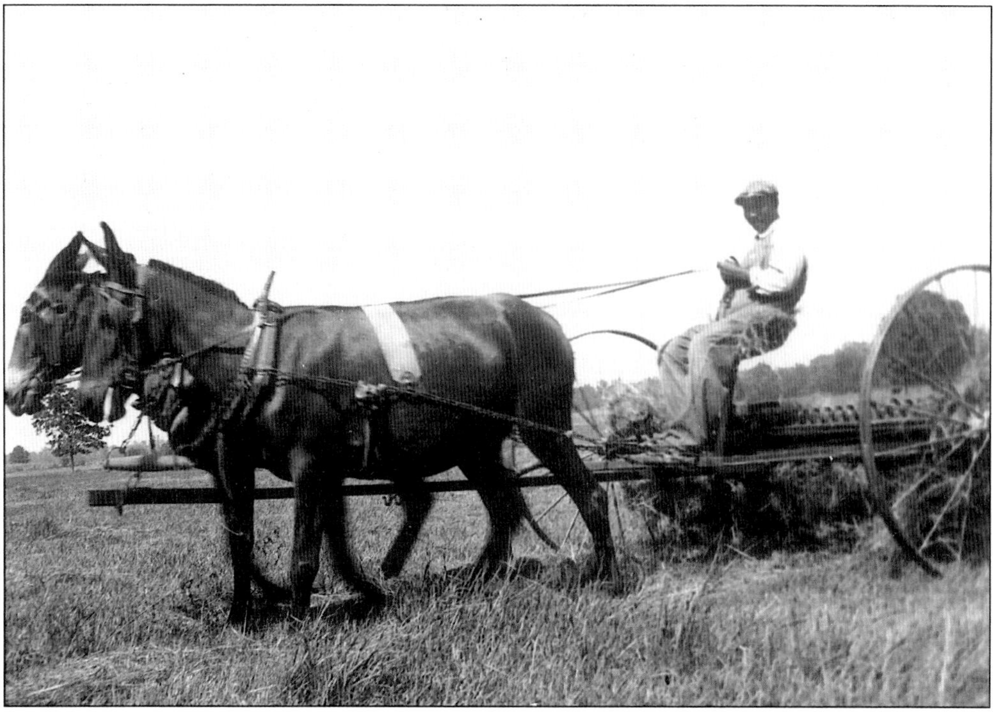

Farmers, like Sammy Gandy, used their mules to work from sun-up to sun-down, hauling in hay. (FB.)

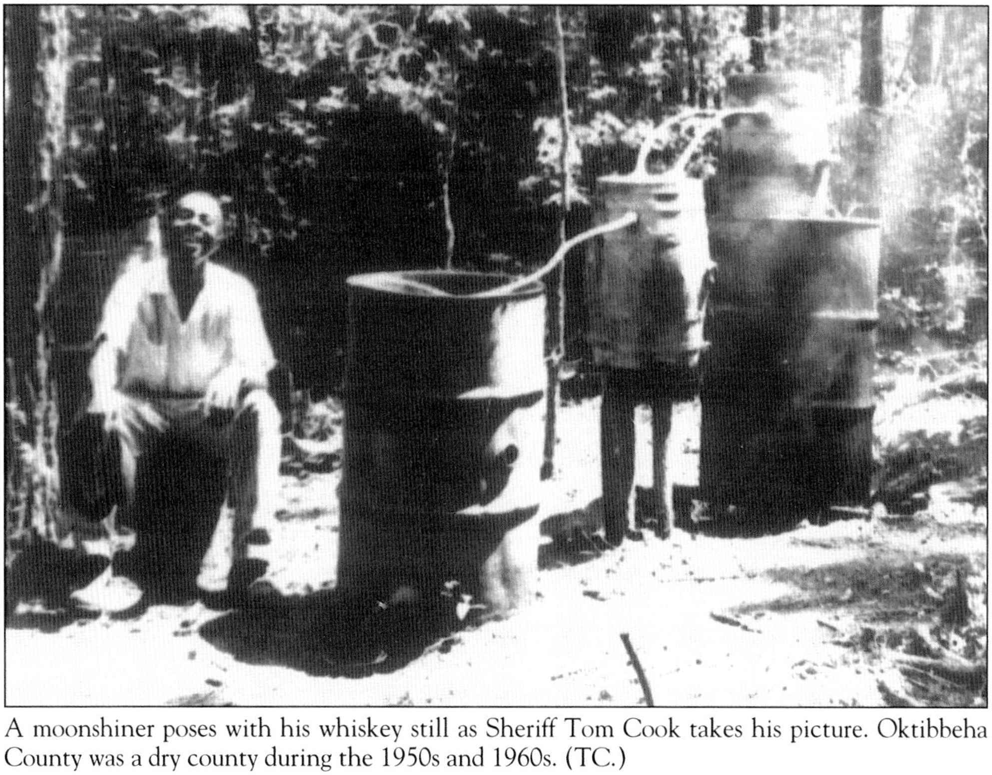

A moonshiner poses with his whiskey still as Sheriff Tom Cook takes his picture. Oktibbeha County was a dry county during the 1950s and 1960s. (TC.)

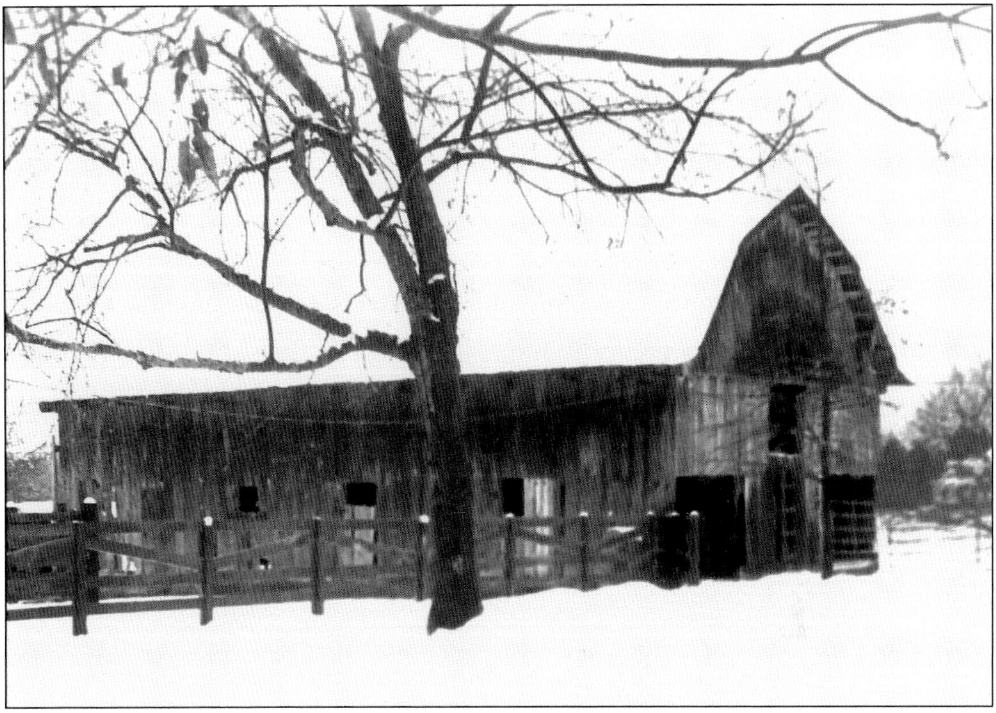

Barns were built as the dairy industry grew in the county. (JSC.)

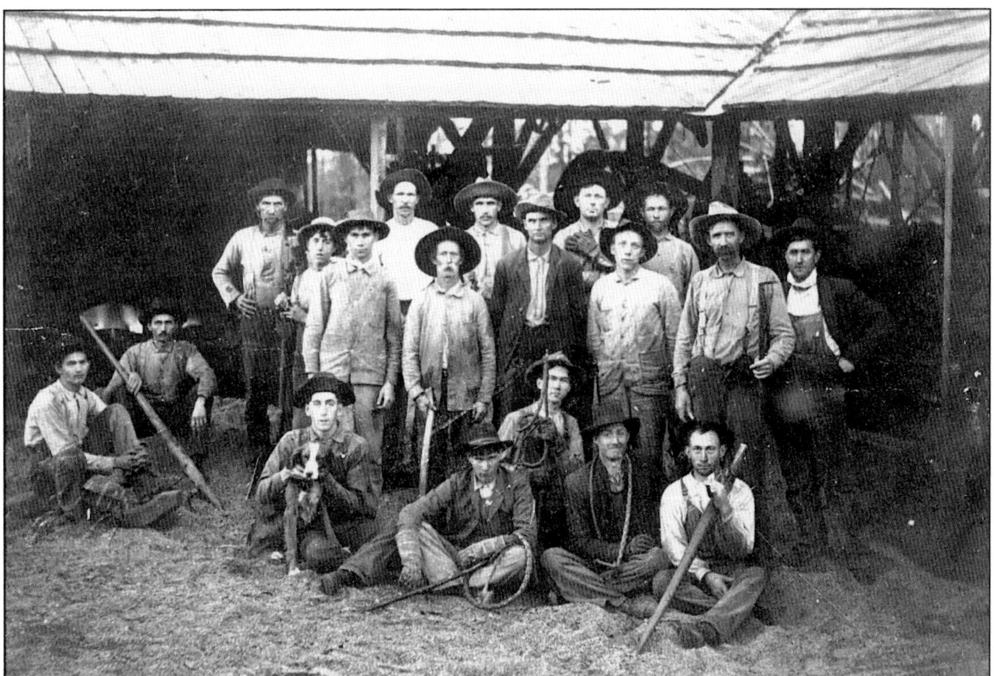

Jack Cotton's sawmill stayed busy with the high demand for wood. (OHM.)

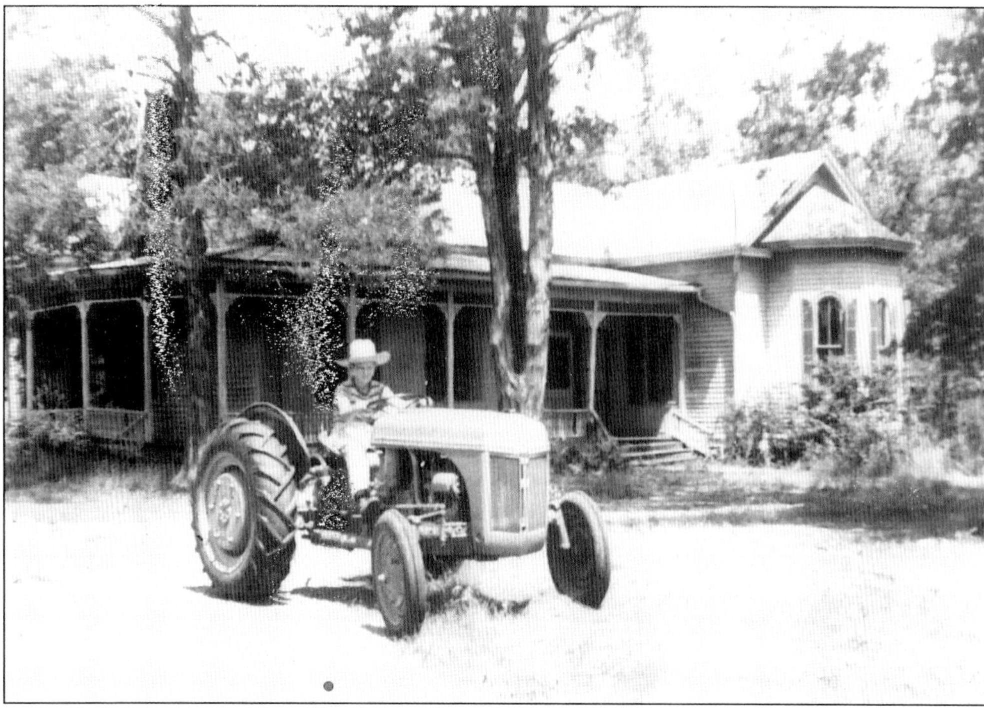

A Ford tractor was used on the Garth Farm, which was located in the northeast section of the county, next to Camp's Airport. (RC.)

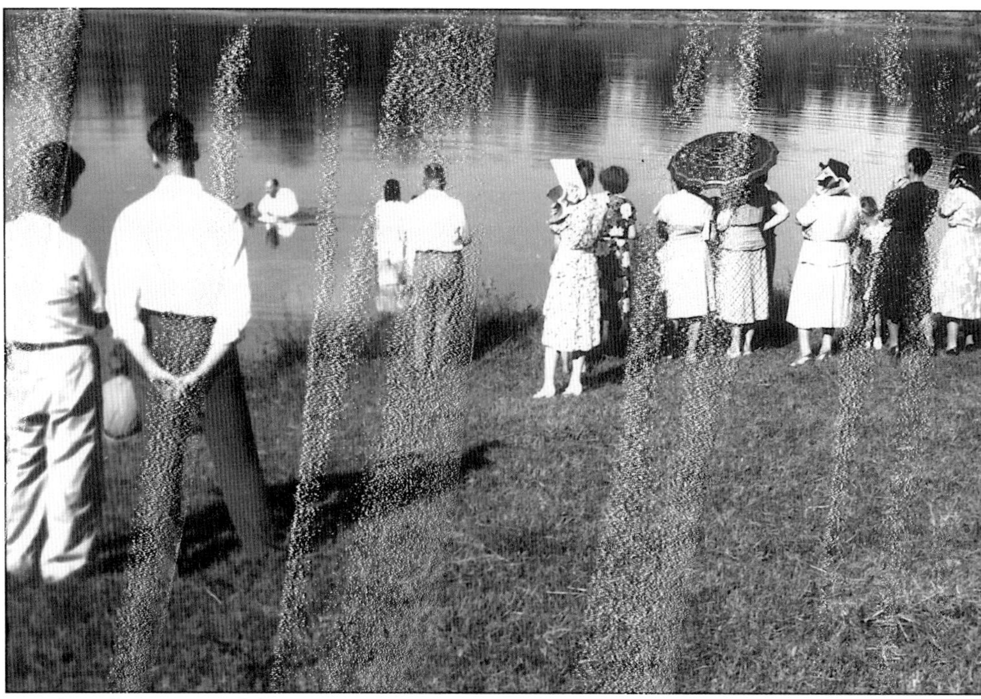

People gather at one of the many Oktoc ponds for a baptism in the early 1960s. (FB.)

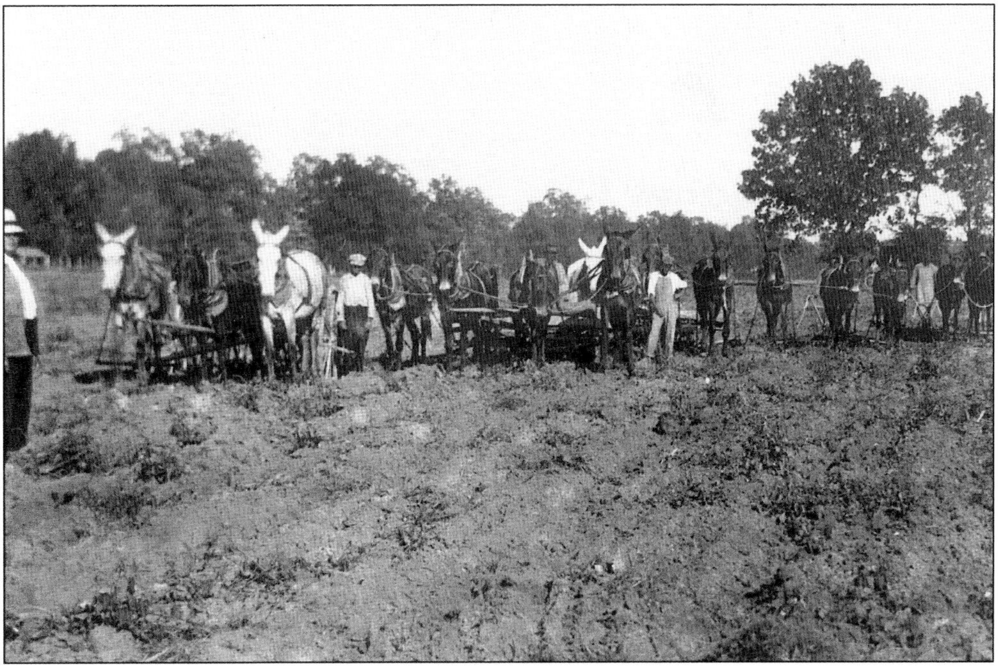

Mules plow the planting fields on the Clardy Farm. In 1919, cotton was sold for 40¢ per pound. The price dropped to 17¢ in 1921. By 1926, when the price for cotton was 10¢ per pound, farmers were thankful to see the Borden plant move to Starkville because it meant opportunities for Oktibbeha County farmers in the dairy industry. (OHM.)

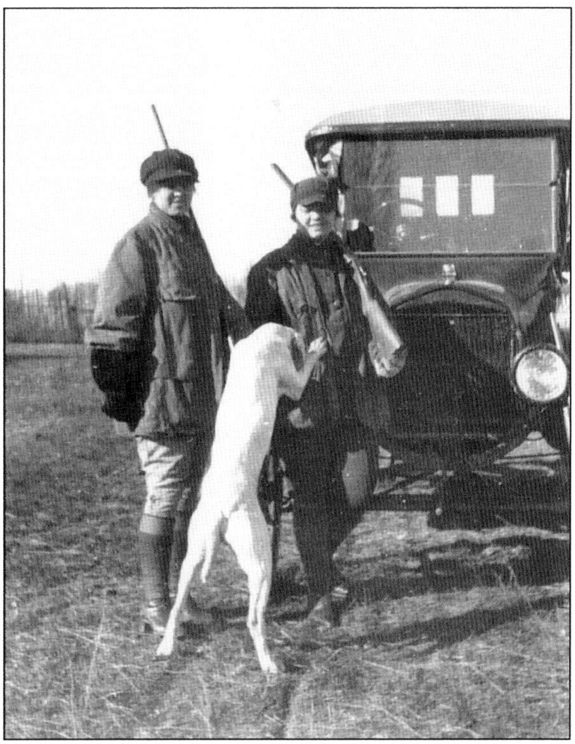

These hunters prepare their dogs for a favorite pastime. (JSC.)

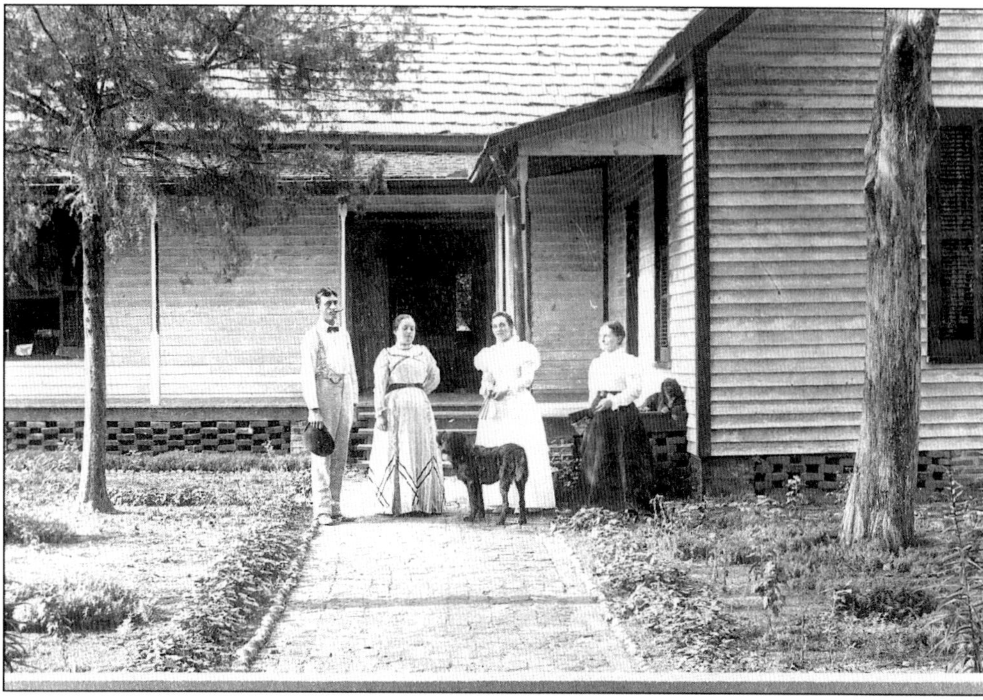

The Sellars Home, which is located in the Bell Schoolhouse community, started as a log cabin in 1823. The porch is believed to be built over a Native American chief's grave. (PS.)

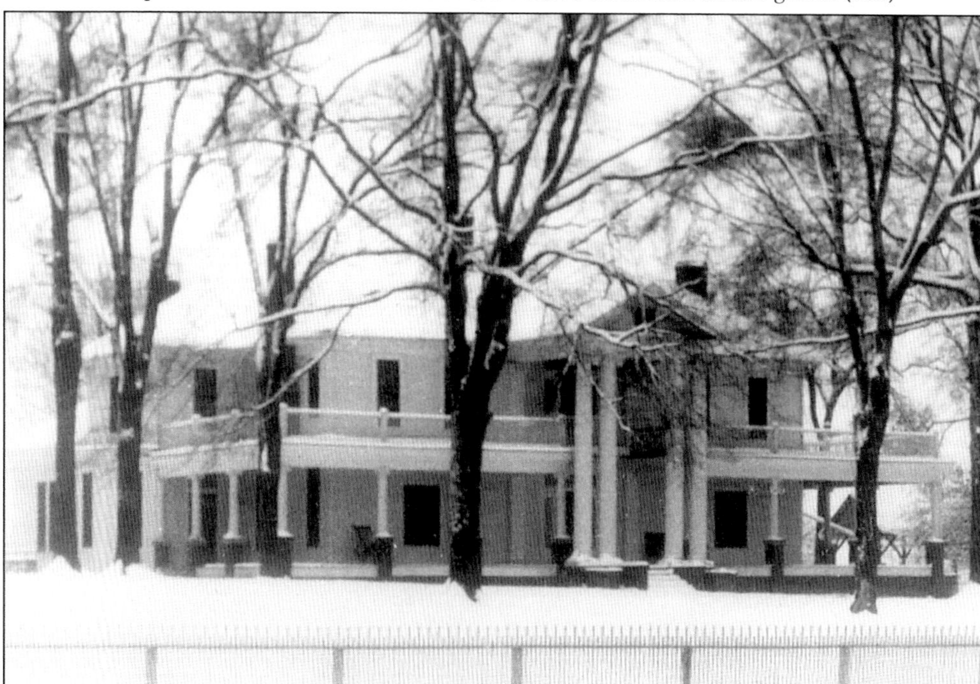

Located in Sessums, the southeast part of the county, the Young Home, later known as the Rogers Home, burned in the early 1960s. After the fire, gold coins that were hid during the Civil War were discovered in the chimney. (OHM.)

L.L. "Moon" Mullins, our late district commissioner, promoted tree farming and initiated Tree Planting Week in Oktibbeha County in 1970. (SM.)

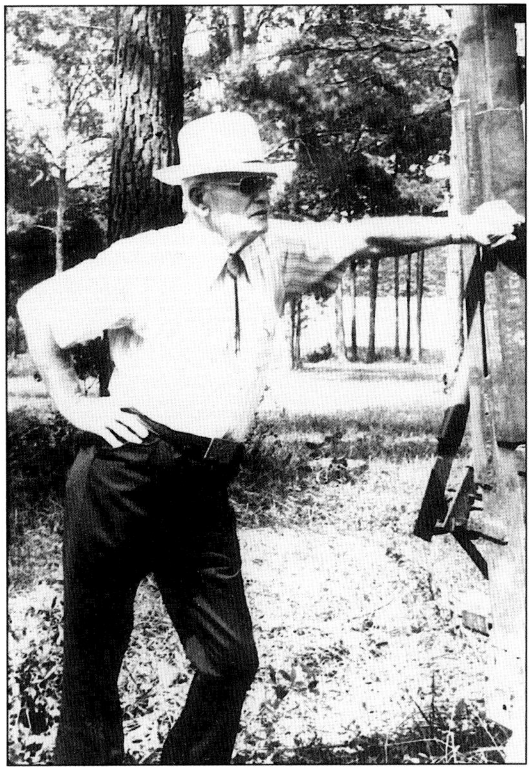

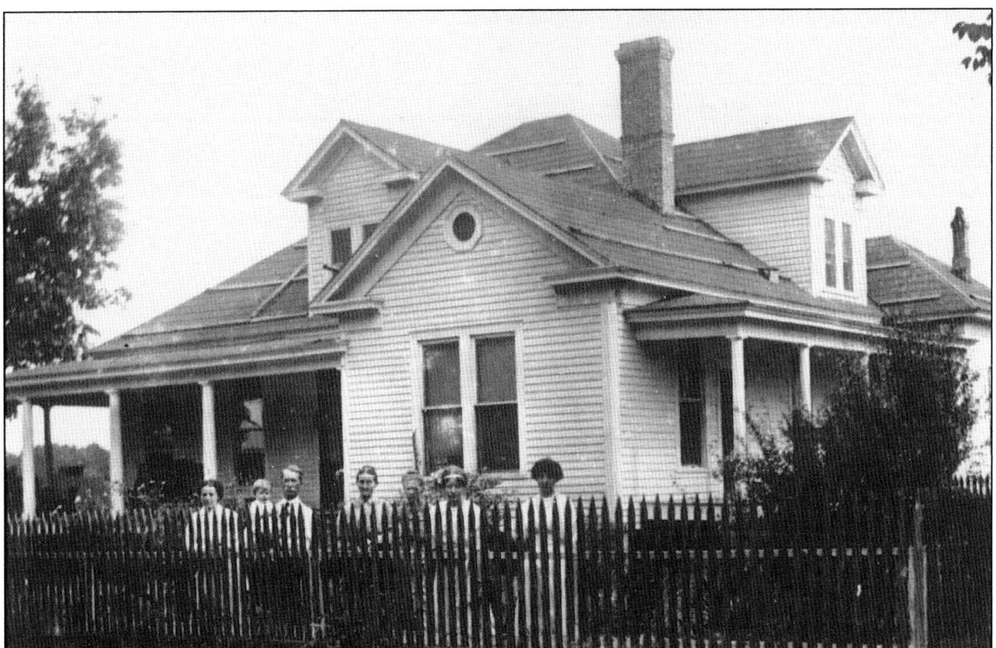

The Jimmy Thomas House, which was located in the Adaton community, was later owned by Memory and Salley Kellum. The house was destroyed by fire in 1938. Slates were often used on steep roofs to help workers keep their footing. (JK.)

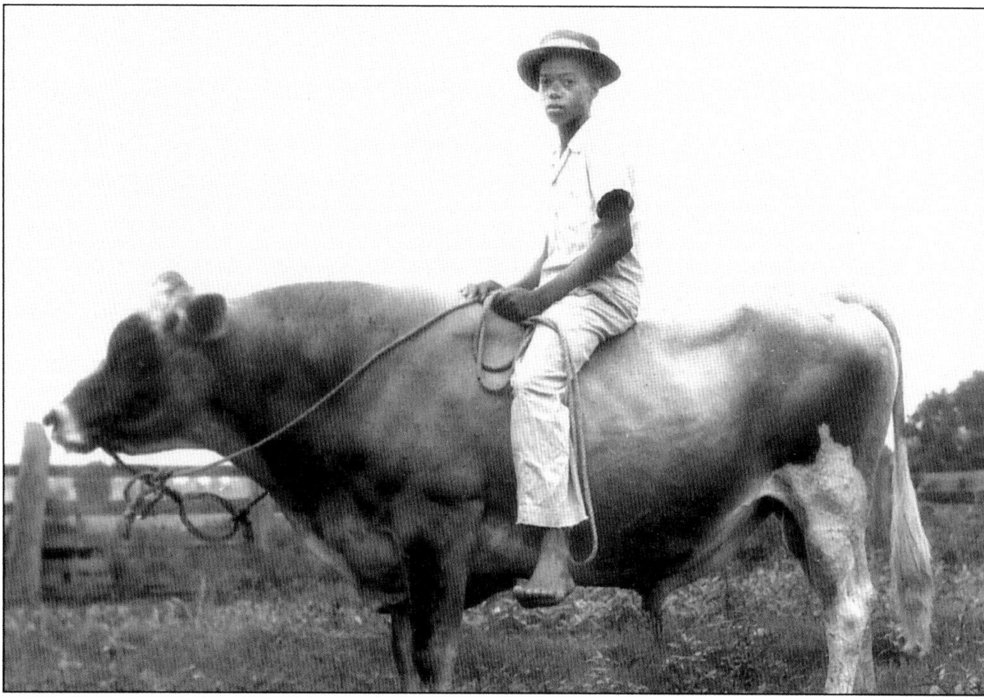

Around 1940, a young man sits bareback on a Jersey bull in the Oktoc community. Riding bulls was a favorite pastime in the county. (FB.)

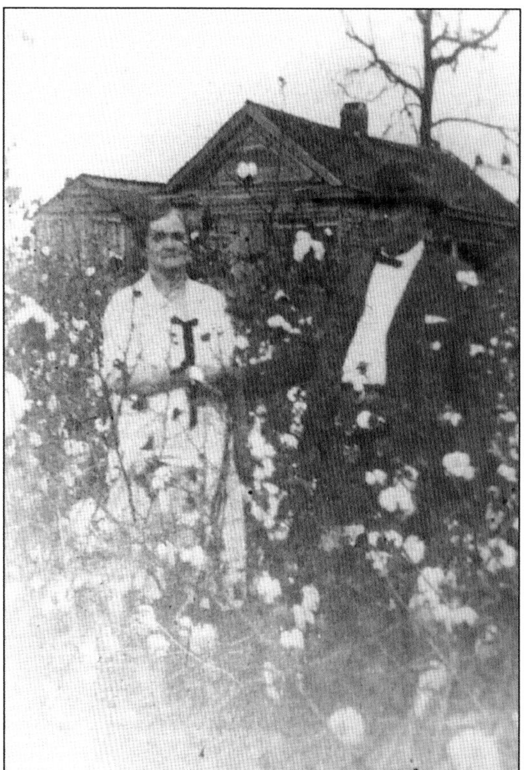

William Henry Sudduth (8/25/1869–11/22/1960) and Eula Temperance Russell (5/6/1876–6/23/1938), who were later married on September 6, 1893, stand in a cotton field on Reed Road, which is located in northwest Starkville. (MB.)

Three

STARKVILLE: THE COUNTY SEAT

First known as Boardtown, Starkville was originally located 2 miles down Reed Road, which is in northwest Starkville. In 1835, Starkville moved to its current location and became the county seat. Even with its bad roads and few existing frame stores, Starkville became the center of activity in the county. After the 1875 downtown fire, Main Street was widened to its present size. When the Mobile and Ohio railroad was built in 1874, Starkville experienced a boost in its economy.

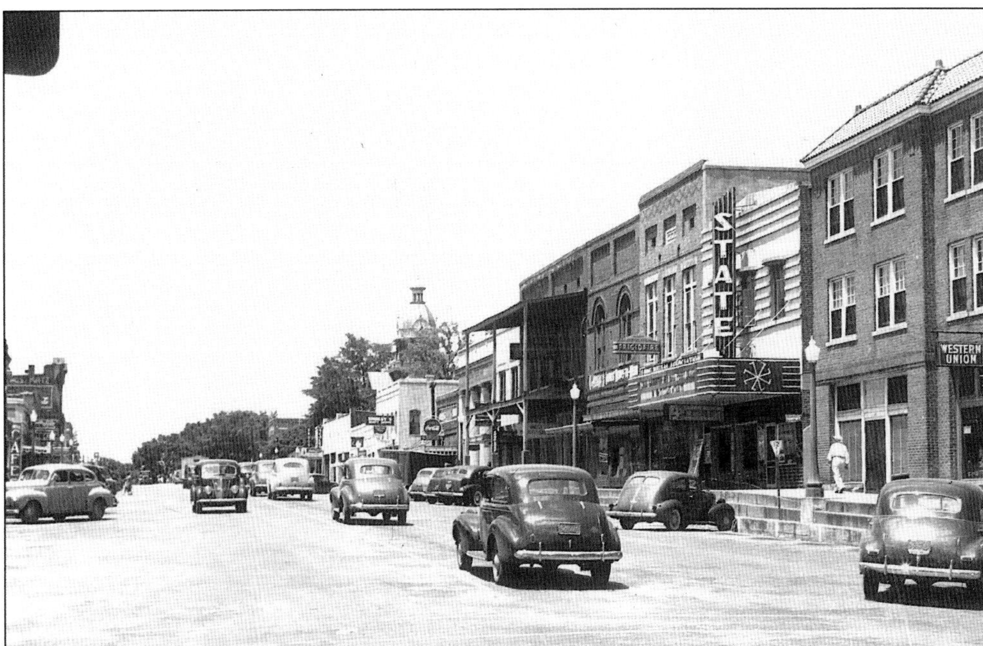

This 1947 picture of Main Street includes the State Theatre, which was built in 1937 at the former location of Rex Theatre and the double-decked awning, which fell January 1947, killing 20-year-old Evelyn Simpson Bullock. Mrs. Bullock's mother was working across the street at the time of the accident. (FB.)

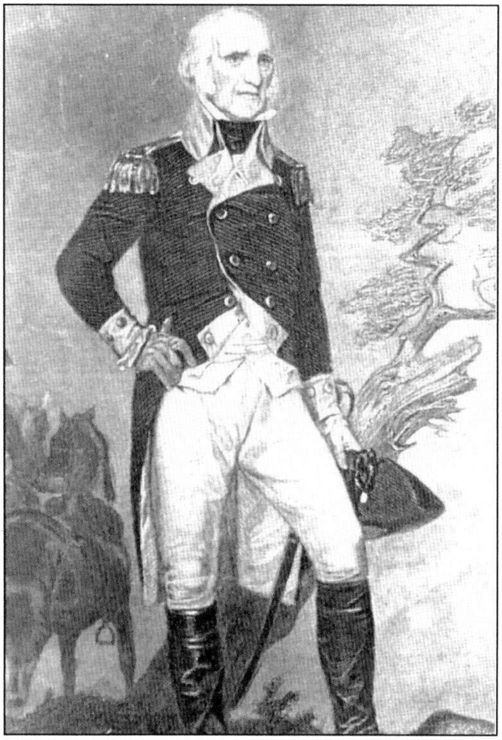

Although the Revolutionary War hero John Stark never visited Mississippi, he still receives credit for Starkville's name. (BS.)

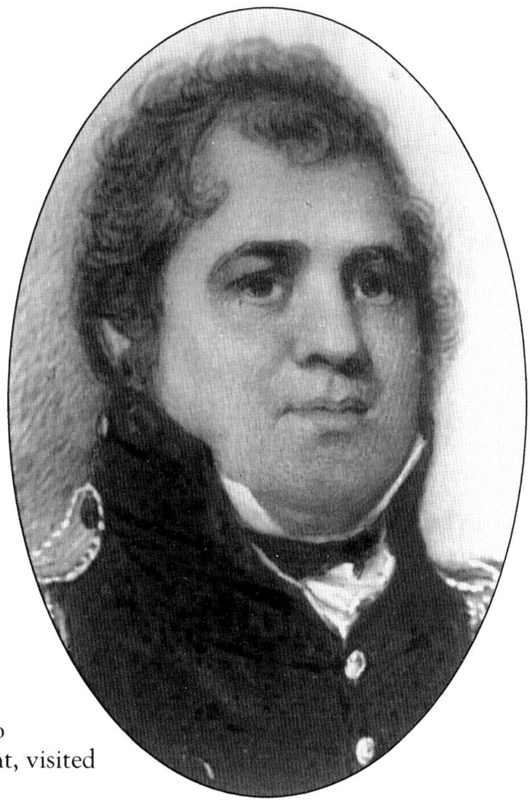

It is more likely that Starkville bears Horatio Stark's name. Stark, a Choctaw Indian Agent, visited this area often. (BS.)

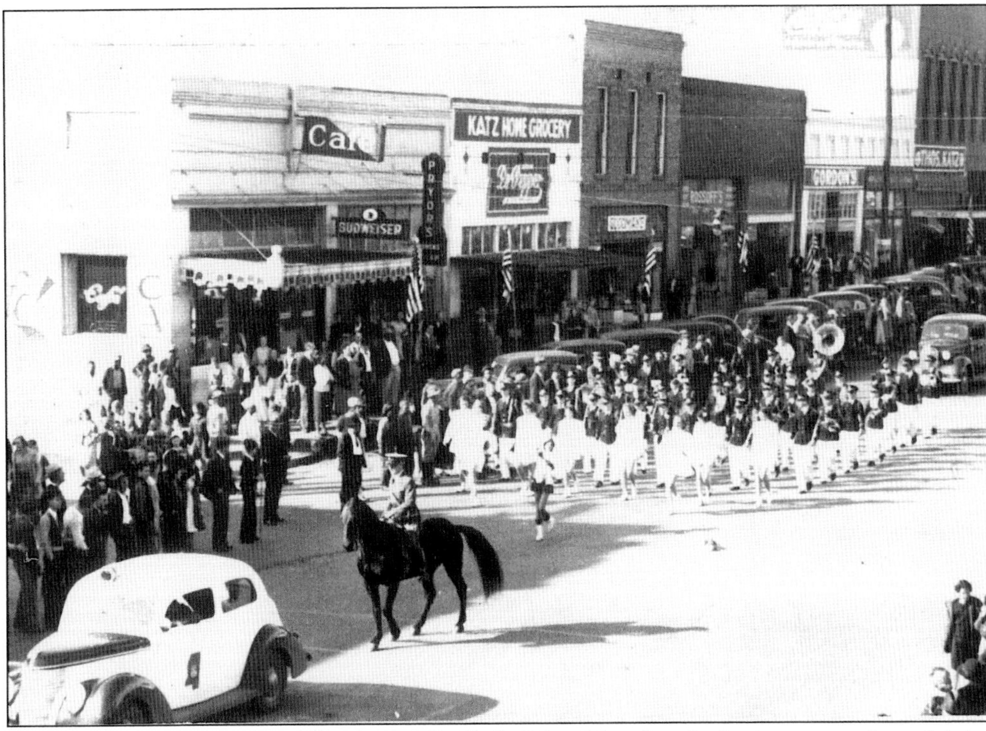

This 1939 parade consists of the Starkville High School band and a highway patrol car. Lining Main Street are many of the Jewish merchants' stores, including Katz, Goodman, Rossoff, Gordon's, and Kleban's. (SM.)

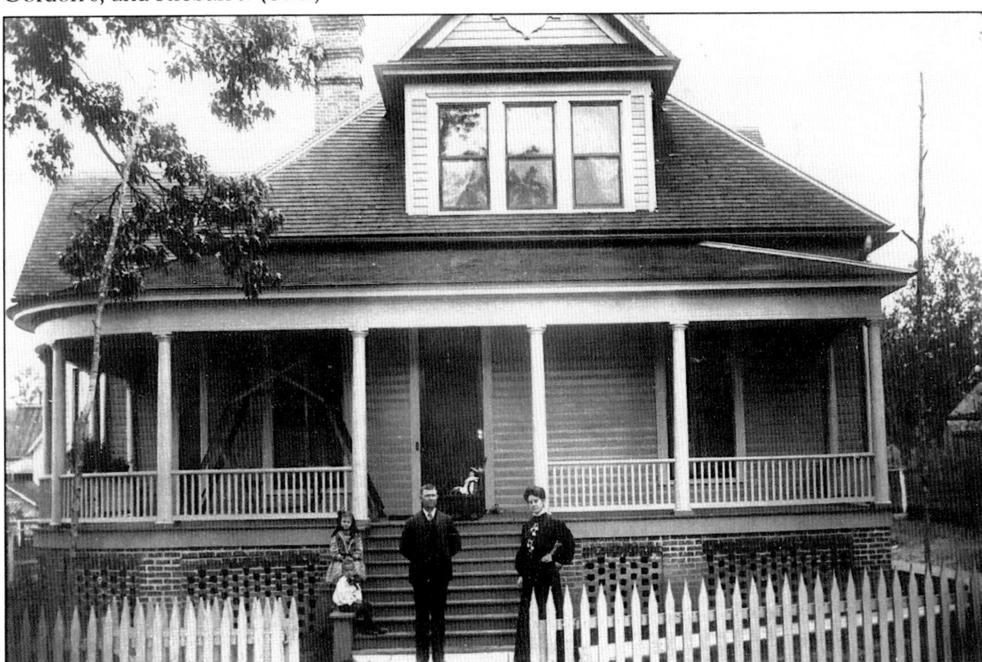

Sumpter Camp's father's home was torn down to build the First Baptist Church parking lot. Standing in front of the home in 1910 are members of the Camp family. (RC.)

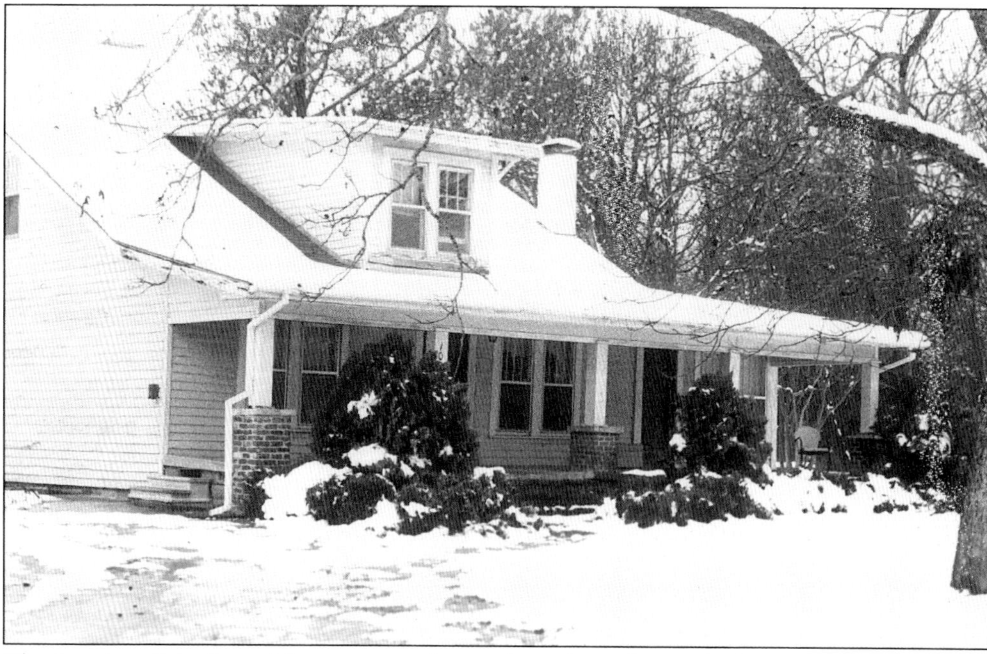

The interior of the Josey House was made up of two log cabins, which were rolled on logs to Reed Road in 1905. One of the cabins was used as the first county courthouse in 1834. Near the courthouse was Starkville's first jail, which had no doors. Prisoners were lowered by rope through a hole in the floor. (JSC.)

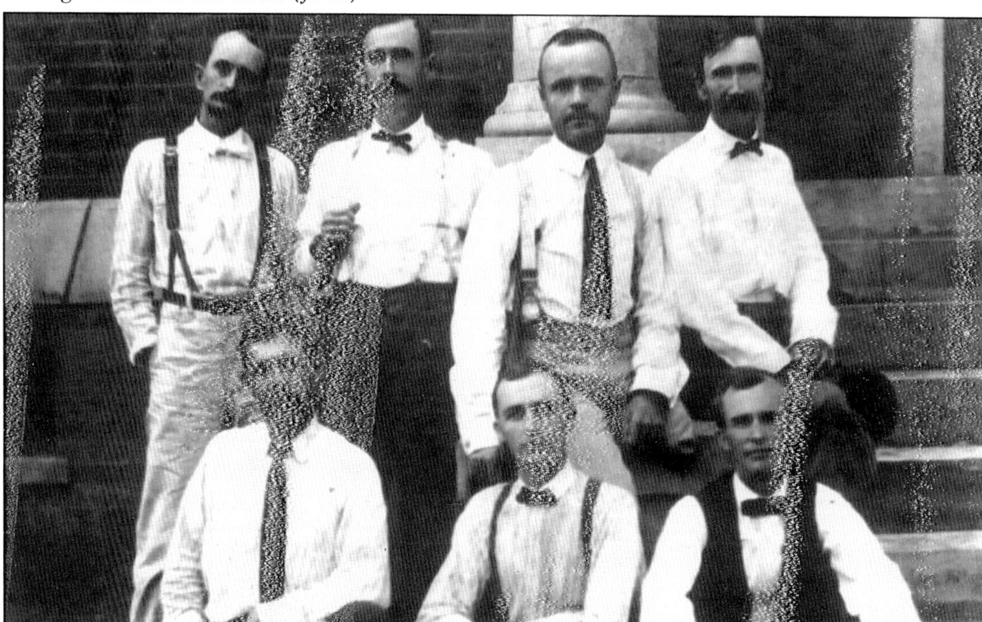

Pictured in front of the courthouse in 1907 are the following, from left to right: (front row) J.L. Lucas, county assessor; E.O. McIlwain, chancery clerk; and Wick Edward, sheriff; (back row) J.H. Welborn, state representative; M.R. Fulgham, circuit clerk; E.A. Buckner, county treasurer; and W.H. Miller, superintendent of education. (EBS.)

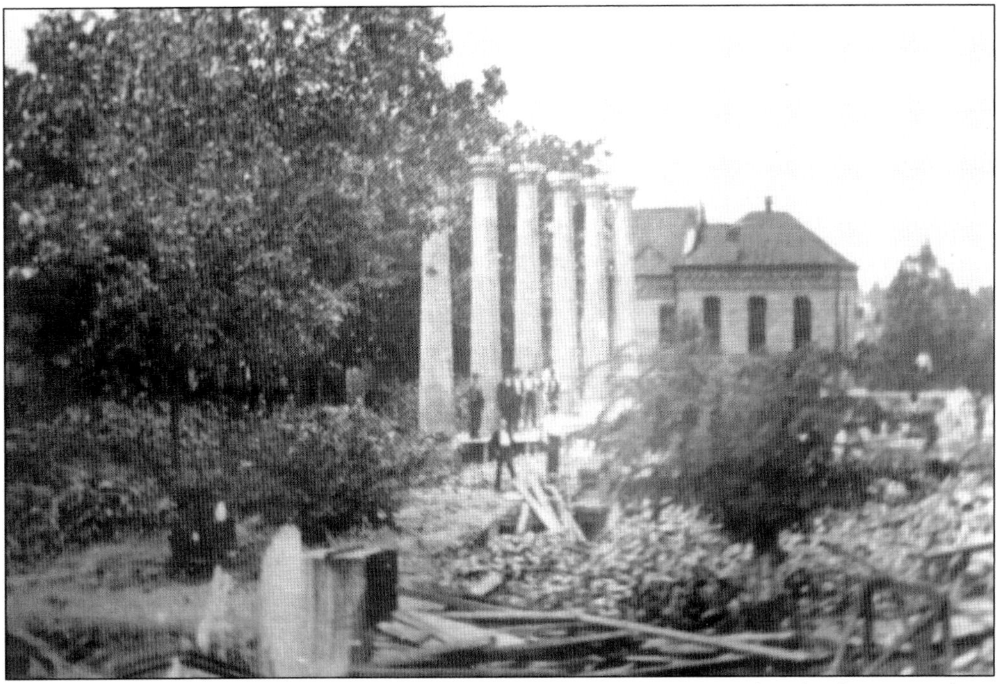

The courthouse and jail are pictured after the 1875 fire. To prevent another fire from spreading, each business donated frontage to widen Main Street. (JSC.)

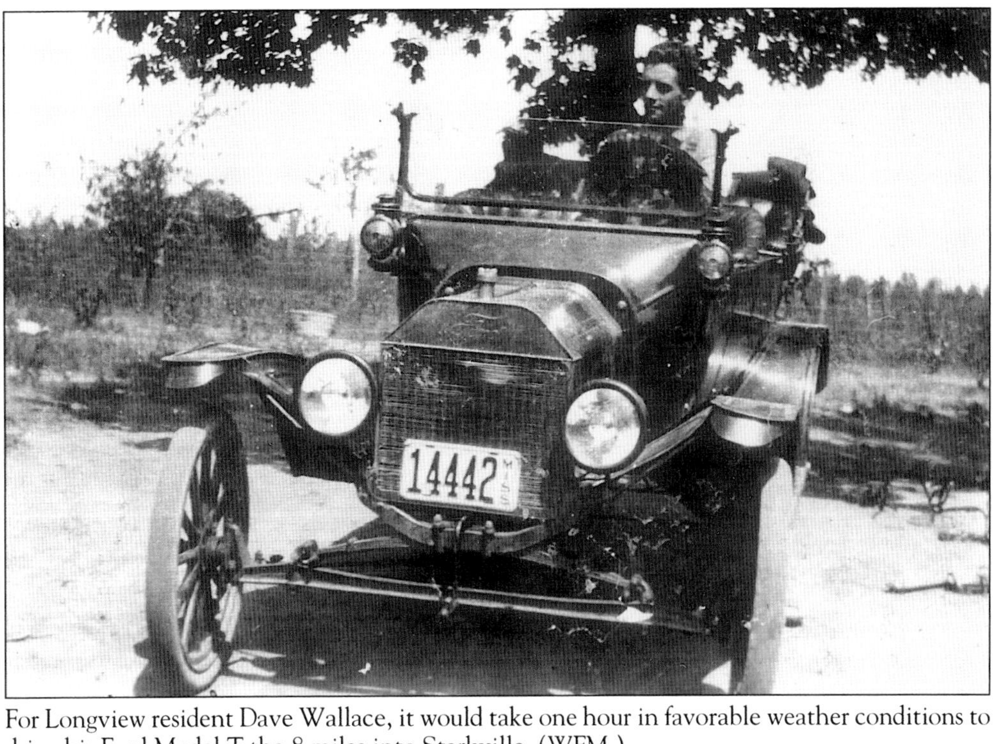

For Longview resident Dave Wallace, it would take one hour in favorable weather conditions to drive his Ford Model T the 8 miles into Starkville. (WFM.)

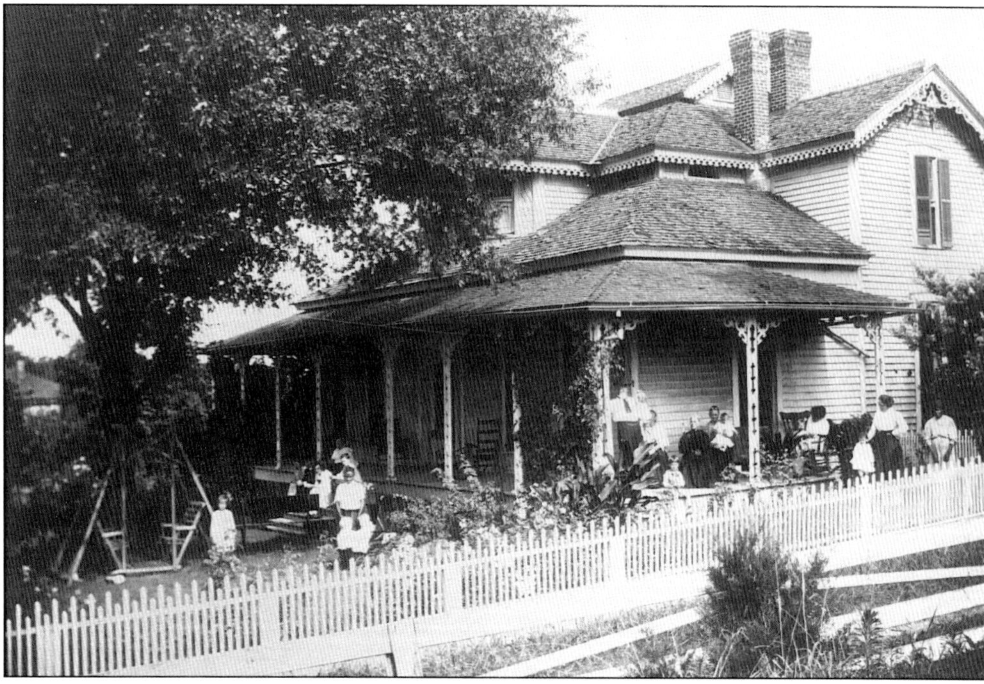

The Reynolds House, which was built in 1869 in front of the Greensboro Center, has remained in the family to this day. (BS.)

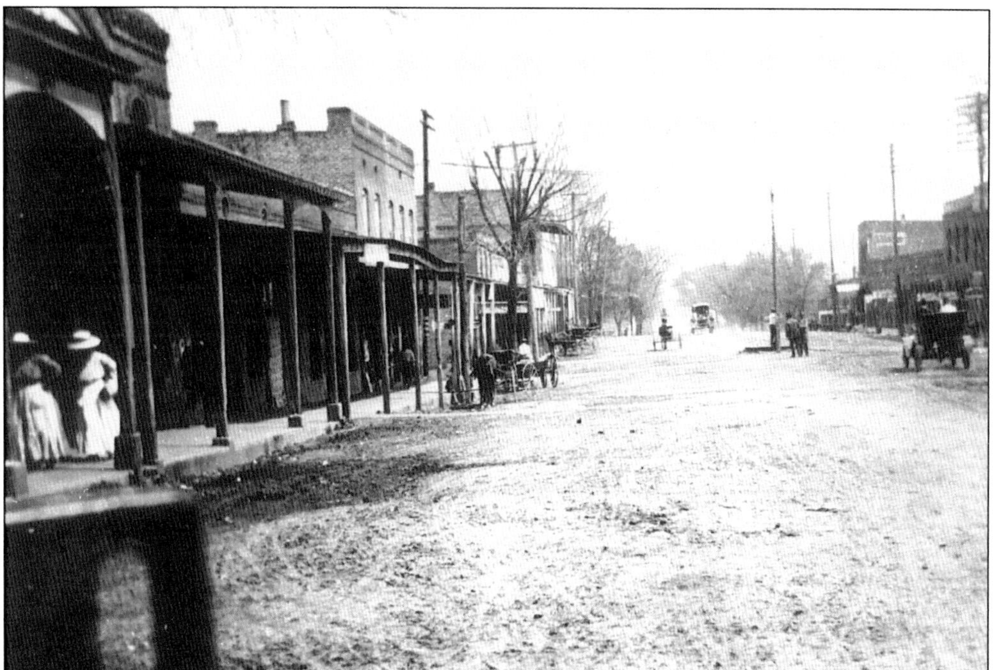

Two water collection systems, one of which is pictured here in the middle of the unpaved street, were used to hold the water that drained from the buildings' roofs on Main Street. Each system held 600 gallons of water in case of fire. In 1893, 128 Starkville residents signed a petition to keep hogs out of the system.

Members of Jewish families such as Philip Goodman, who started as a peddler, opened businesses on Main Street after the 1875 fire. Mr. and Mrs. Goodman's three sons, Raymond, Arthur, and Louis, graduated from A&M College. (BG.)

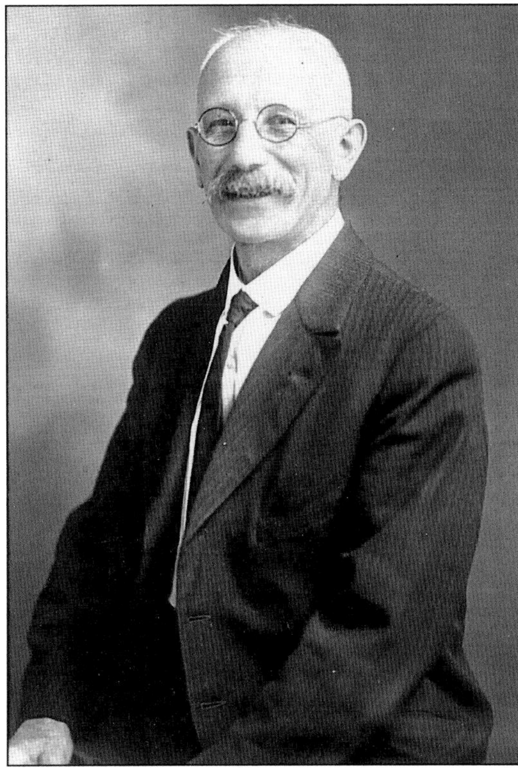

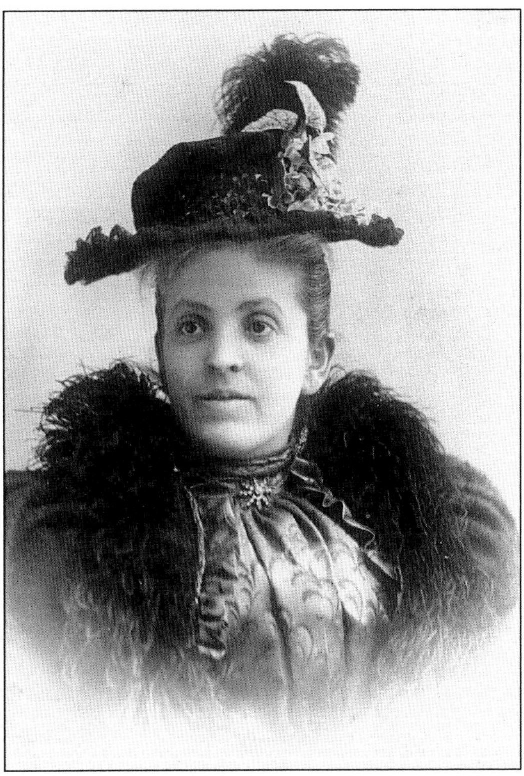

Pictured is Helen Goodman, the wife of Philip Goodman. Their home sat on the corner of Main and Jackson Streets. (BG.)

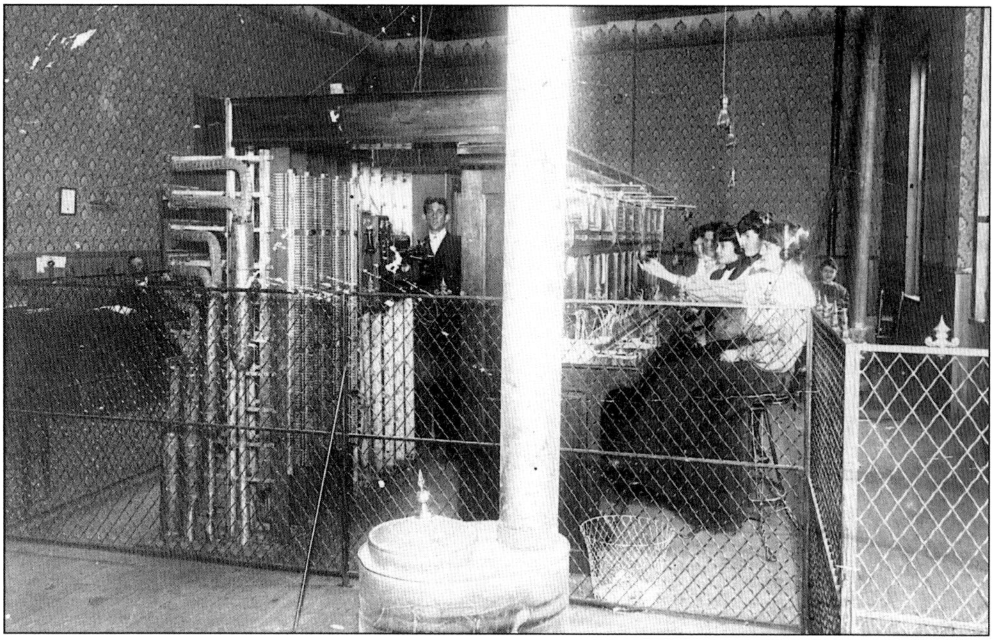

The first phone service, which was owned by R.K. Weir, was located on the corner of Main and Montgomery Streets. The Cumberland Telephone Company purchased the service in 1905. In 1927, the name was changed to Southern Bell. "The tuneful jingle of your telephone bell is a welcome reminder that there is NO LONELINESS IN THE HOME WITH A TELEPHONE." This is from the back cover of Starkville's 1938 telephone directory. (OHM.)

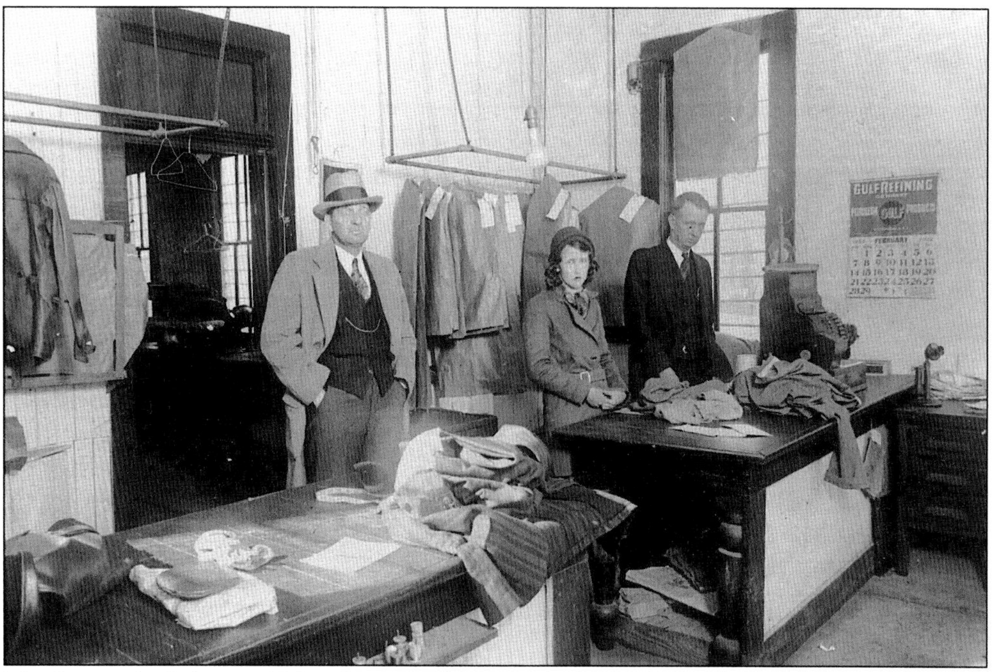

Mr. Cooper (right) owned New Process Cleaners, which was located on the west end of Main Street. Also standing behind the counter is Frank Thompson (left). Starkville's 1952 telephone directory listed New Process Cleaners phone number as 511. (OHM.)

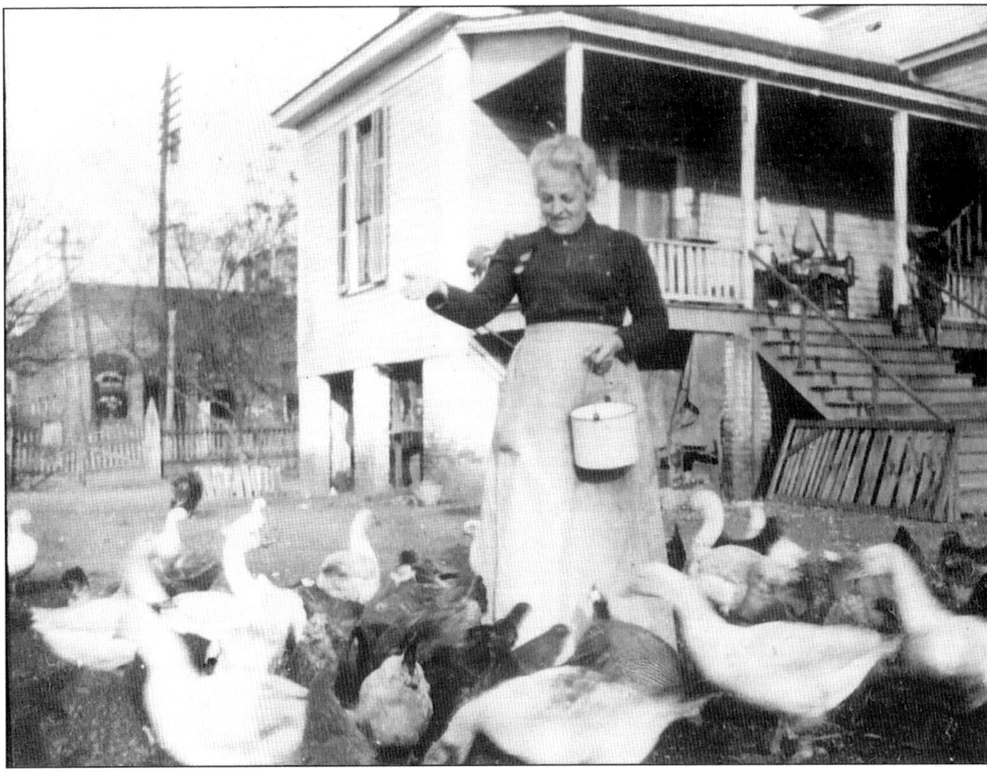

Mrs. Goodman (see page 53) is shown here feeding her geese. She was also known to buy pigeons for a dime from Sam Polk, who caught the pigeons in Mr. Page's barn. (BG.)

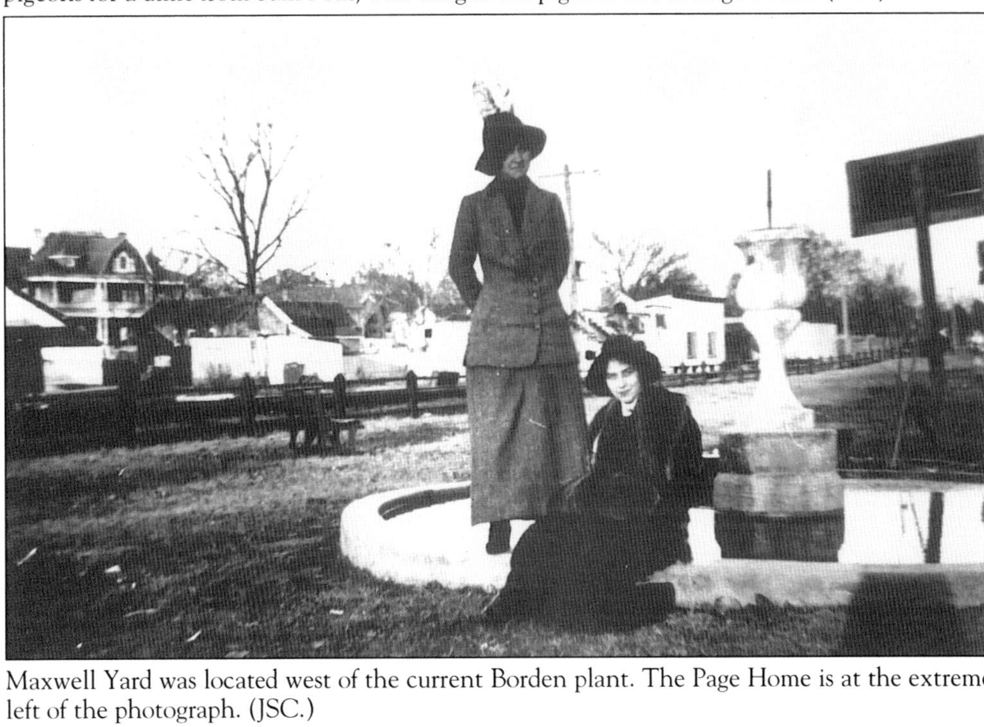

Maxwell Yard was located west of the current Borden plant. The Page Home is at the extreme left of the photograph. (JSC.)

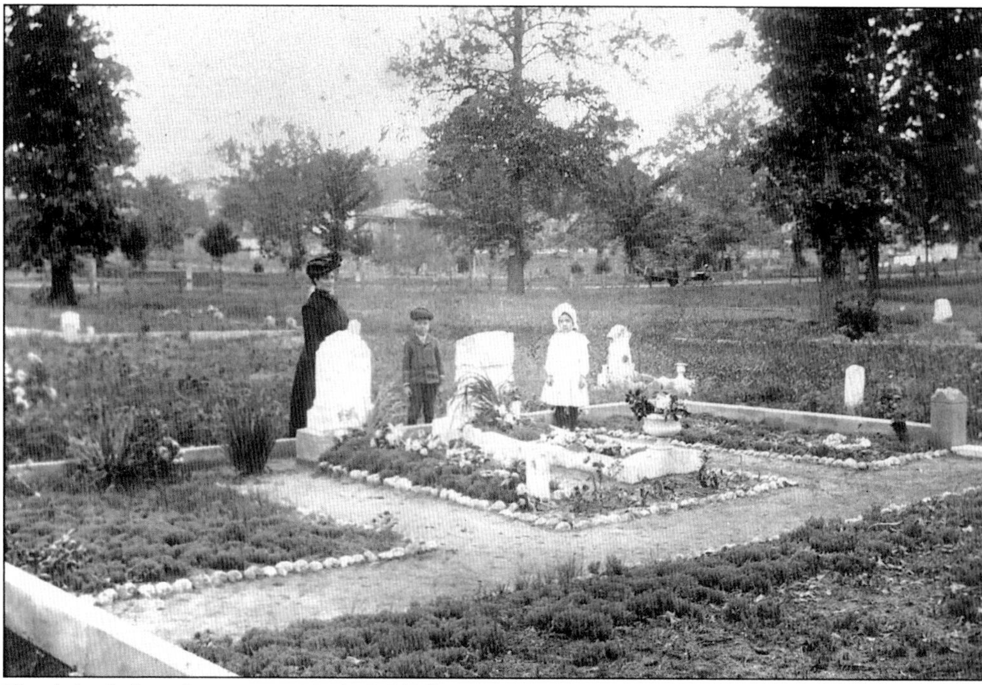

Until deeded to the city in 1946, Oddfellow Cemetery was owned by the Independent Order of Oddfellows. Oktibbeha County has more than 160 cemeteries. The gravesite visitors are members of the Sellars family. (PS.)

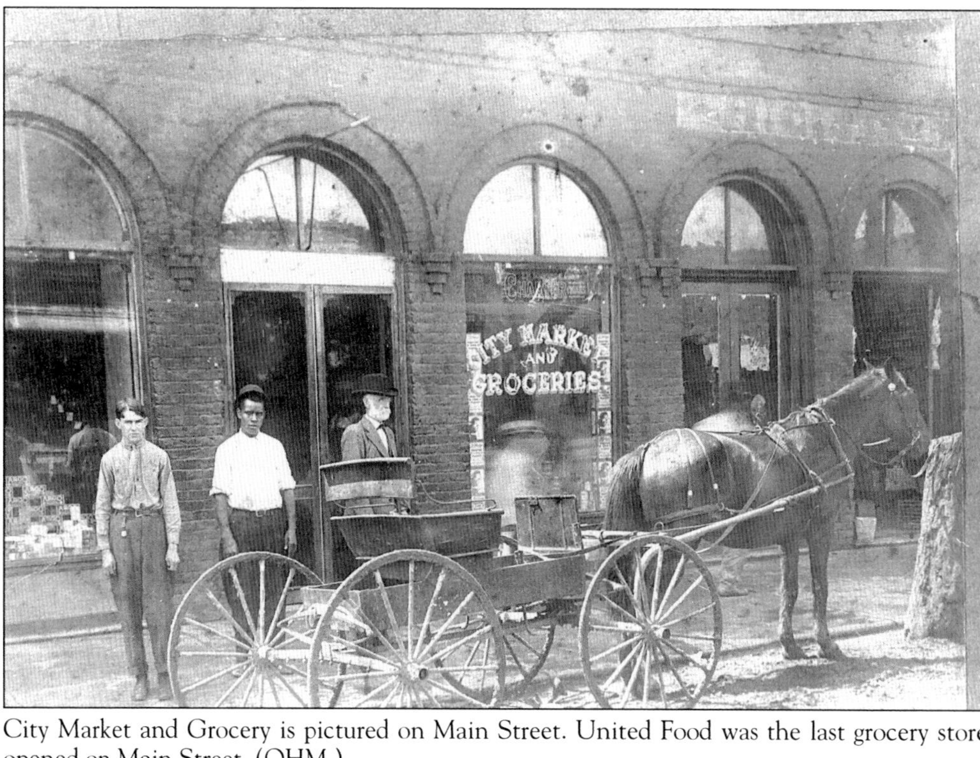

City Market and Grocery is pictured on Main Street. United Food was the last grocery store opened on Main Street. (OHM.)

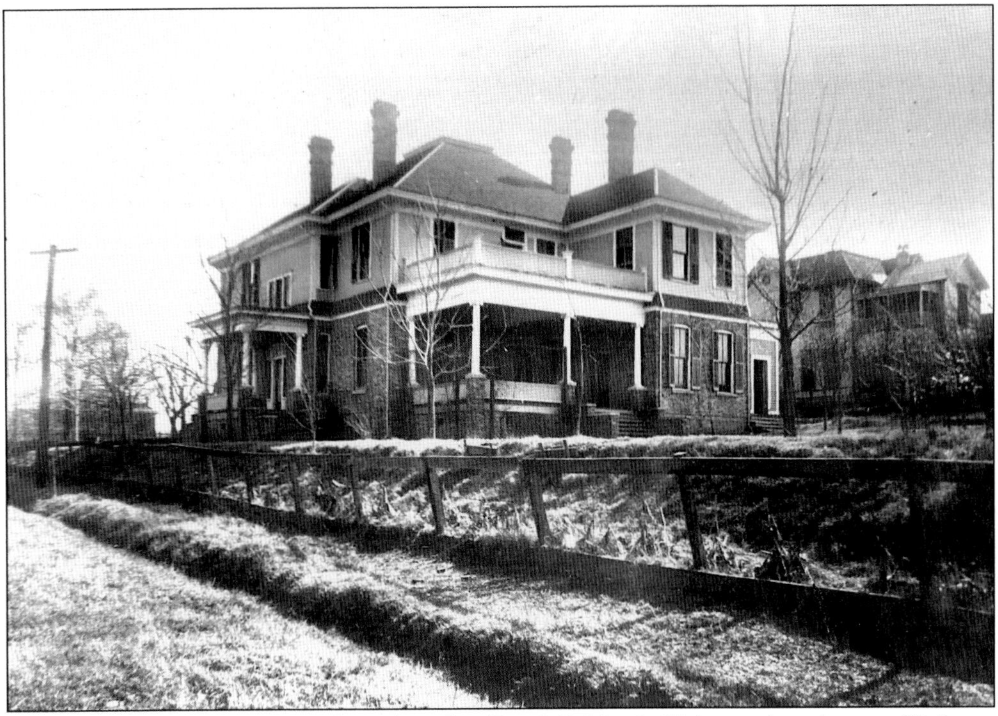

Lee Street, a dirt road running along the side of Dr. C.B. Mitchell's home, later became Highway 82. (JSC.)

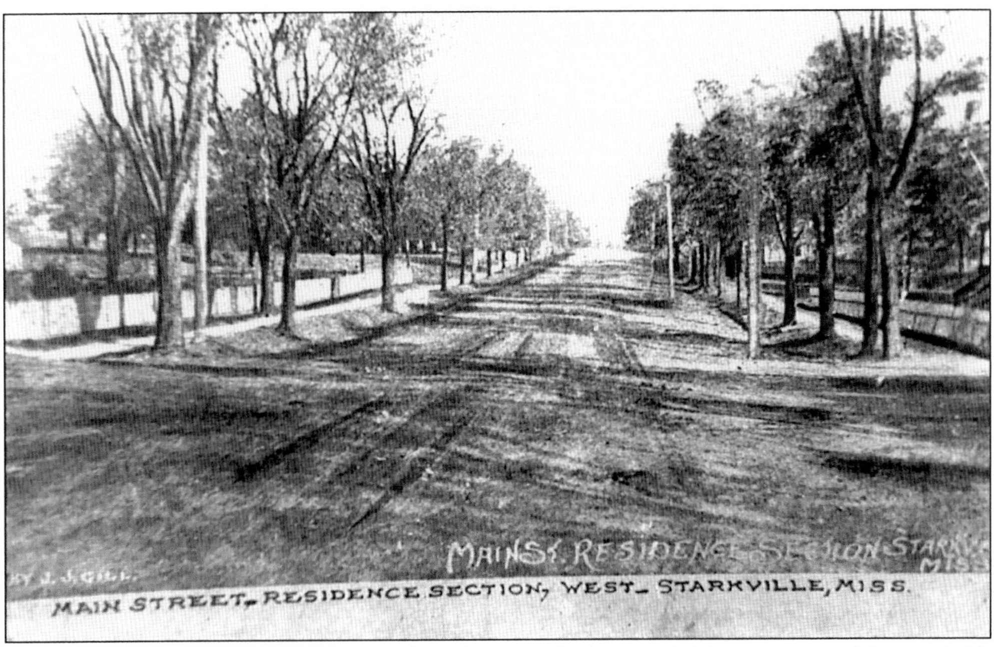

"Starkville has it all—paved streets, sidewalks, and shade trees." This was quoted from a 1929 Louisiana newspaper article. The sidewalk that linked Starkville to A&M College cost $16,000 to build in 1913. (JSC.)

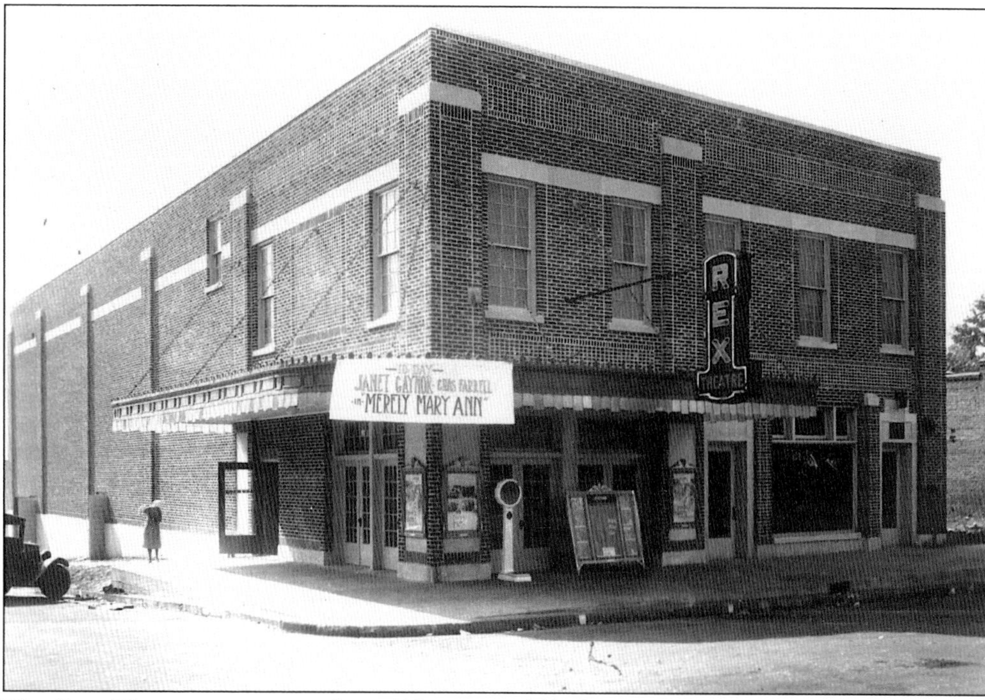

The Rex Theatre was pictured in 1931 at its fifth location, on the corner of Main and Washington Streets. When the Rex opened in 1912, it had 150 bench seats. (BG.)

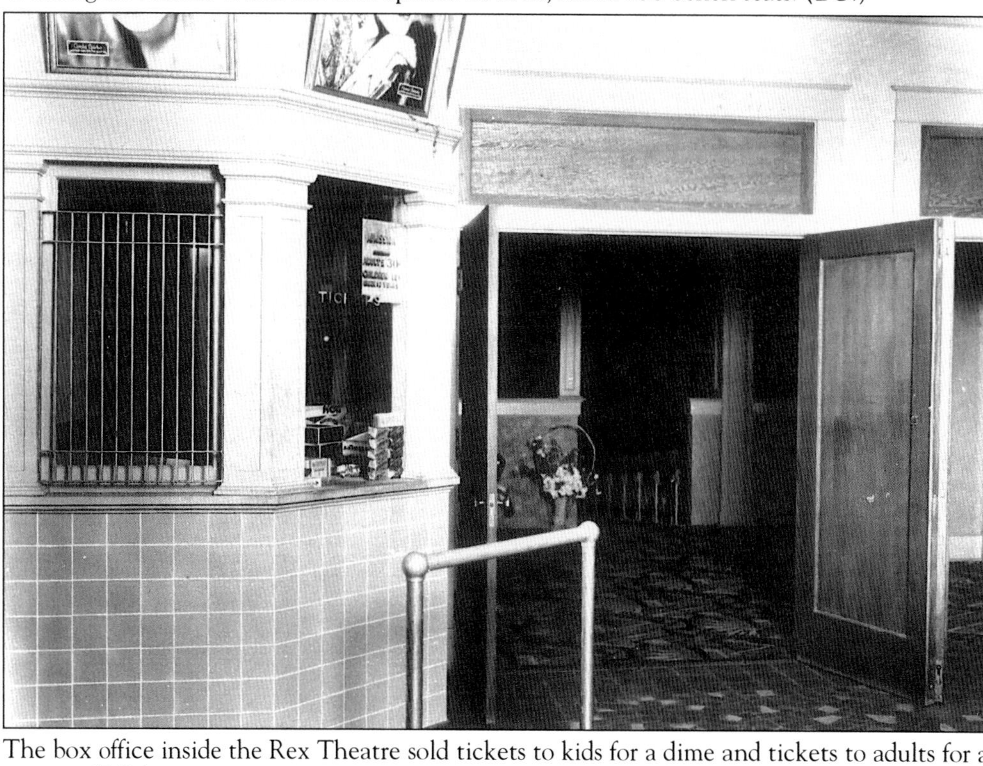

The box office inside the Rex Theatre sold tickets to kids for a dime and tickets to adults for a quarter. (BG.)

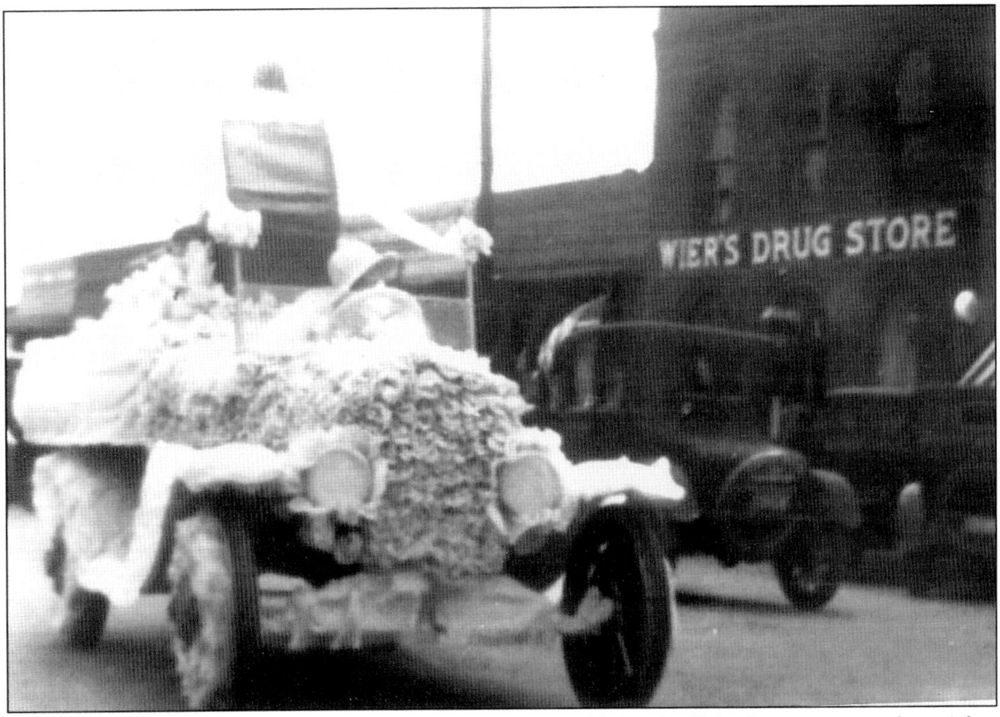

This early automobile has been decorated for one of Starkville's frequent parades. After buying out Davenport and McDowell "Drug Store" in 1889, Wier's Drug Store stopped selling liquor. (JSC.)

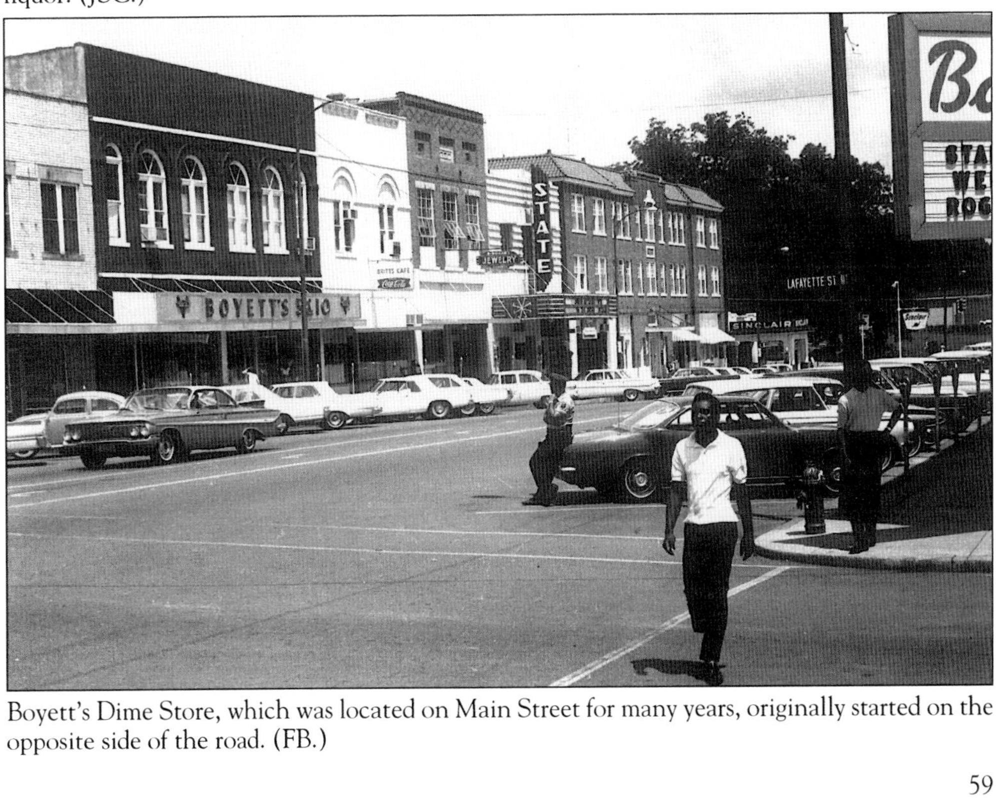

Boyett's Dime Store, which was located on Main Street for many years, originally started on the opposite side of the road. (FB.)

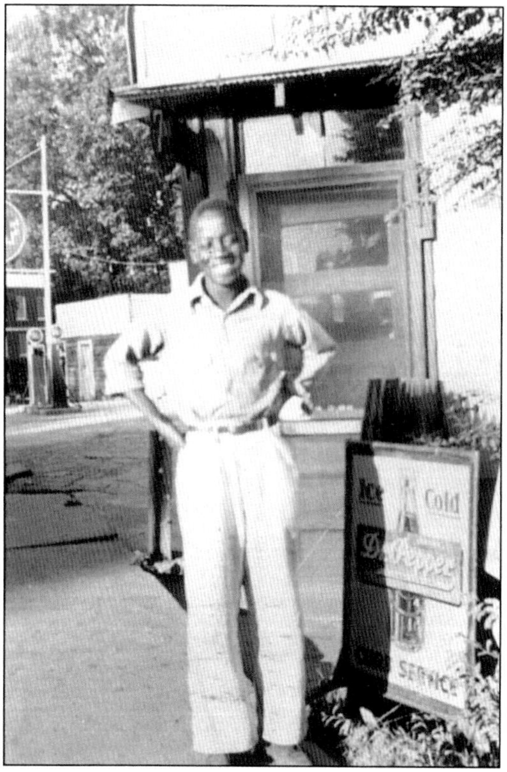

The man known as "Snowball" stands in front of Temp's Cafe, which was the first drive-in restaurant in Starkville. Temp's was in the same location as the current Starkville Electric Department. In the background is the Gulf Station. (EB.)

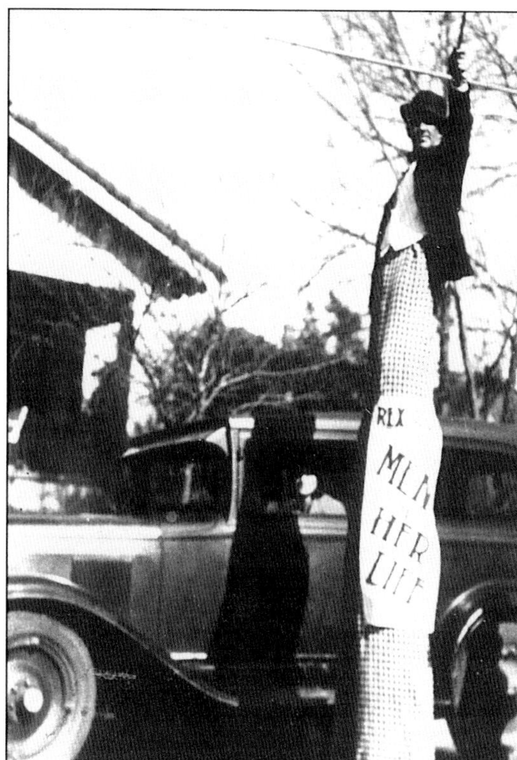

A man on stilts promotes a movie showing at the Rex Theatre. (BG.)

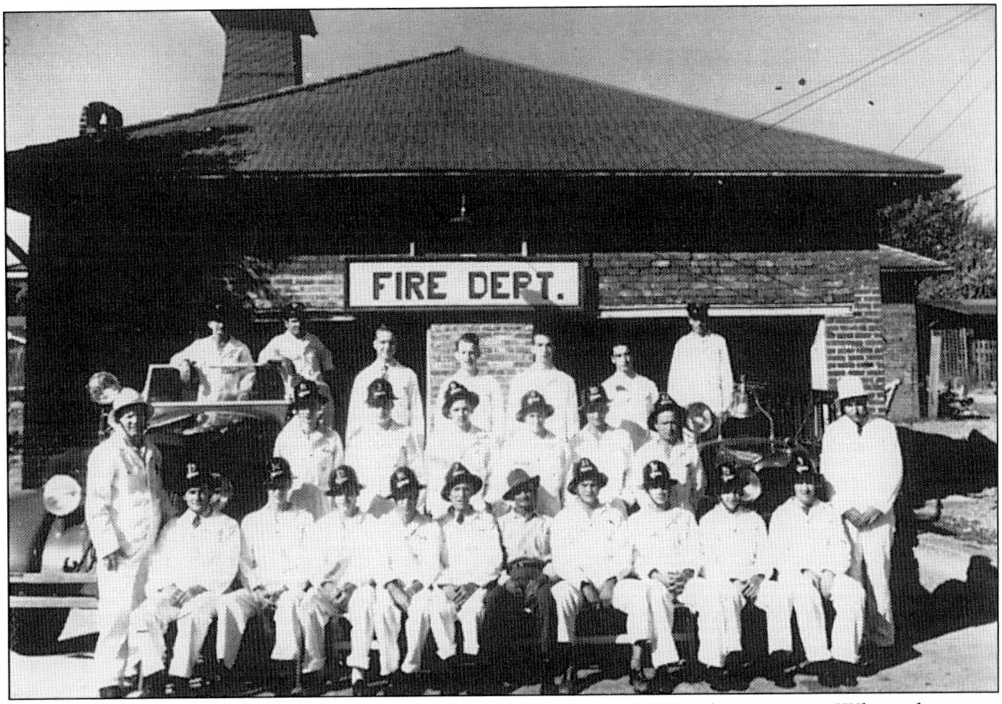

Firemen, many who were volunteers, stand in front of the old fire department. When the siren on the water tower sounded, the volunteer firemen would tune in their radio to find out the location of the fire. (JSC.)

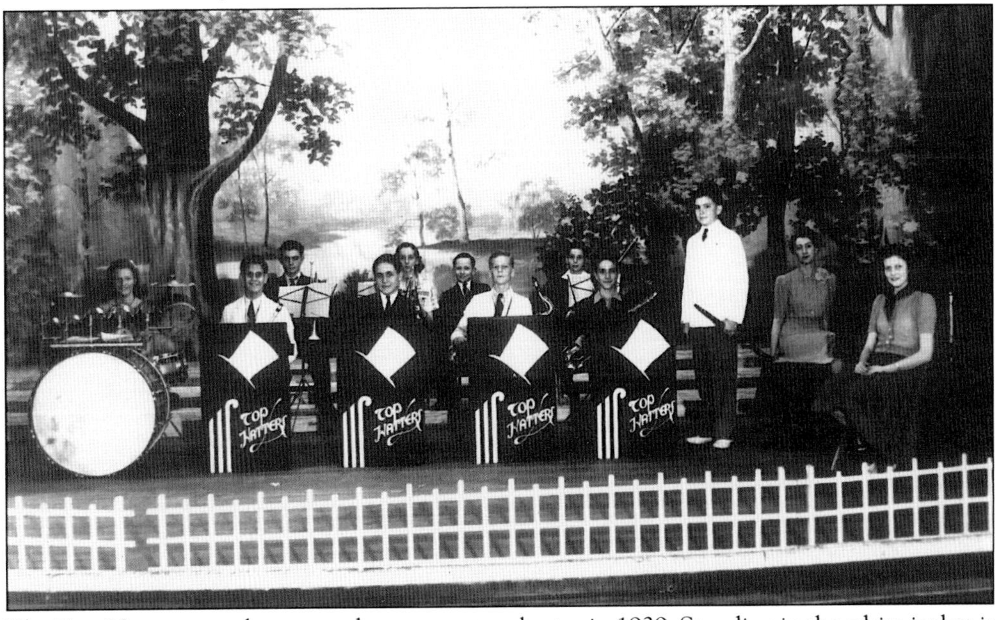

The Top-Hatters were known as the youngest orchestra in 1939. Standing in the white jacket is Jimmy Hartness. Pictured are the following, from left to right: (front row) Ralph Katz, Stanley Hart, Stuart Johnson, and Leon Tallichet; (back row) Billy Beall, Carolyn Beattie, Herman Gordon, and Jerome Rossoff. The drummer is Lorena Johnson. Mrs. Hartness and Evelyn Redus sit to the far right. (JSC.)

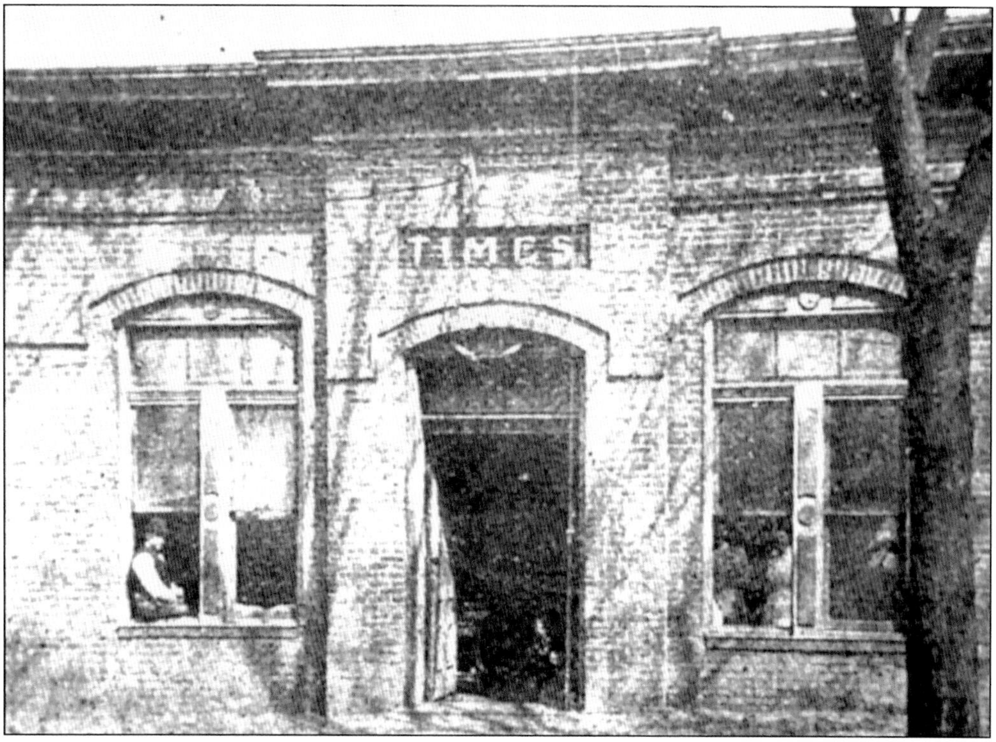

The *East Mississippi Times* newspaper was opened in 1866 by William Ward. The business also sold stationary and business cards. (JSC.)

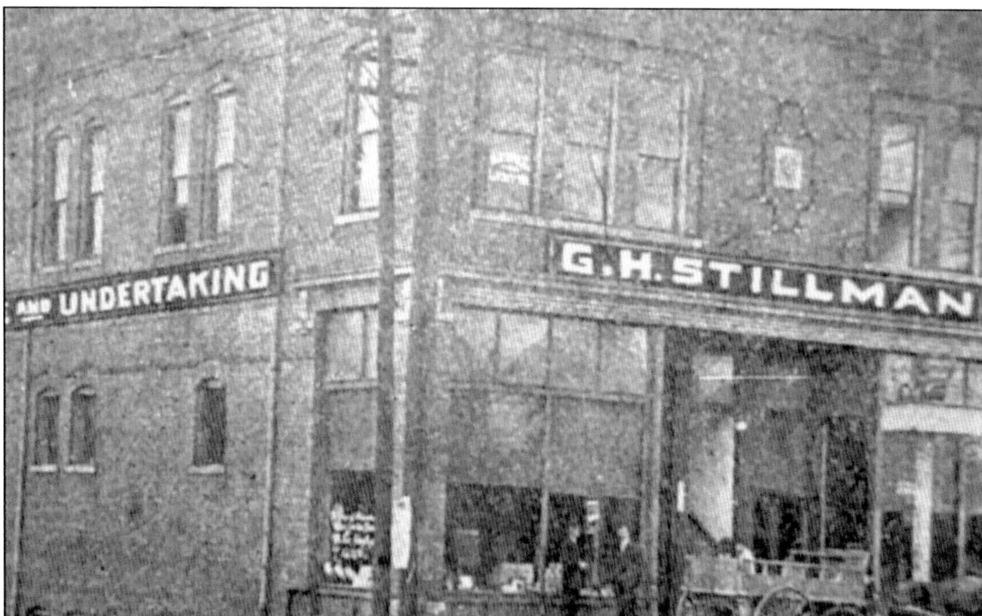

Stillman's five and dime, furniture, and undertaking business is pictured in 1913. When the building burned in 1930, it was owned by the Masons, who lost two previous buildings to fire. When they reconstructed the building, it was rented to the Rex Theatre. (JSC.)

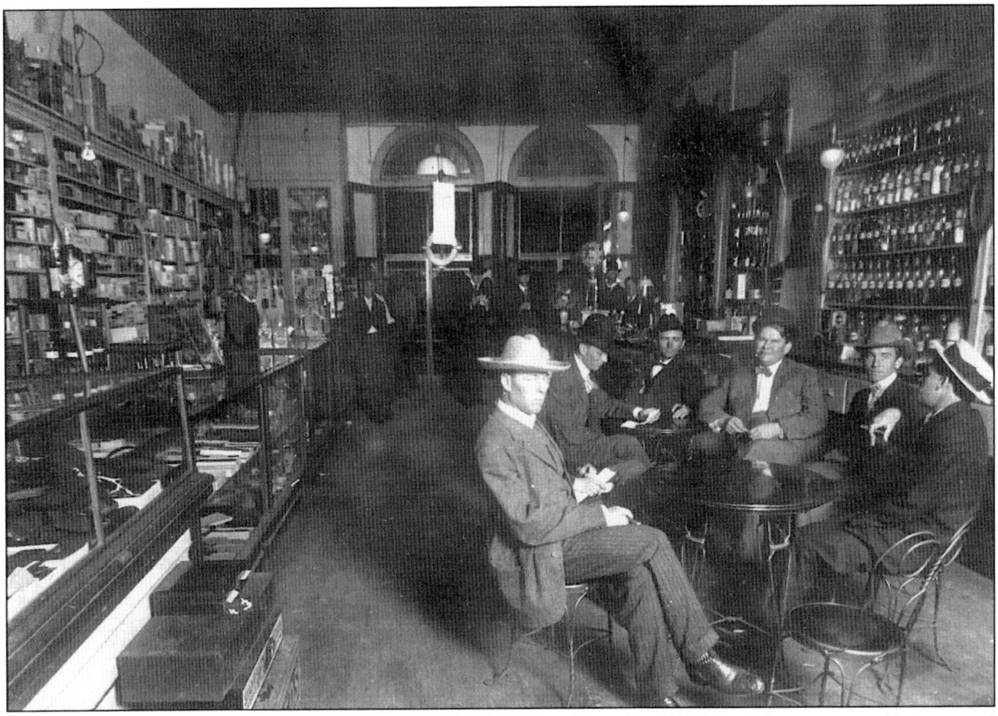

Men gather at a table in Gill's Drugstore, which opened in the 1860s on the corner of Main and Lafayette Streets. (OHM.)

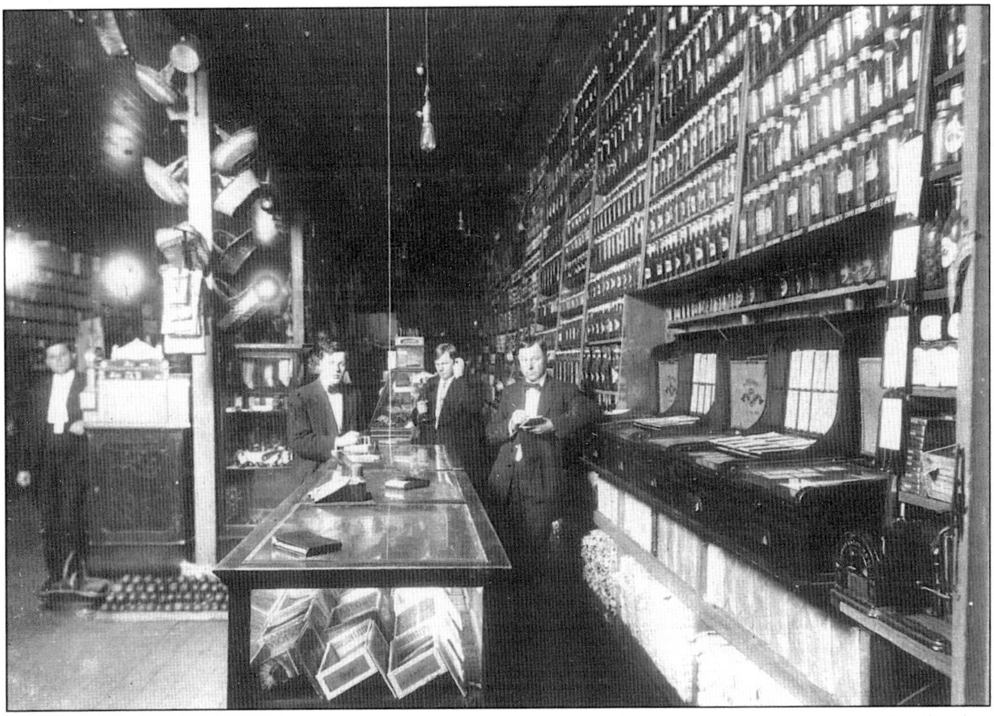

Duff Clardy's Drygoods was opened and is pictured in 1906. Notice the cigar boxes in the display case and an early example of electric lighting. (OHM.)

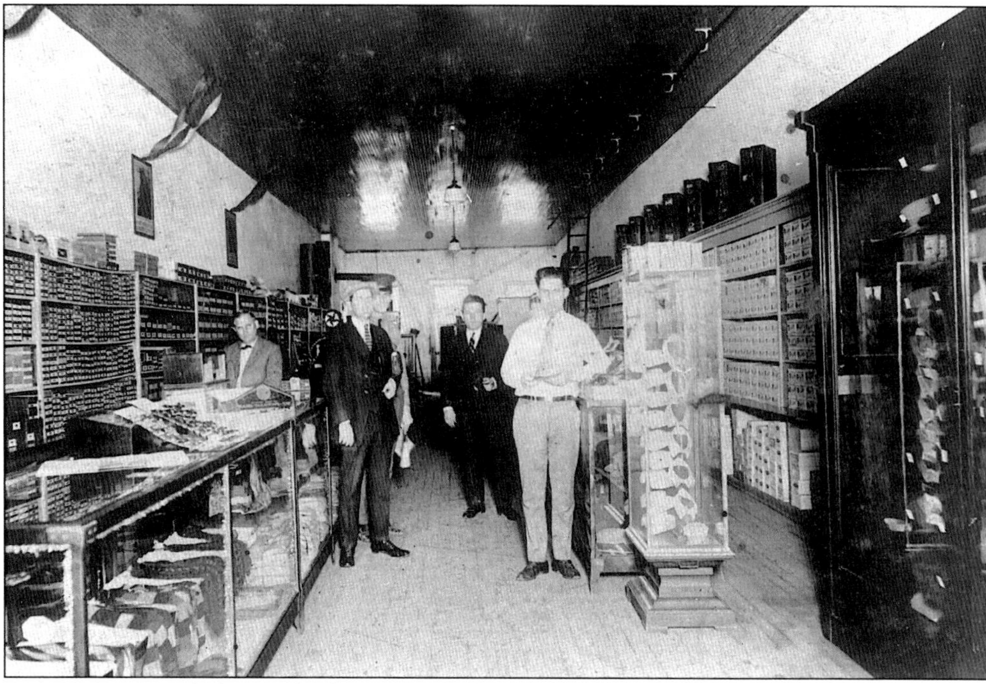

Harrison Men's Clothing, which was pictured in 1920, was located on the southwest corner of Main and Lafayette Streets. The vertical display case at center right contains shirt collars and cuffs. (OHM.)

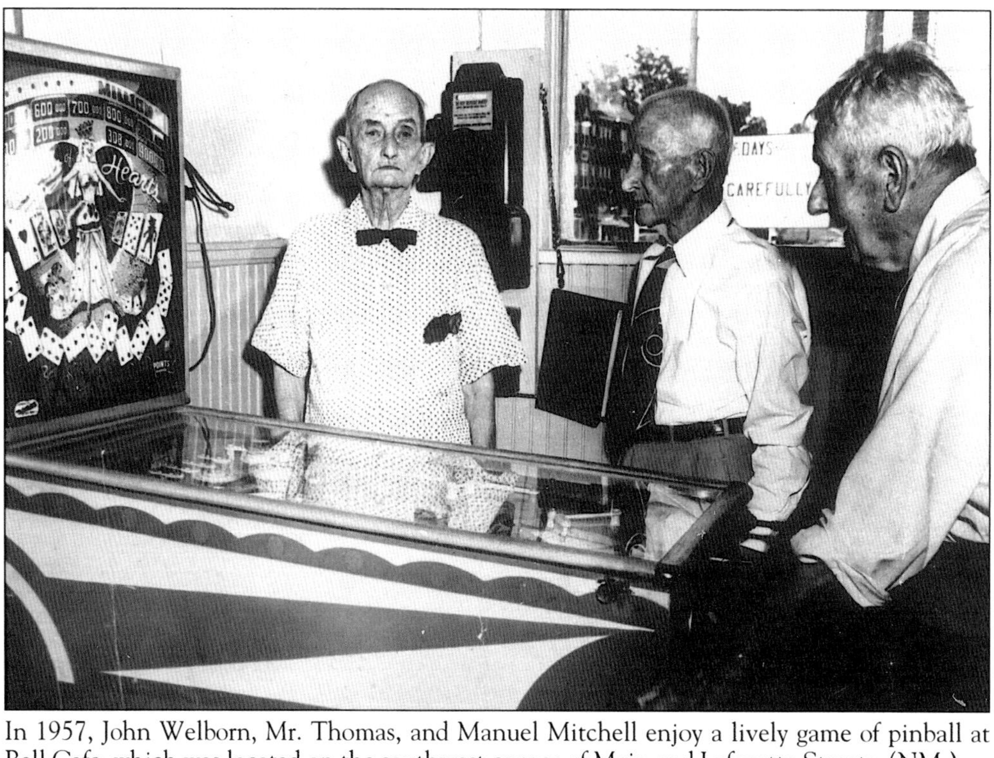

In 1957, John Welborn, Mr. Thomas, and Manuel Mitchell enjoy a lively game of pinball at Bell Cafe, which was located on the southwest corner of Main and Lafayette Streets. (NM.)

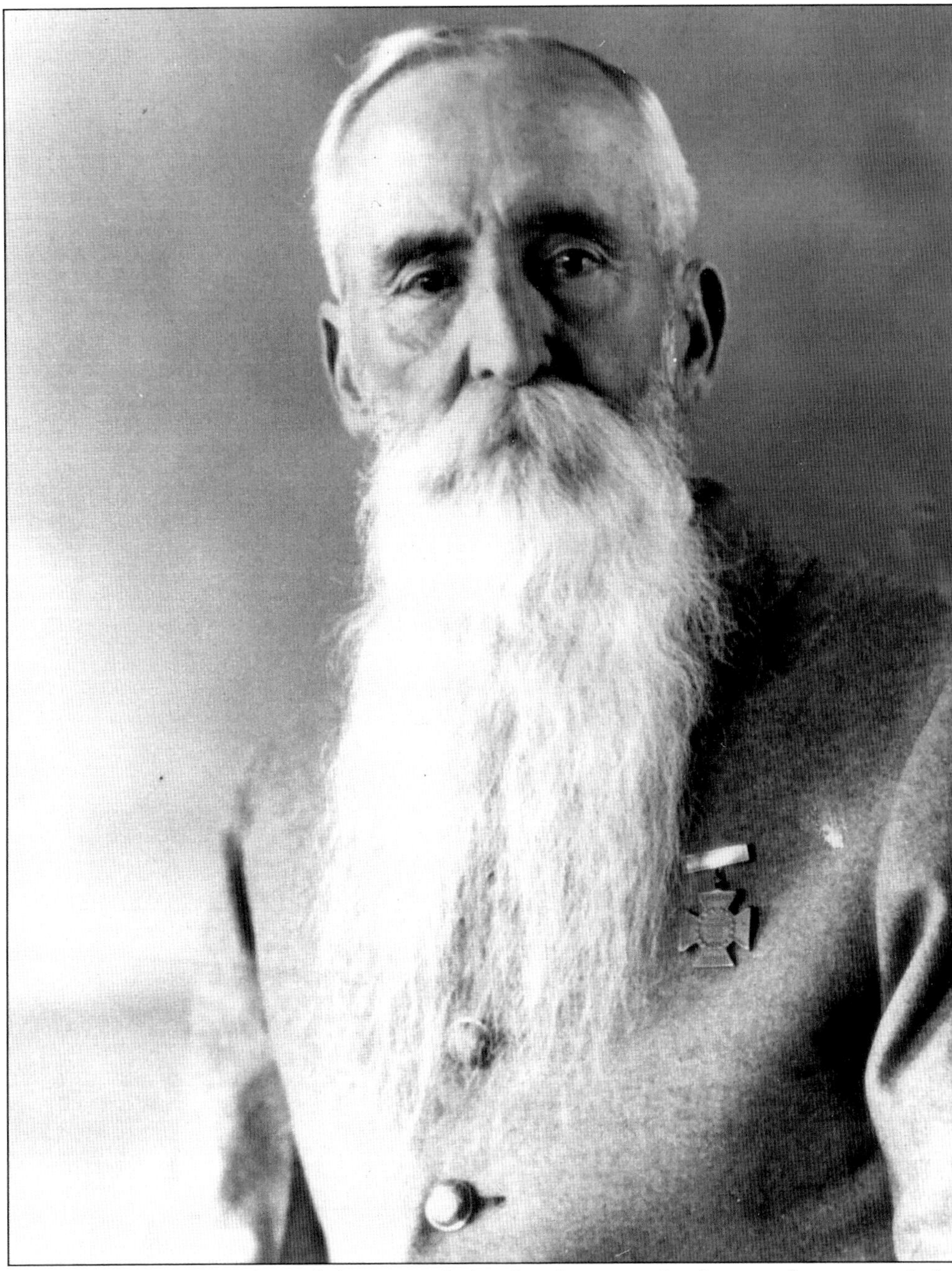

General J.A. Glenn, whose father owned the first house with glass windows, joined the Confederate Army at age 15. He was assigned to the 6th Mississippi Cavalry, Company I, under the command of Capt. C.A. Johnston in Columbus. After the war, Glenn was an active member of the Veterans Association and rose in rank from private to general. Laid to rest in his uniform at age 95, he was one of the last Civil War veterans in the county. Together, he and his father served as clerks for the First Baptist Church for nearly 100 years. Like many Confederate veterans, Glenn proudly wears the Southern Cross of Honor medal, presented by the United Daughters of the Confederacy. (OHM.)

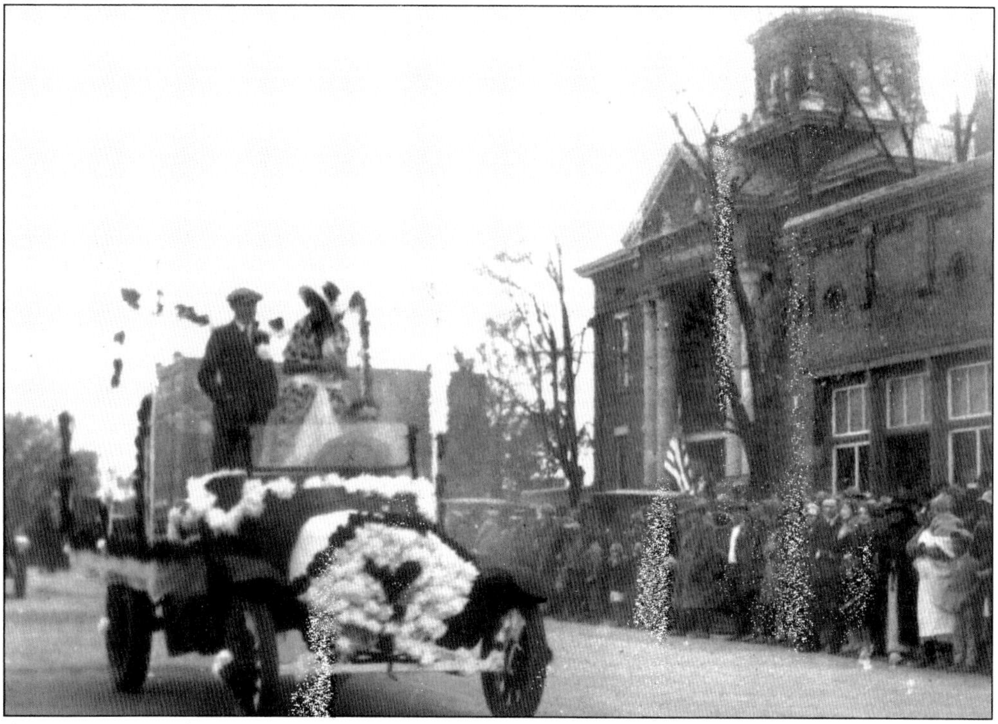

A car promoting the WWI victory parades down the street. Because of his gymnastic background at West Point Academy, Lt. W.M. "Bud" Miley was assigned for more than a year to the first Army Circus, which promoted Army Relief in the eastern states. (JSC.)

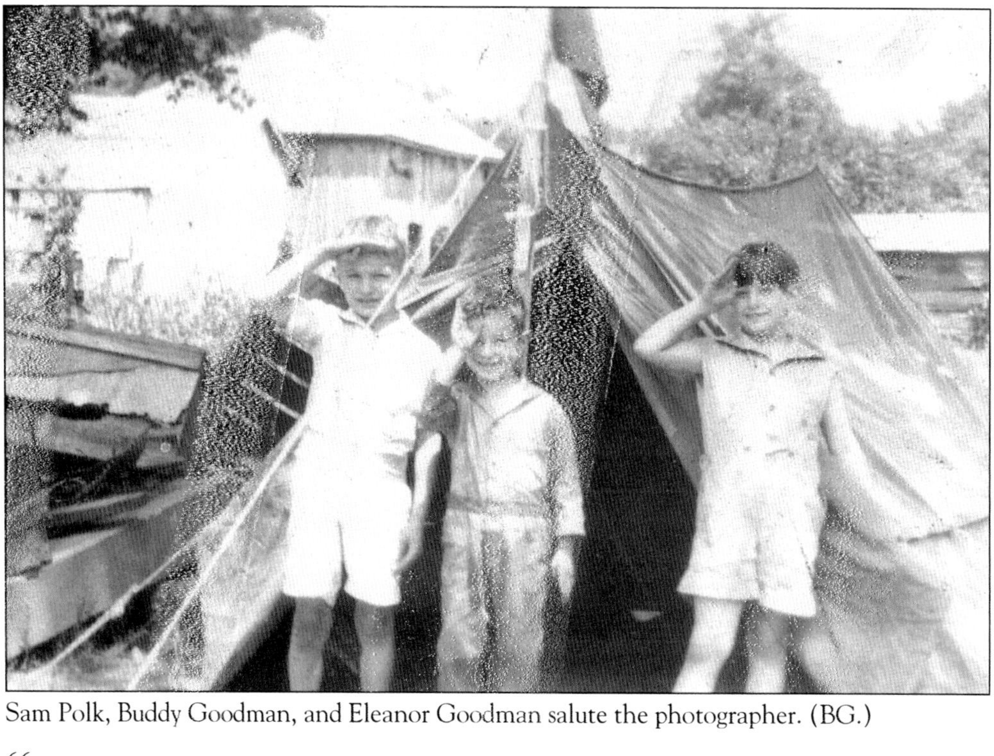

Sam Polk, Buddy Goodman, and Eleanor Goodman salute the photographer. (BG.)

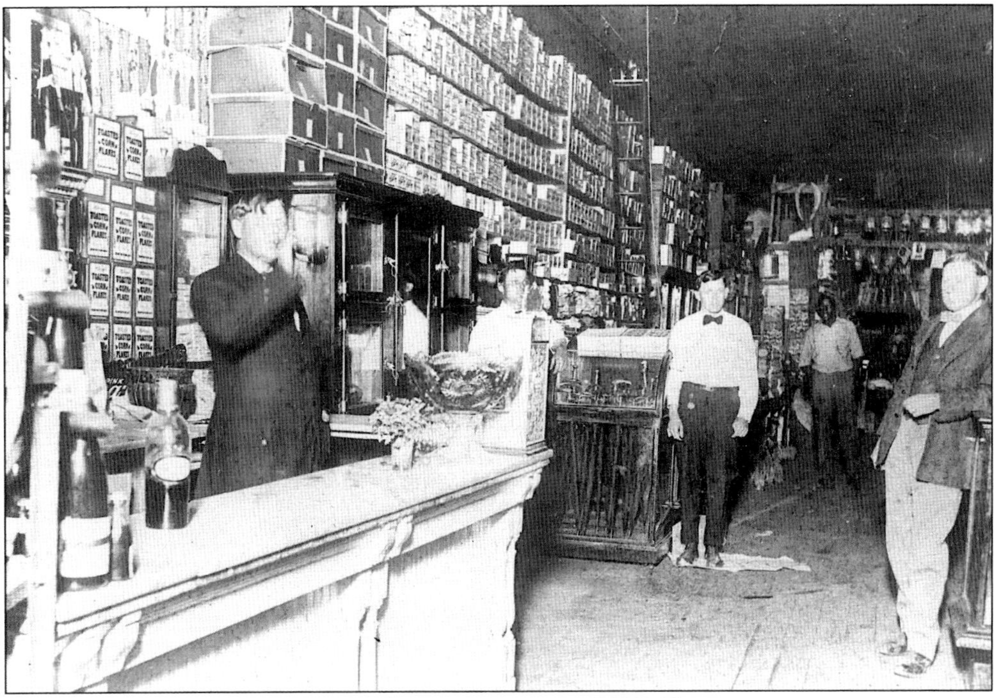

The Clardy General Store was open from 1900 to 1906. (OHM.)

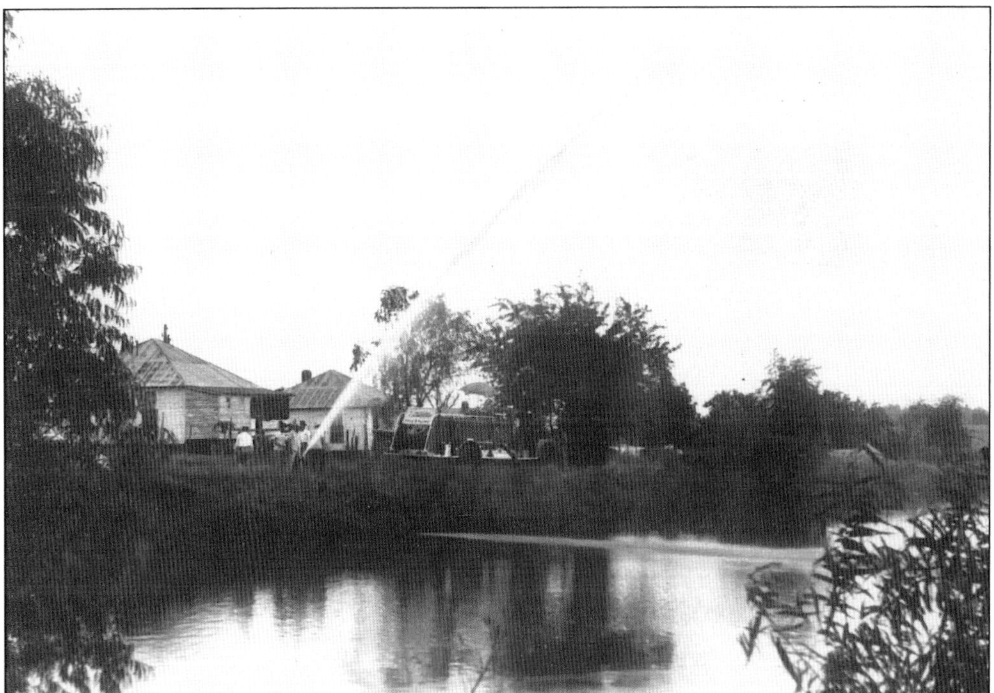

Firemen test water pressure on a 1937 fire truck sitting behind the cotton mill. In 1913, 75 families moved into the area around the cotton mill and lived in houses such as those pictured in the background. The pond was called "Snakey Pond" by the kids in the neighborhood. (CR.)

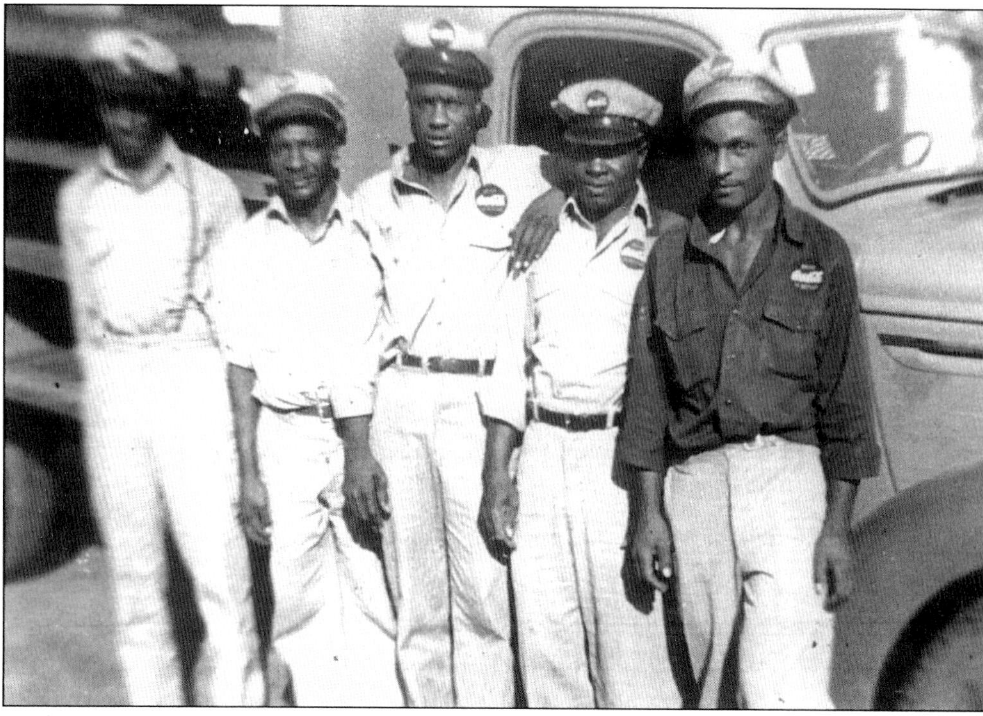

Starkville Coca-Cola Bottling Company started in 1928 with three trucks and eight employees. Their slogan was, "It had to be good to get where it is." (EB.)

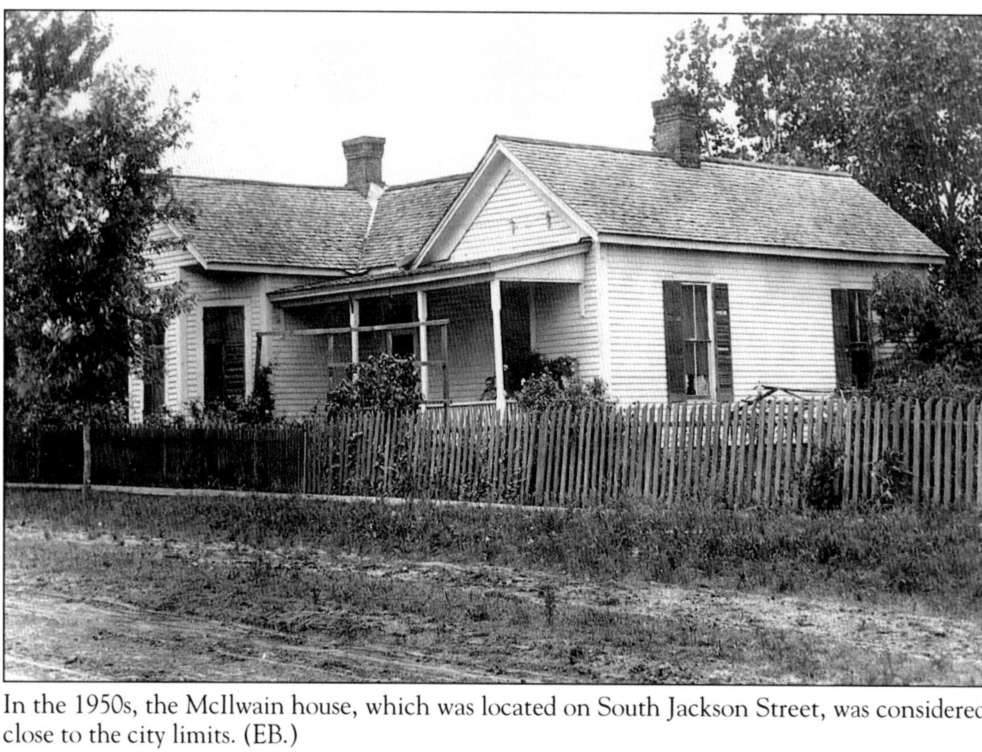

In the 1950s, the McIlwain house, which was located on South Jackson Street, was considered close to the city limits. (EB.)

Dr. Jim Eckford opened his practice in 1896. He and his son, Dr. Freddie Eckford, contributed many years of service to this community. (BG.)

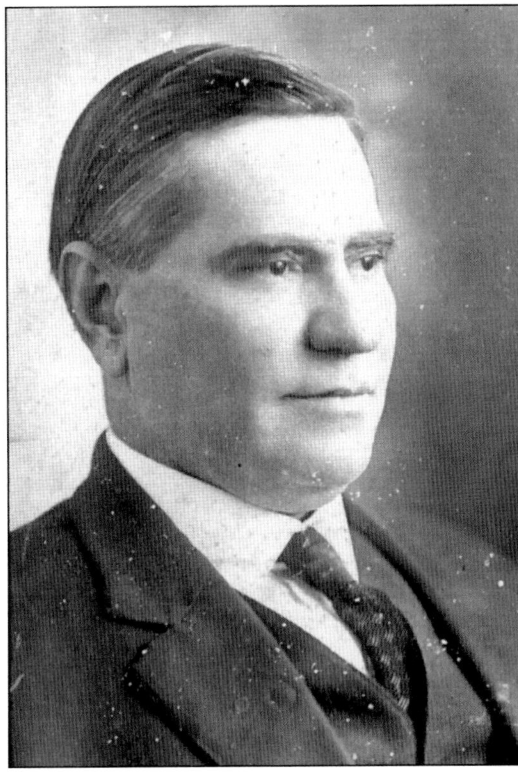

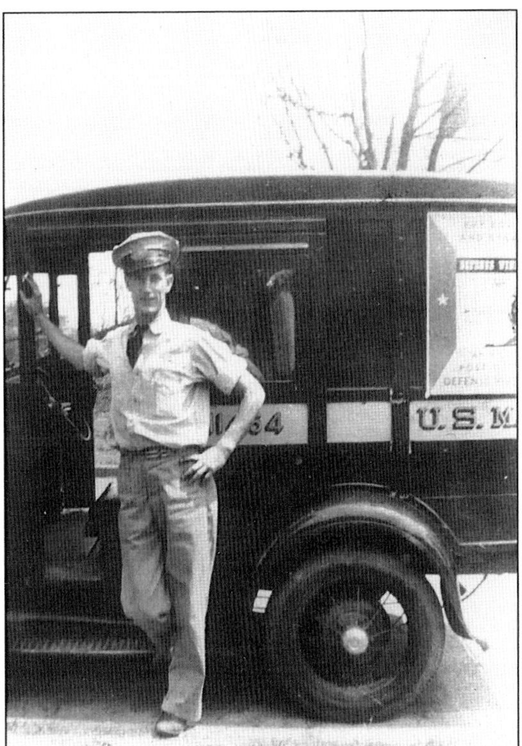

Postman John R. Thompson, who later became postmaster, poses next to a Ford Model A mail truck. (EB.)

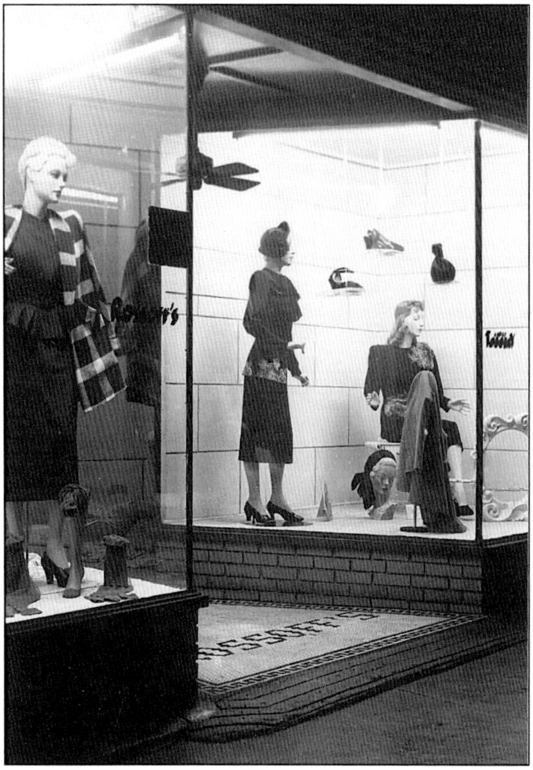

Rossoff's Dress Shop, which was owned by one of Starkville's Jewish families, was located on Main Street. (FB.)

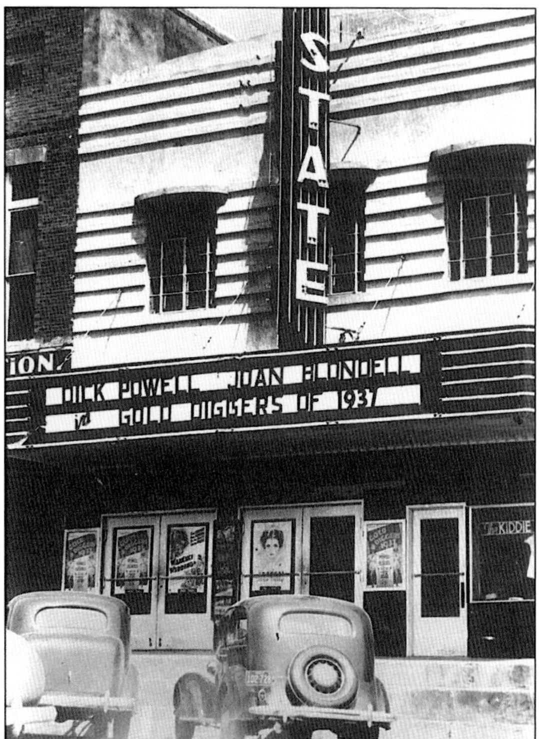

In January 1947, Dr. Rankin took over Dr. Oakley's dental practice, which was located over the State Theatre on Main Street. This picture was taken in 1937. (BG.)

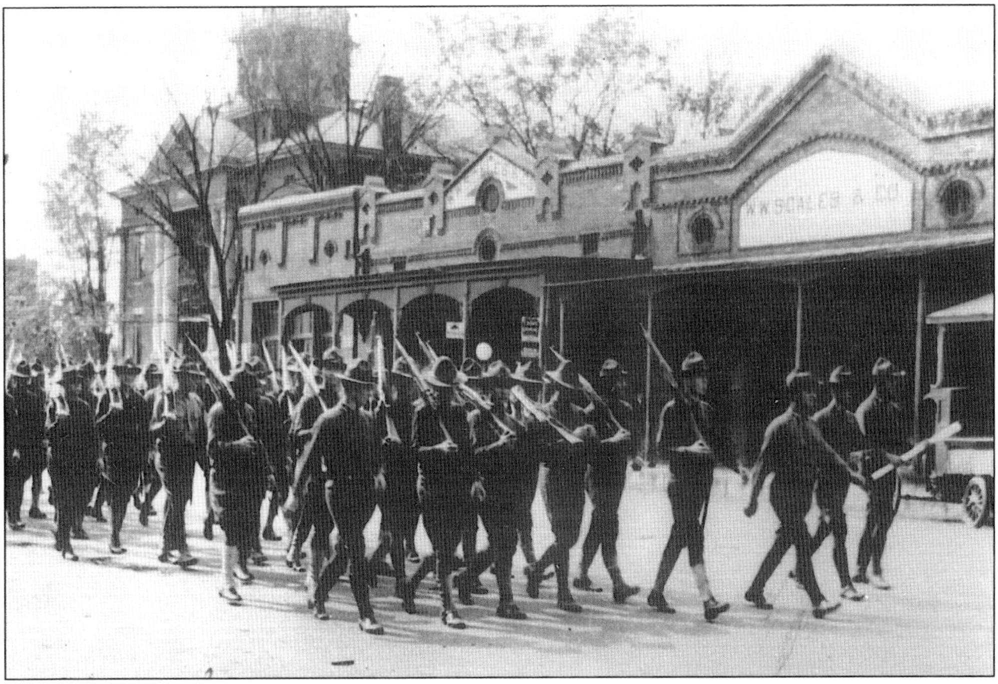

In this photograph, the State Guard marches down Main Street in 1924. Scales Company, which is pictured in the background, first opened in Crawford in 1845 before another branch opened in Starkville in 1866. After the 1875 downtown fire, Scales closed their Crawford location and moved their merchandise to Starkville. (JSC.)

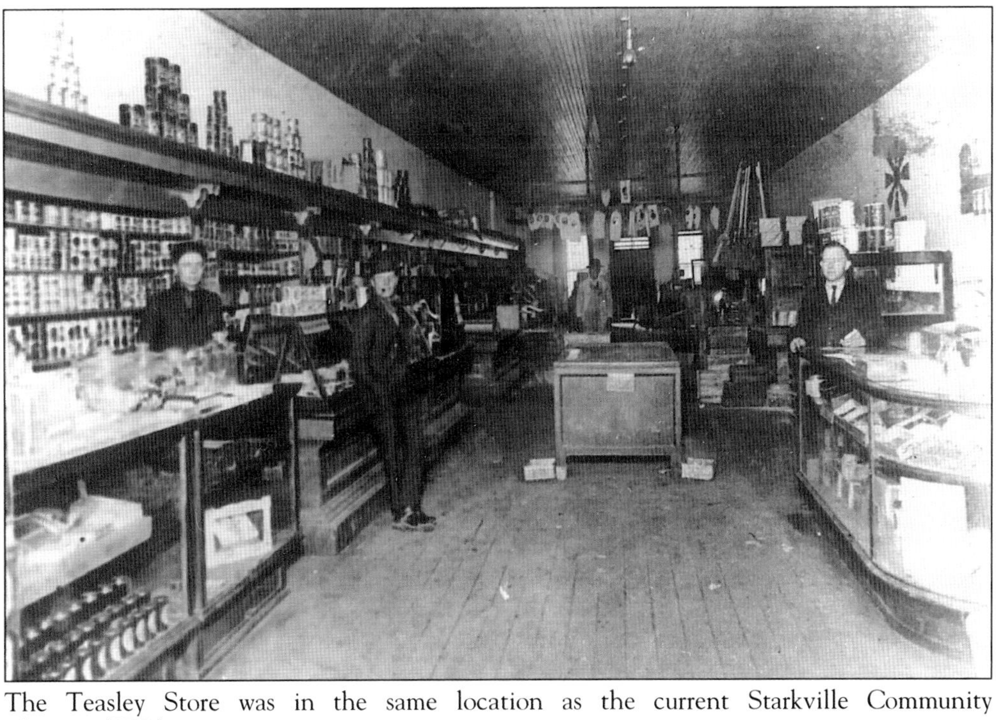

The Teasley Store was in the same location as the current Starkville Community Theatre. (HT.)

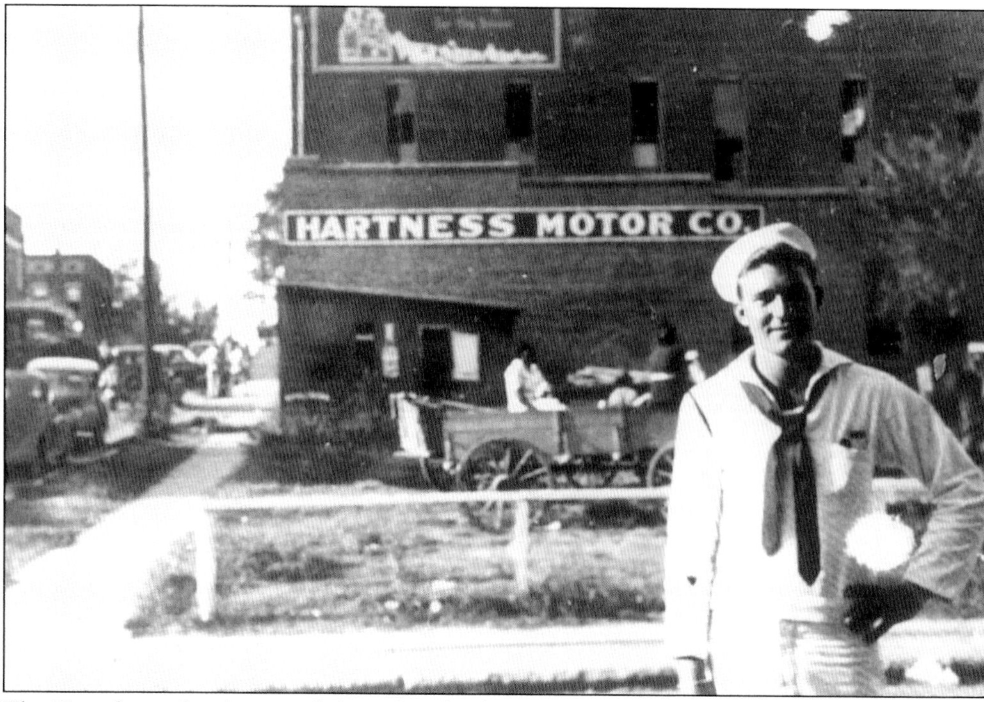

The Templeton family started their Overland and Pontiac dealership in the Hartness Motor Company building. The Big Apple Restaurant, which served hamburgers, is pictured behind the wagon. (EB.)

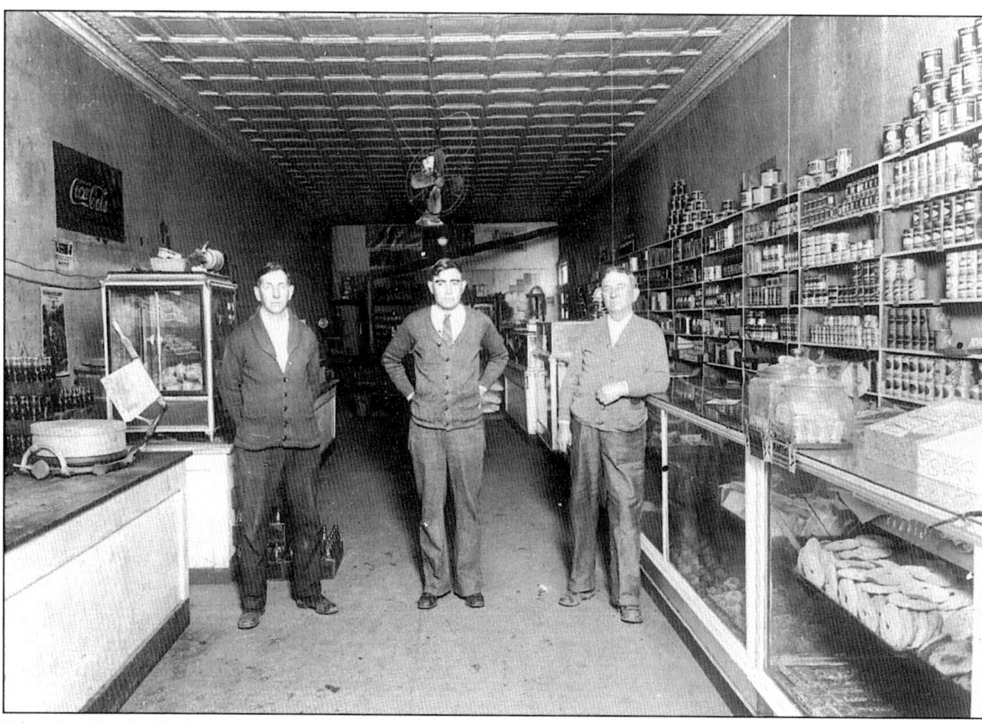

The Starkville Bakery is pictured here. (OHM.)

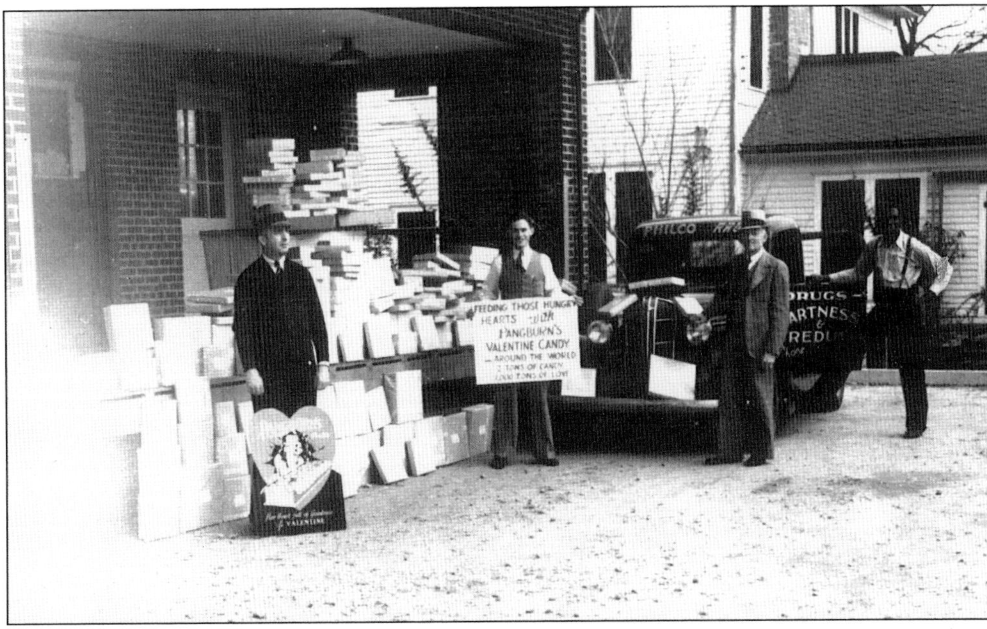

Here, men prepare to ship Valentine candy to the WWII soldiers. This picture was taken behind the post office in the current location of Reed's. (JSC.)

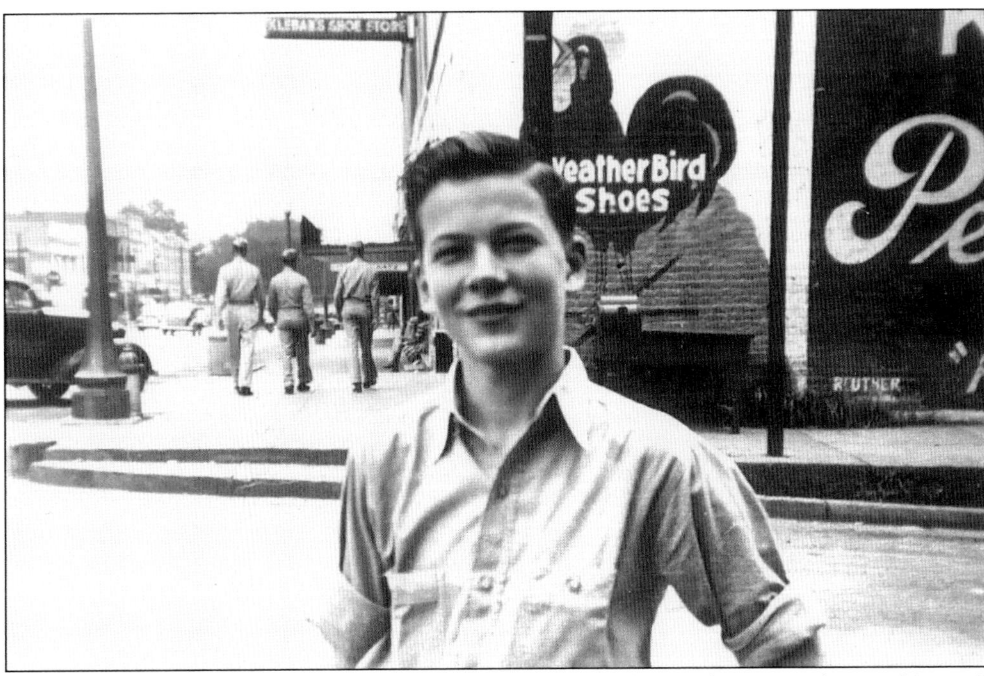

Harry Teasley was known as "Firehorse Harry" because during the movie he would notify volunteer firemen of a fire by blinking the foot lights on the stage of the Rex Theatre. (BG.)

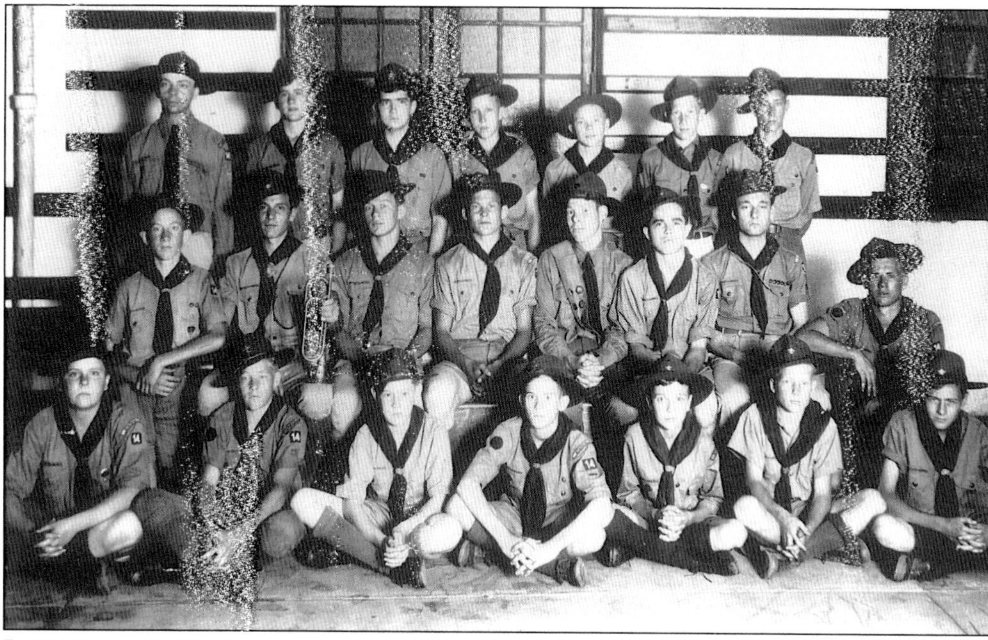

Boy Scout Troop 14 is pictured around 1935. From left to right are as follows: (front row) Jimmy Lloyd, Ted McKecknie, Arthur Harned, Dr. Steve Hester, Leon Tallichet, Billy Green, and Leon Denson; (middle row) Duncan Bracken, Sid Adams, Buster Bobbit, Edward Turner, James Long, Laughlin Magruder, Alfred Walker, and James Thaxton; (back row) Mr. Burdine, Charlie Lloyd, William Magruder, Felix Odom, Goat Lewis, John Roberson, John Robert Arnold, Henry Reynolds, and John R. Thompson. (JW.)

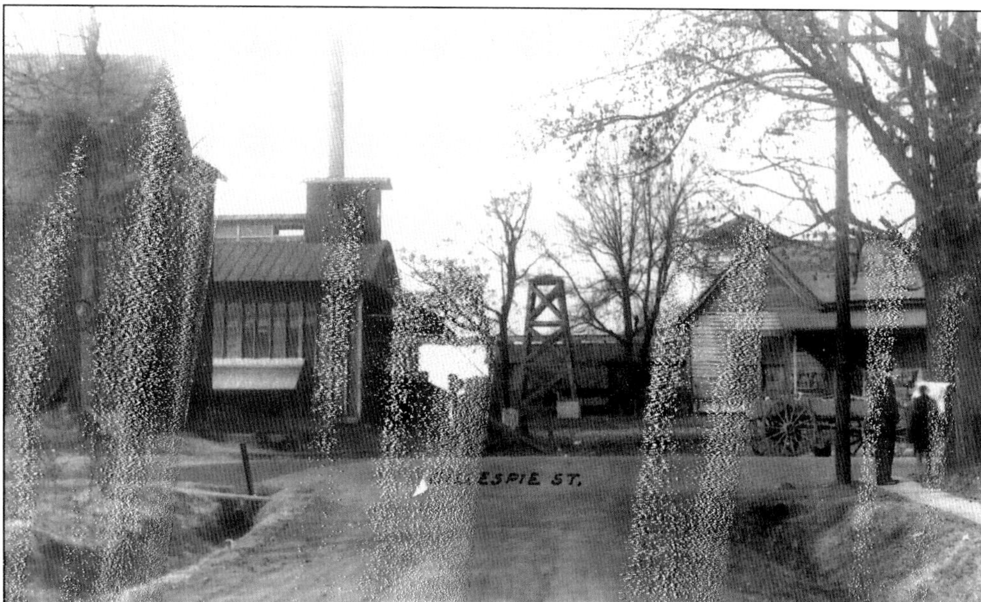

The Starkville Cotton Oil Company, which was located across from the Big Star grocery store on Russell Street, was established in 1900. The company also ran an ice plant, with 35 employees and delivery wagons that ran daily. (MG.)

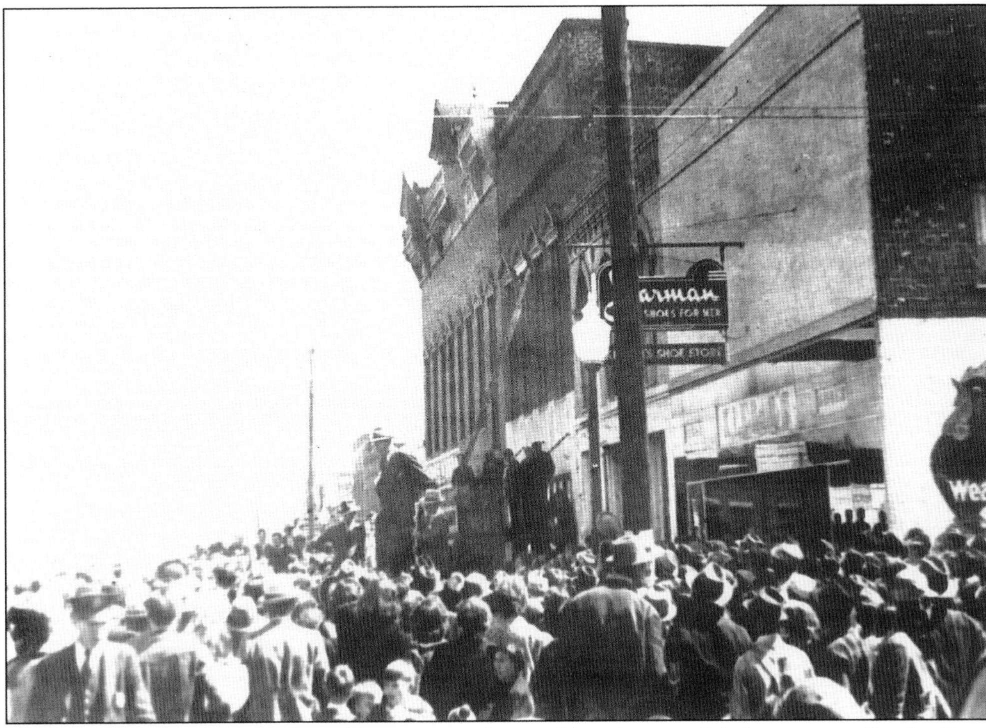

Robert Wardlaw, who was the tallest man in the world with a size 34 shoe, was in Starkville to help with one of Kleban's shoe promotions. (HT.)

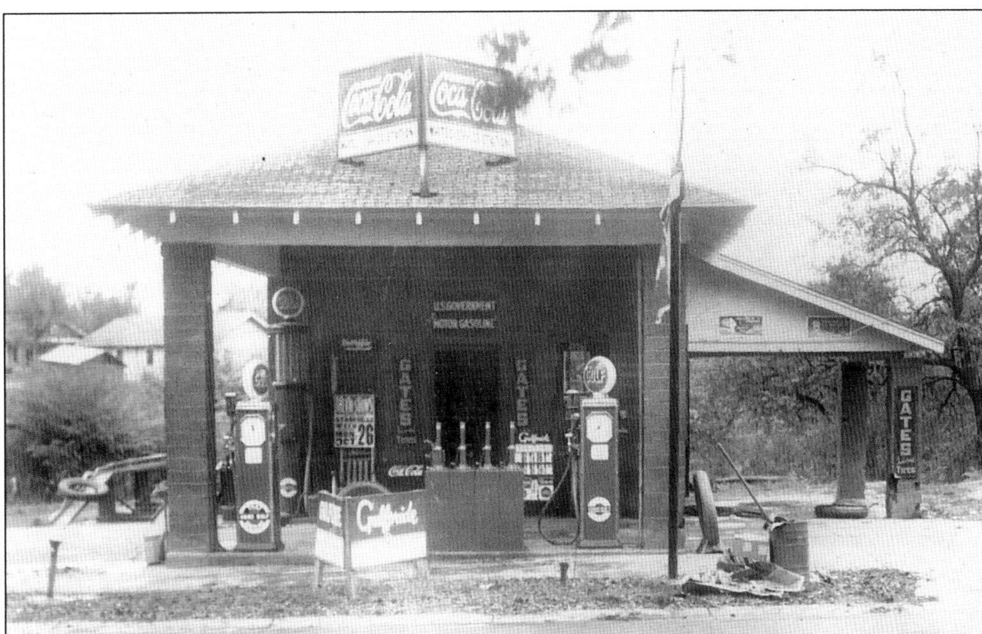

Gulf Station, pictured in the 1930s, sat in Dr. James Long's current office location. Highway 12, which ran in front of Gulf Station, was heavily traveled. (EO.)

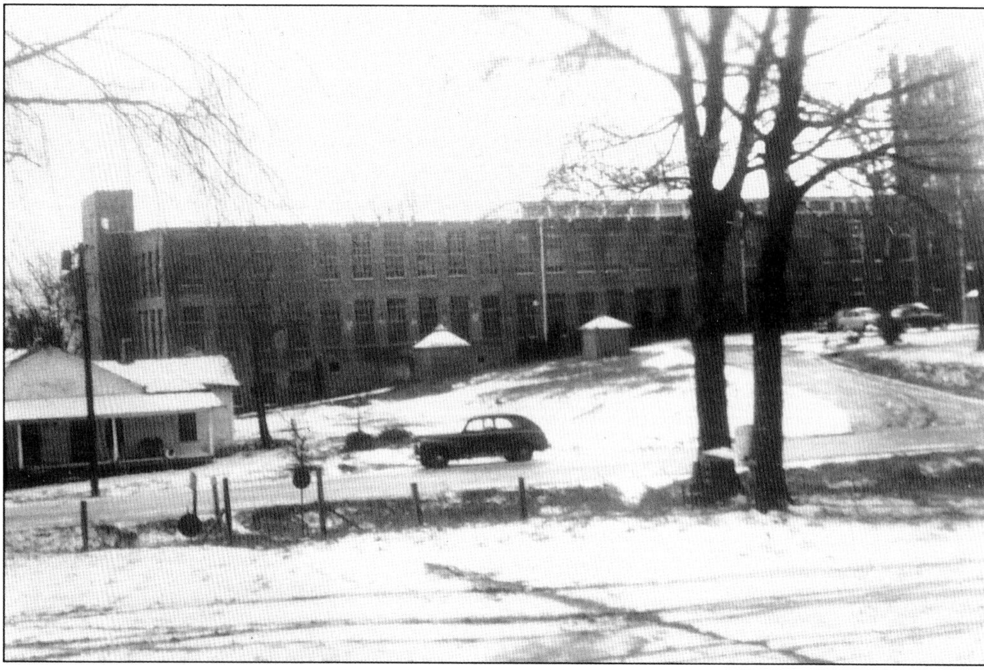

Mr. W.W. Scales served as president of the John M. Stone Cotton Mill, which was established in 1902 on the Mobile and Ohio Railroad. The mill employed 75 workers, who ran 150 looms and 5,360 spindles. (EB.)

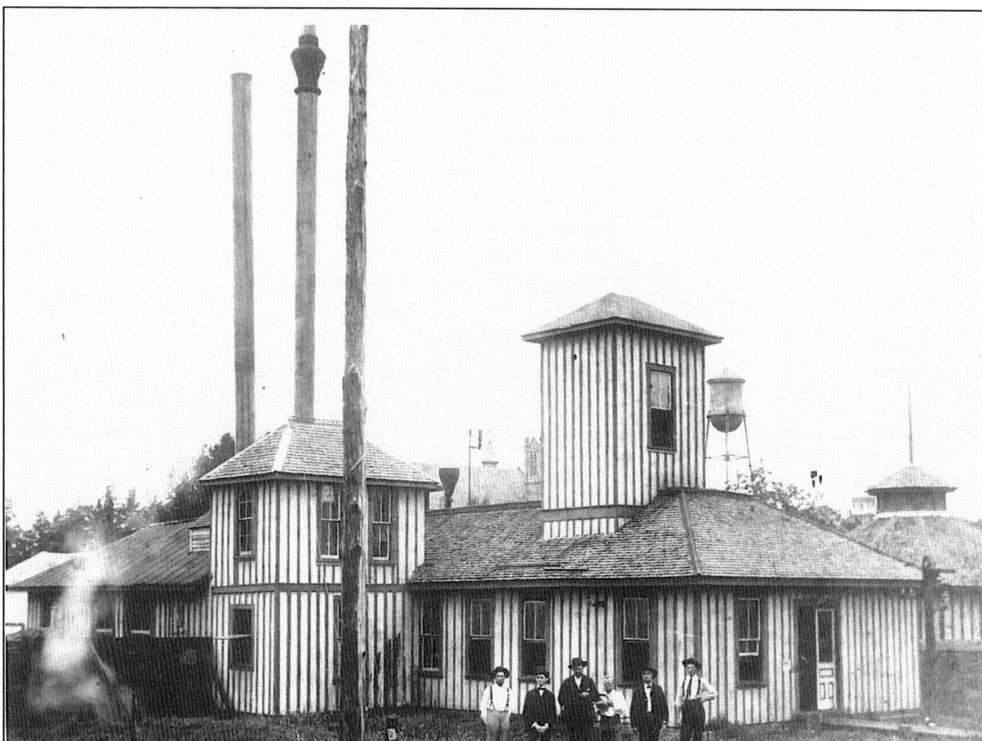

Shown in 1909 are the fire department, water works, and power plant on Jackson Street. (HB.)

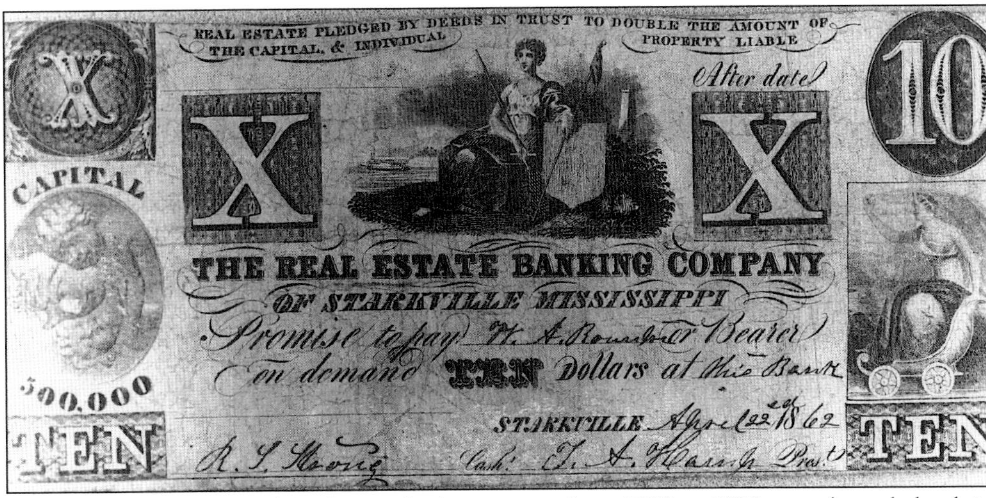

Starkville Real Estate and Banking, which was open from 1835 to 1839, was the only bank in Starkville that printed money. Many types of money with different values were being used in the county. This bill was probably used during the Civil War. (BFH.)

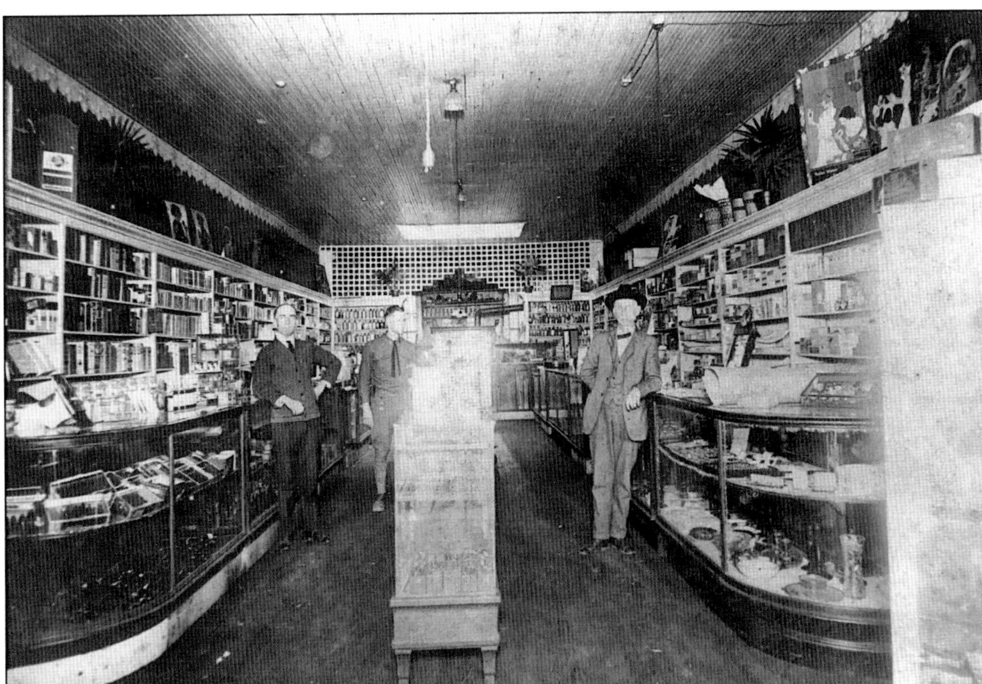

The Hartness and Redus Drugstore was one of the largest candy distributors in the United States. (OHM.)

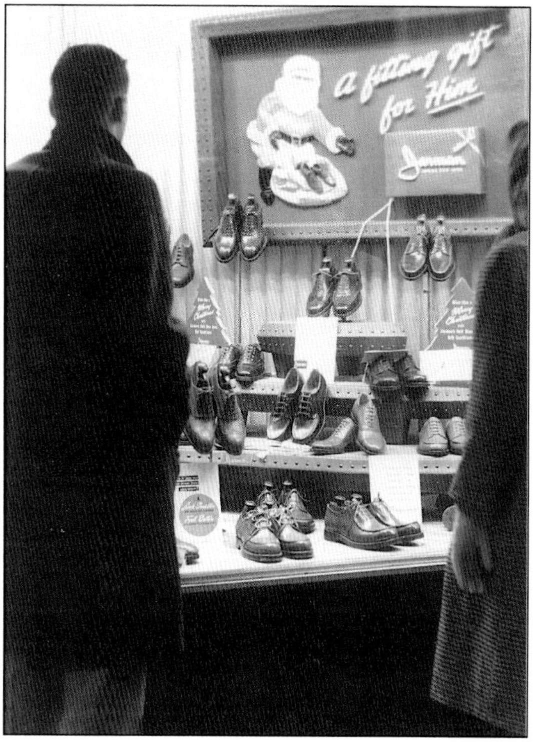

These people, who are pictured in front of Kleban's Shoes, spend time window shopping, a popular pastime in the 1950s. (FB.)

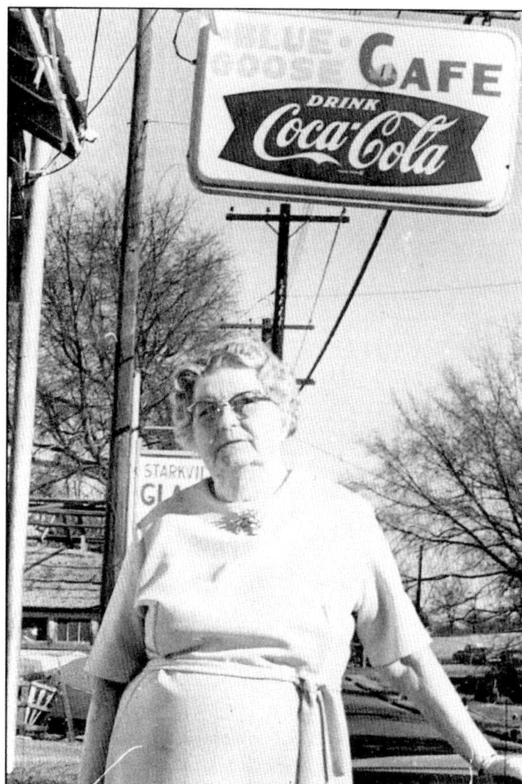

Mrs. Raines owned the Blue Goose Cafe, which was located in the "Needmore Area" near the old cotton mill. (PR.)

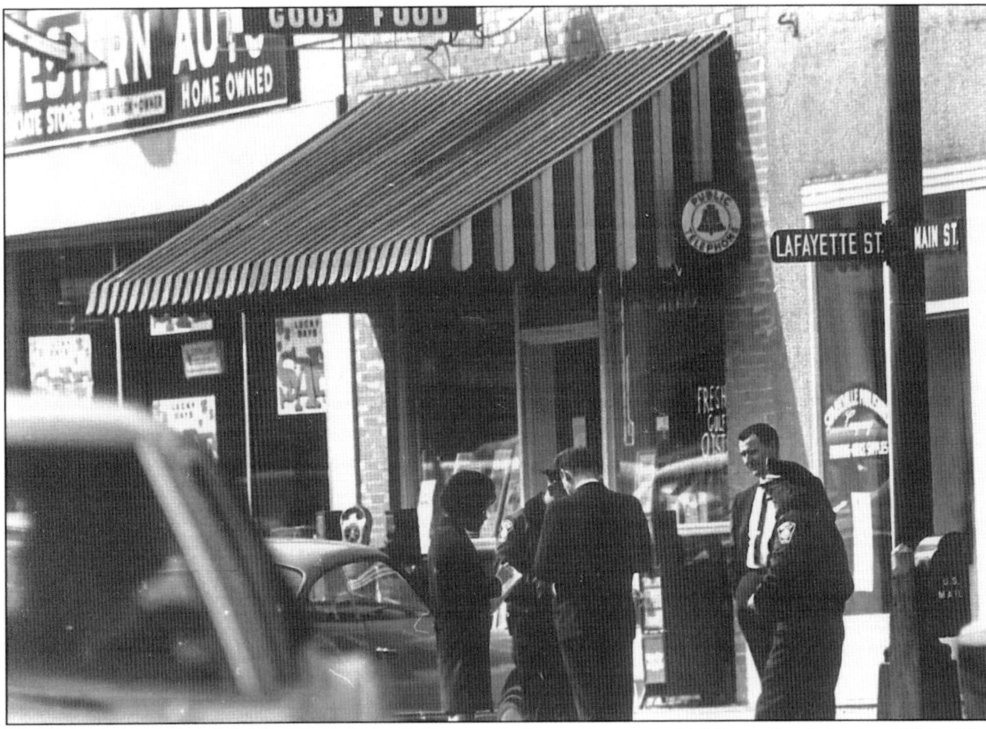

Mitchell and Marmaduke opened the Peoples Cafe in the early 1920s and sold it in 1972. The cafe employed all black, male waiters. The town's favorite waiter was Blue Billups, who never wrote his orders down and never got them wrong. (FB.)

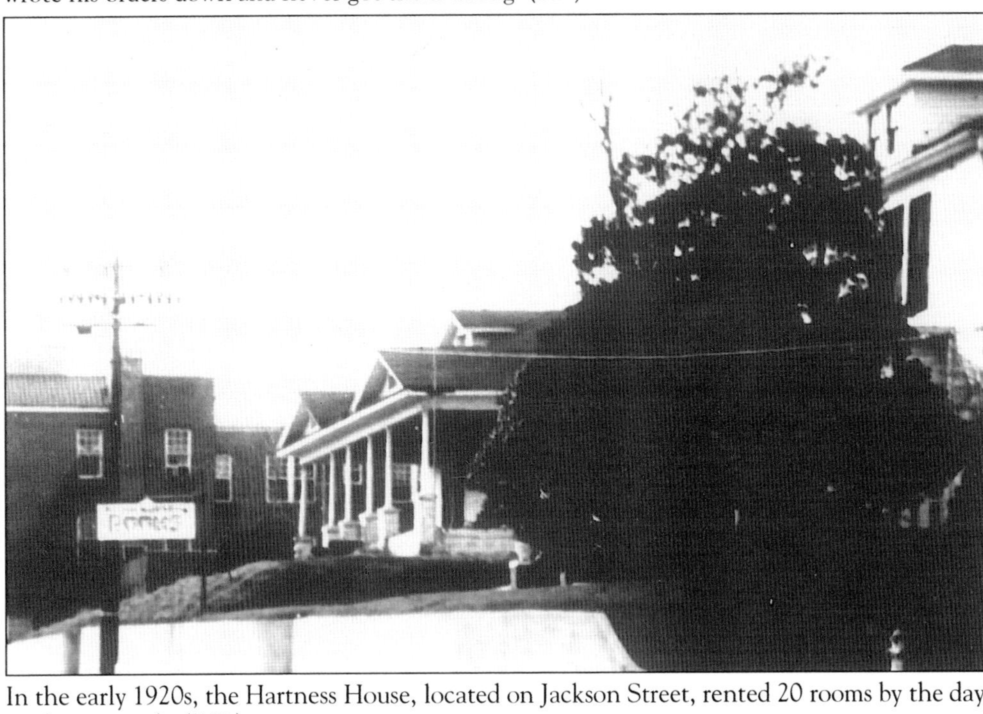

In the early 1920s, the Hartness House, located on Jackson Street, rented 20 rooms by the day, week, or month. (BG.)

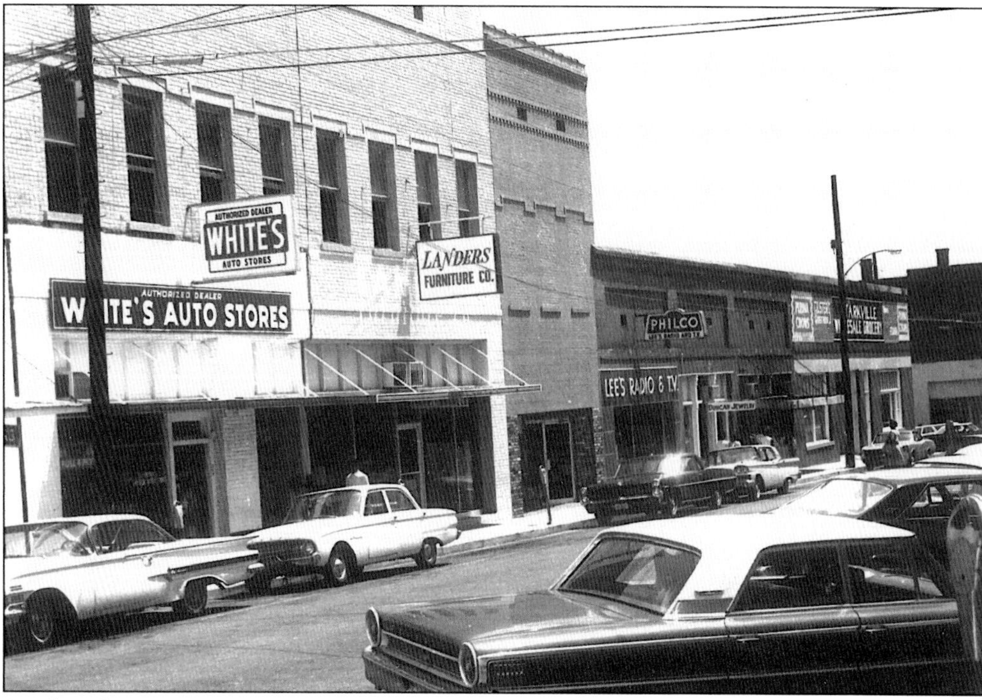

South Lafayette Street is pictured in the 1960s. (FB.)

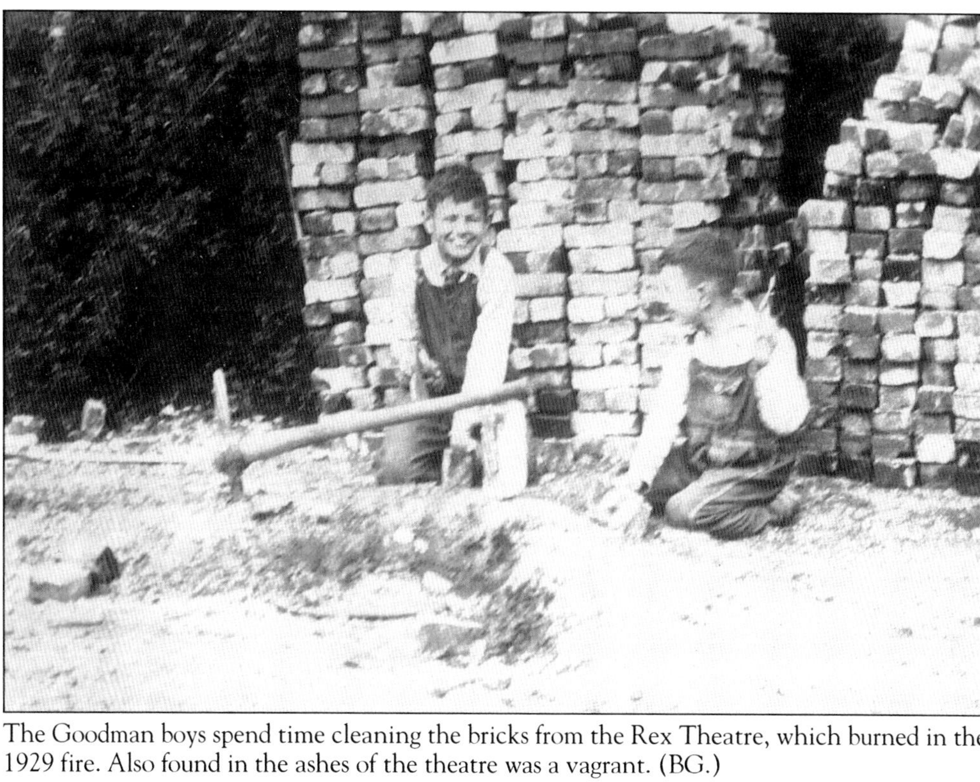
The Goodman boys spend time cleaning the bricks from the Rex Theatre, which burned in the 1929 fire. Also found in the ashes of the theatre was a vagrant. (BG.)

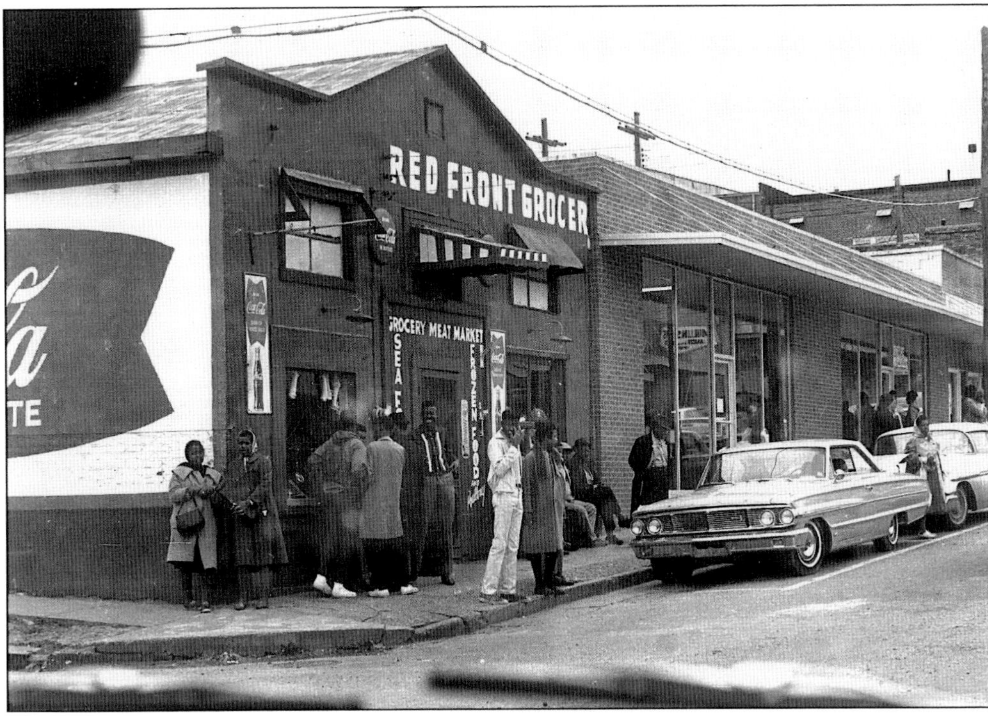

The Red Front Grocery, which was located on North Lafayette Street, had a picture of James Arness, who played Matt Dillon on the television show *Gunsmoke*. Arness was known to visit friends in Starkville. (FB.)

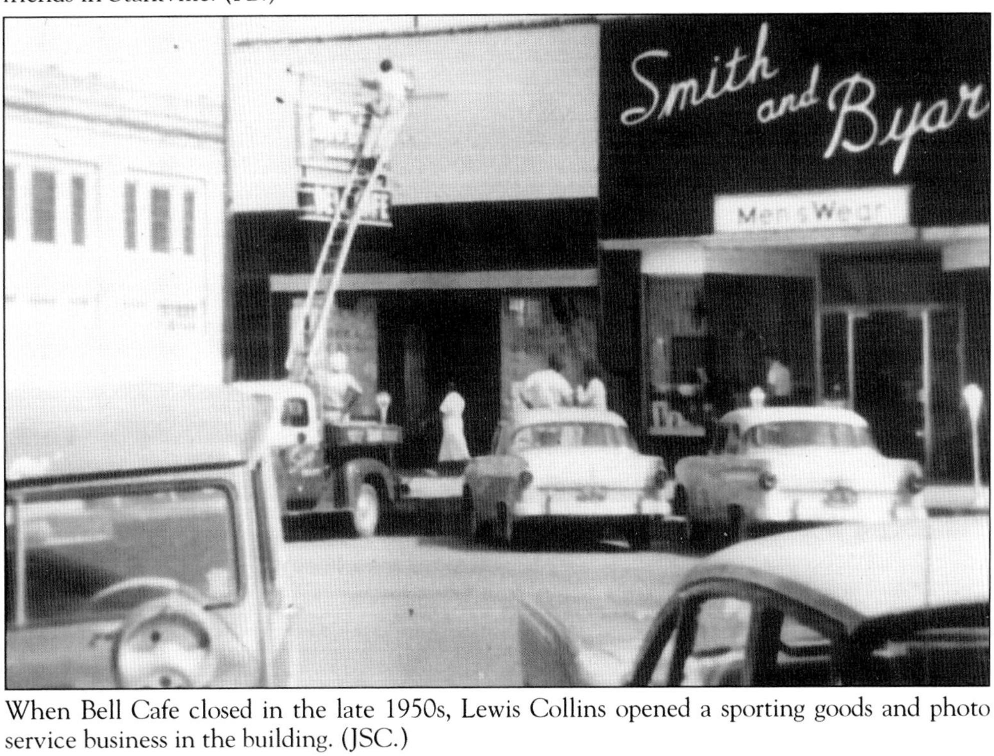

When Bell Cafe closed in the late 1950s, Lewis Collins opened a sporting goods and photo service business in the building. (JSC.)

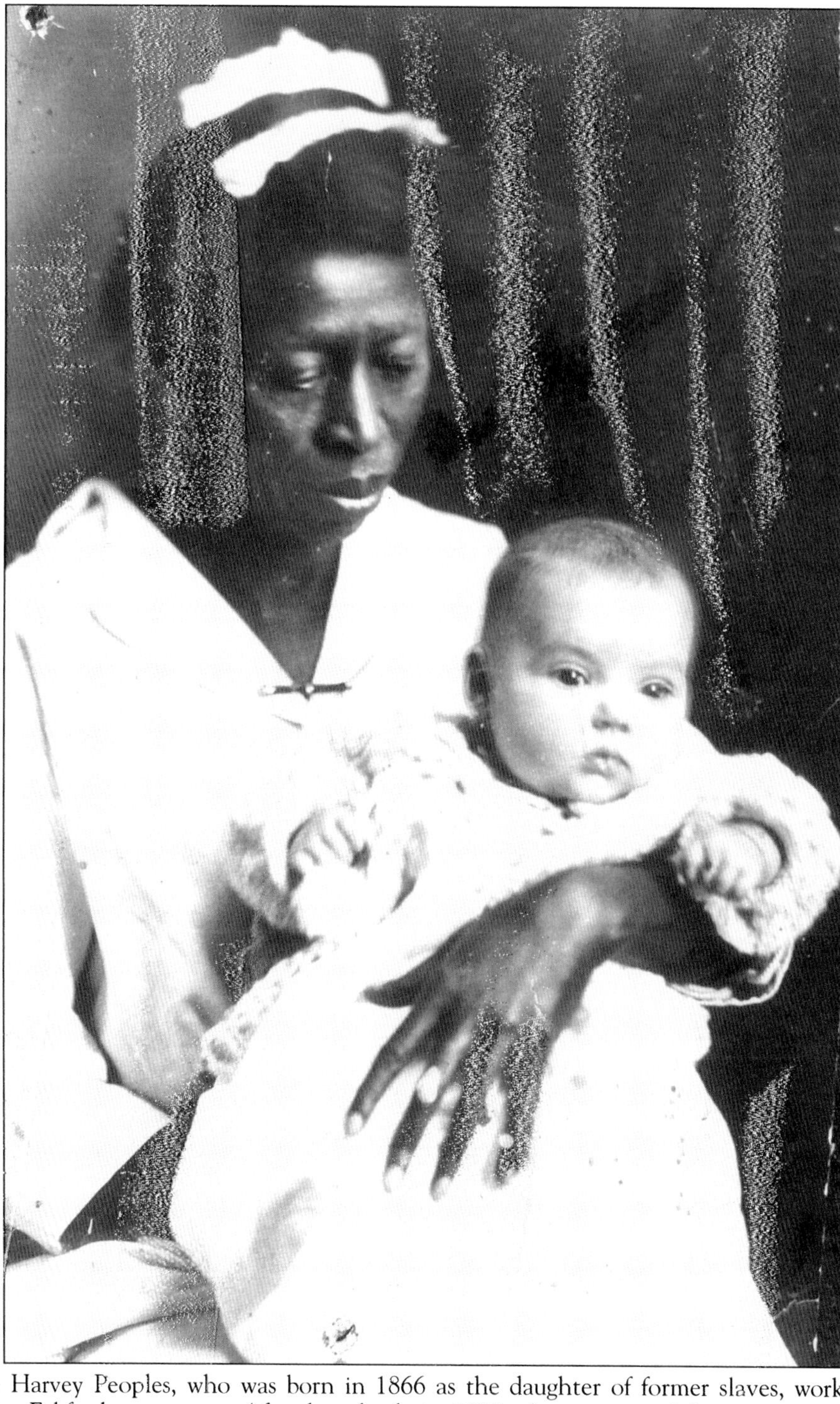

Grace Harvey Peoples, who was born in 1866 as the daughter of former slaves, worked for Dr. Jim Eckford as a nurse. After her death in 1930, the women of the county erected a monument in appreciation of her faithful service. Inscribed on the monument are the words, "A faithful servant and nurse—dedicated in gratitude by her white friends whom she loved and served." (BS.)

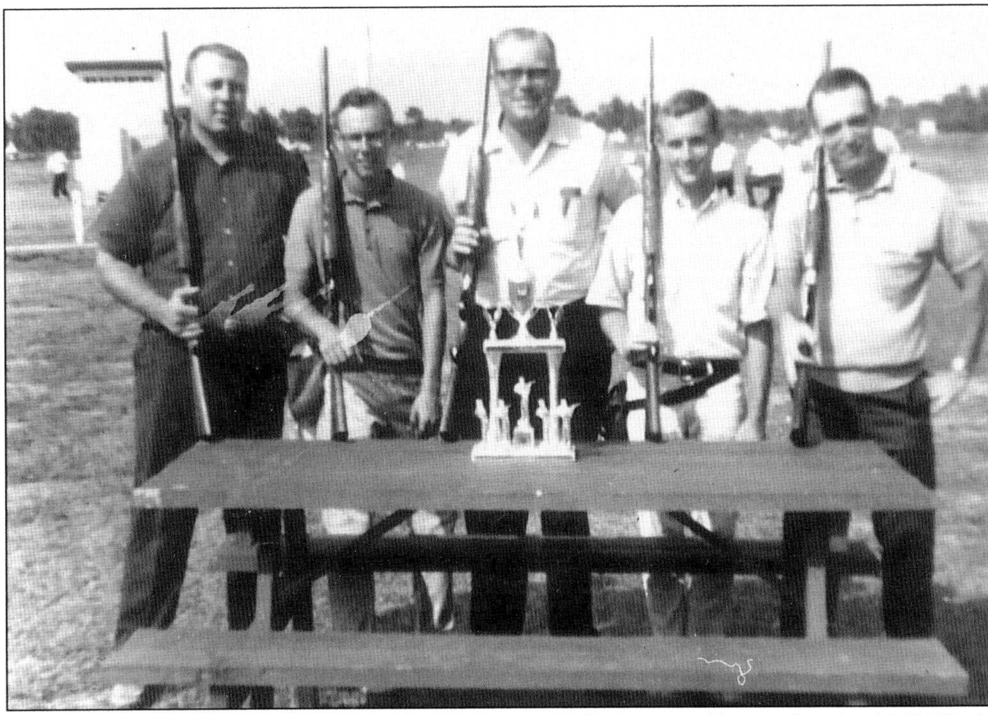

Starkville Gun Club's five-man team set the 20-gauge shotgun world record at the 1965 World Championship. Pictured are team members Bob Crawford, Tony Rosetti, Dan Hester, David Smith, and Gary Smith. (MS.)

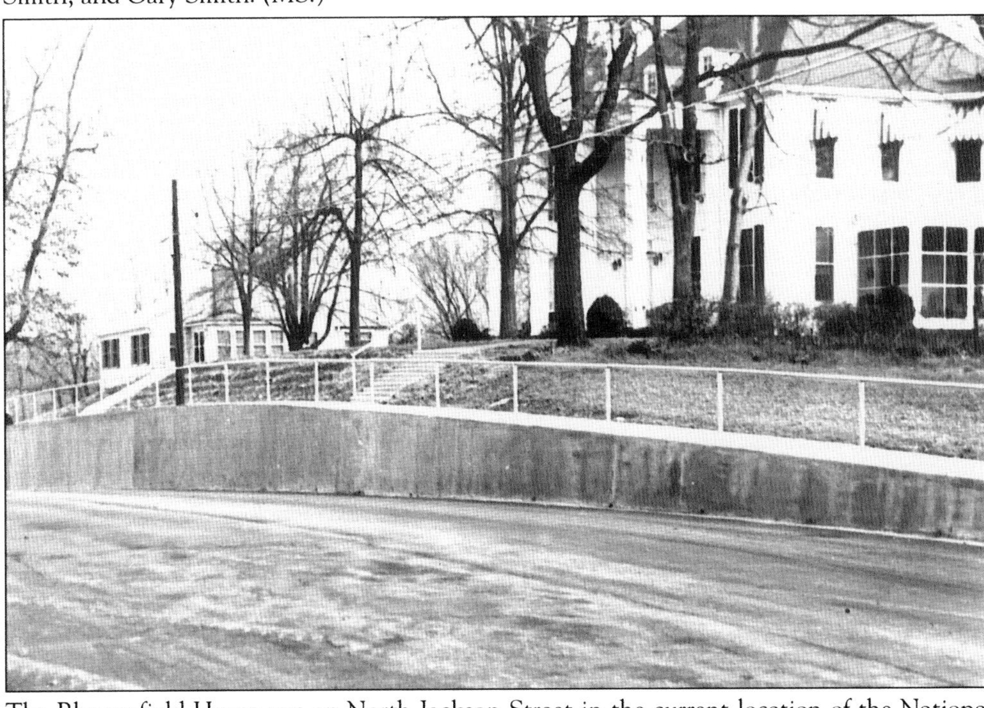

The Blumenfield House was on North Jackson Street in the current location of the National Bank of Commerce parking lot. (BG.)

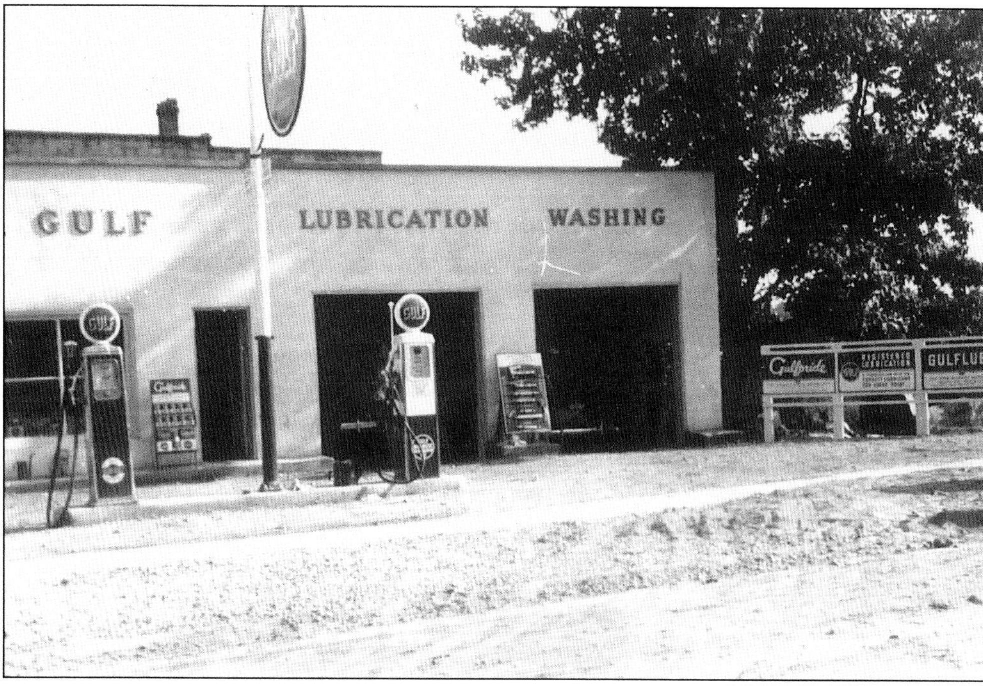

During the late 1930s, College Drive Gulf sat on Highway 12, which was the second busiest street in Mississippi. (EO.)

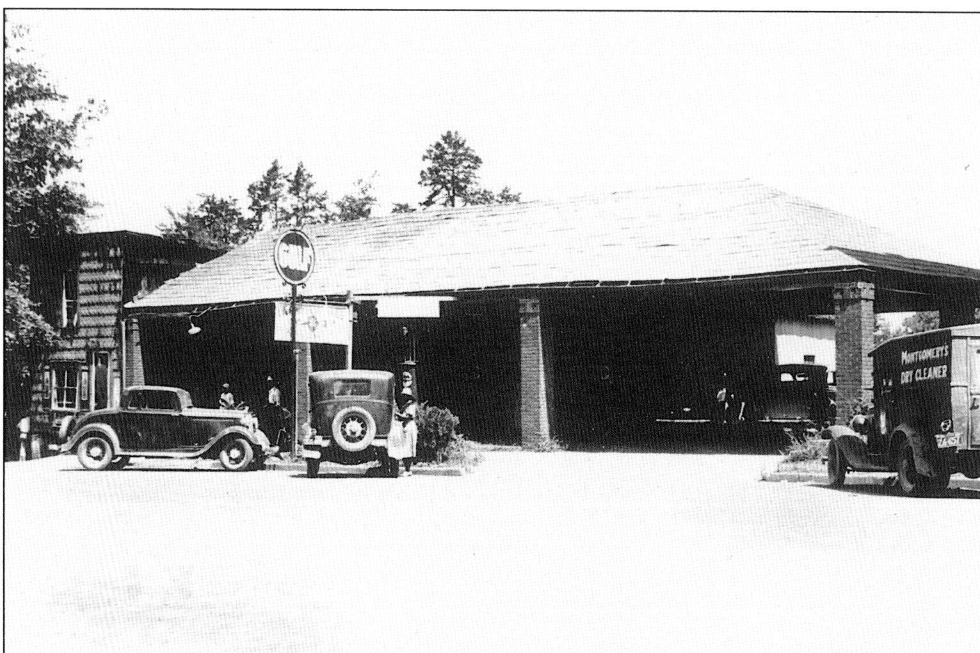

A Montgomery Dry Cleaner van parks to the right of the Gulf Station, which was located west of Ben Hilbun's office on Main Street. (EO.)

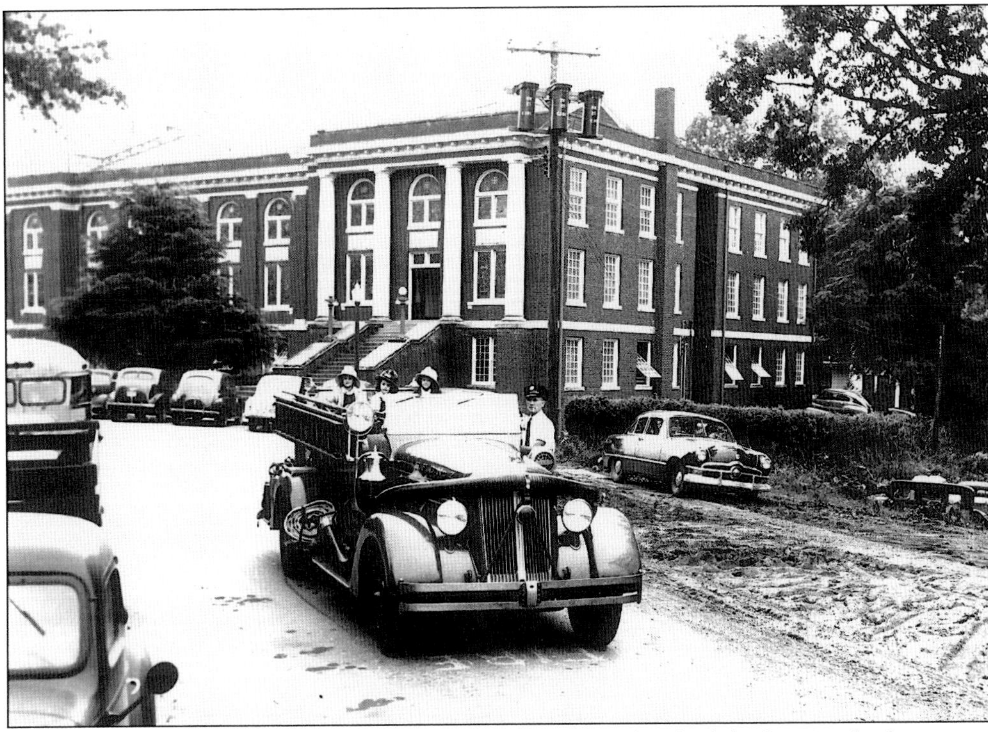

Three youngsters take a ride on the 1937 Seagrave fire truck, which had a 12-cylinder engine, duel ignition, and 24 spark plugs. The truck, which was the fastest in the state, could reach speeds as high as 95 miles per hour. Pictured in the background is First United Methodist Church. (CR.)

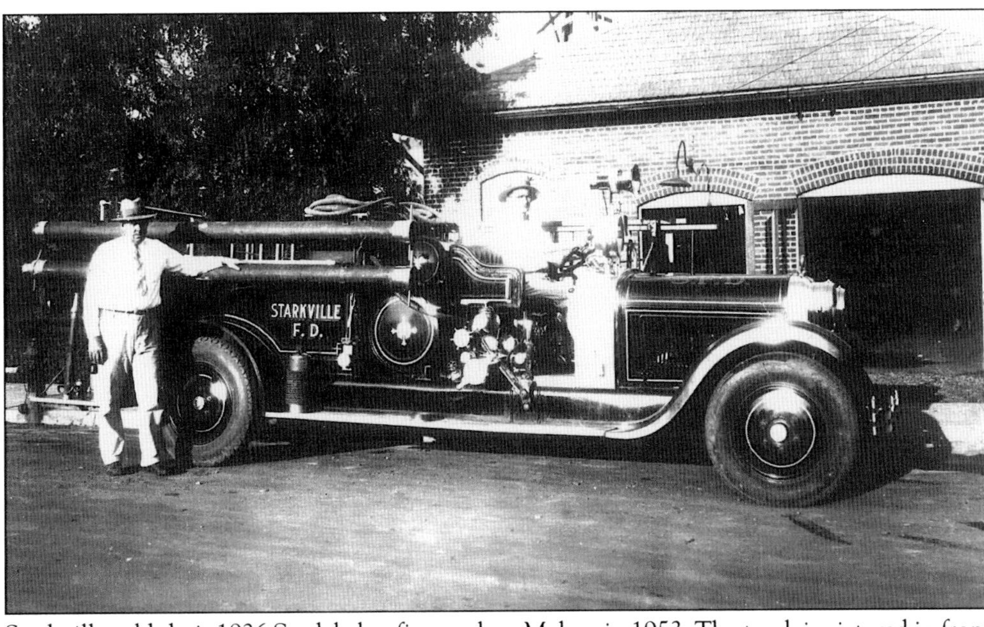

Starkville sold their 1926 Studebaker fire truck to Maben in 1953. The truck is pictured in front of the firehouse on Jackson Street. (CR.)

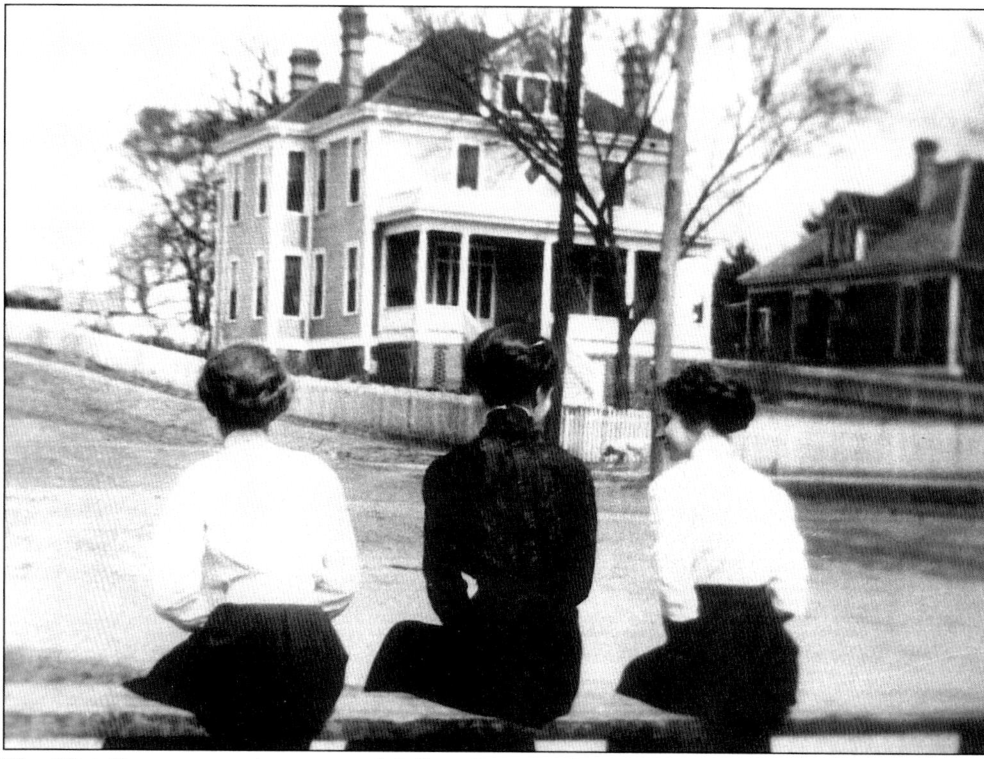

The Weir House sat on the corner of College Drive and Montgomery Street. Located across the street from the Wier House was the Cumberland Telephone Company, which was originally owned by Mr. Wier. The three women sitting on the bench could be telephone operators on break (see page 54). (JSC.)

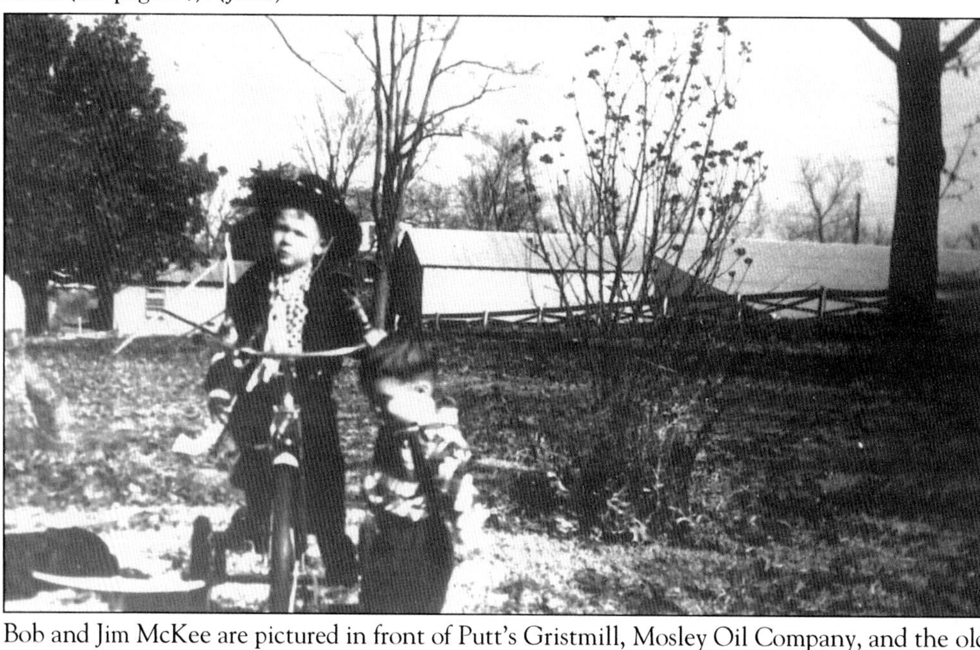

Bob and Jim McKee are pictured in front of Putt's Gristmill, Mosley Oil Company, and the old cotton warehouse. This is the current location of College Park Shopping Center. (JM.)

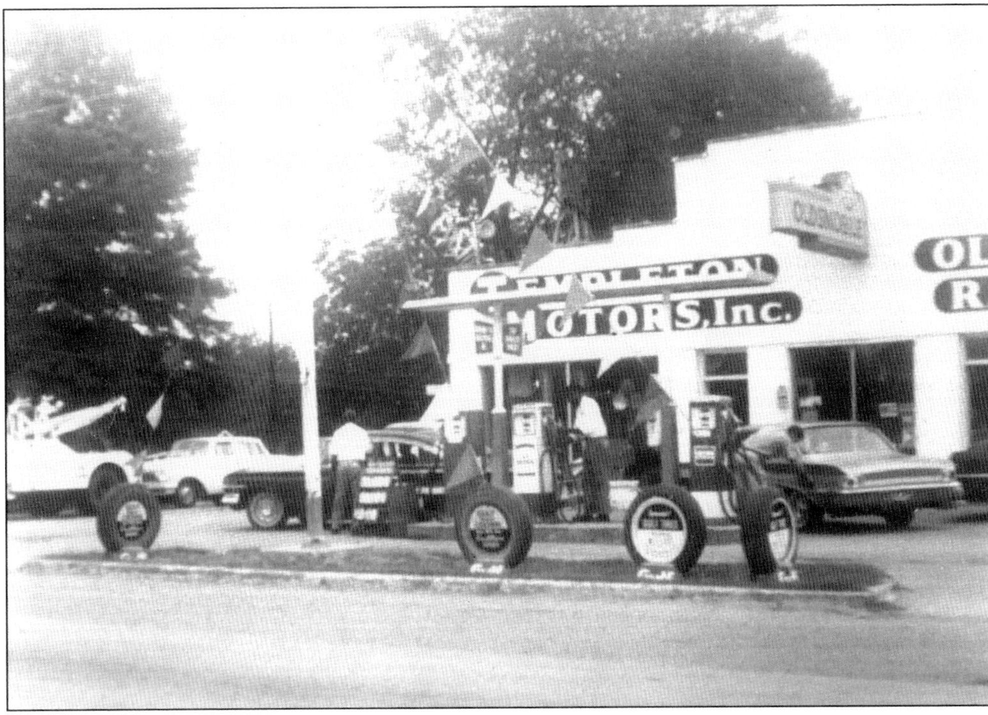

When Templeton Motors moved from the corner of Montgomery Street and Highway 12 in 1965, Holiday Inn, now Ramada Inn, built on the location. (EO.)

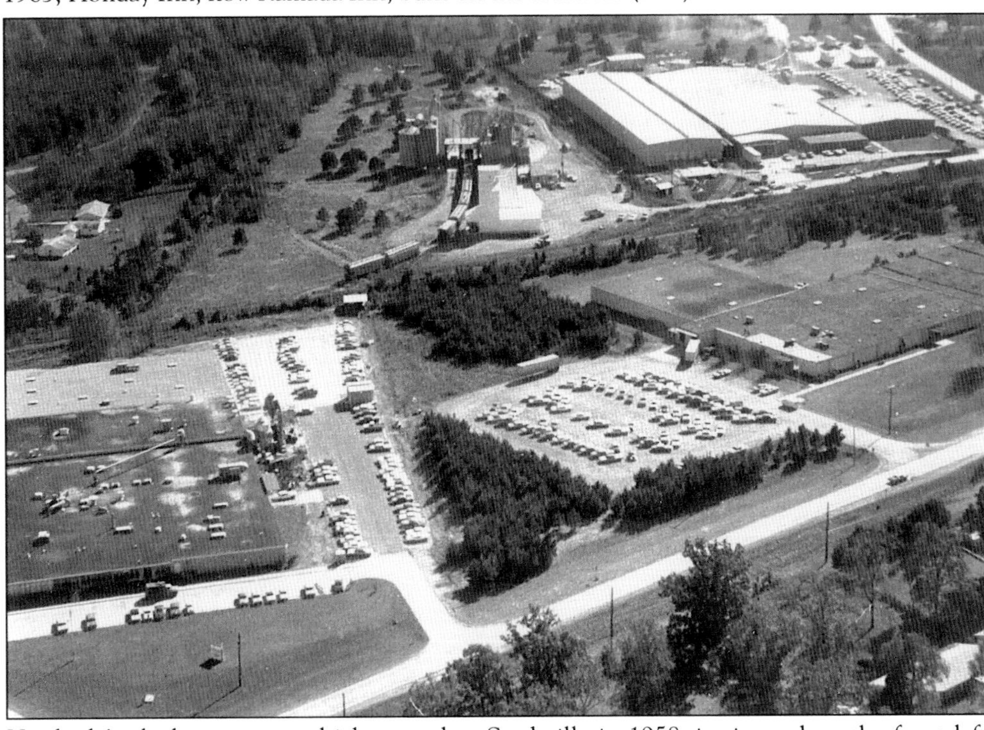

Hershede's clock company, which moved to Starkville in 1958, is pictured on the front left. Garan's shirt factory is on the front right, and Howard Furniture is on the back right. (SC.)

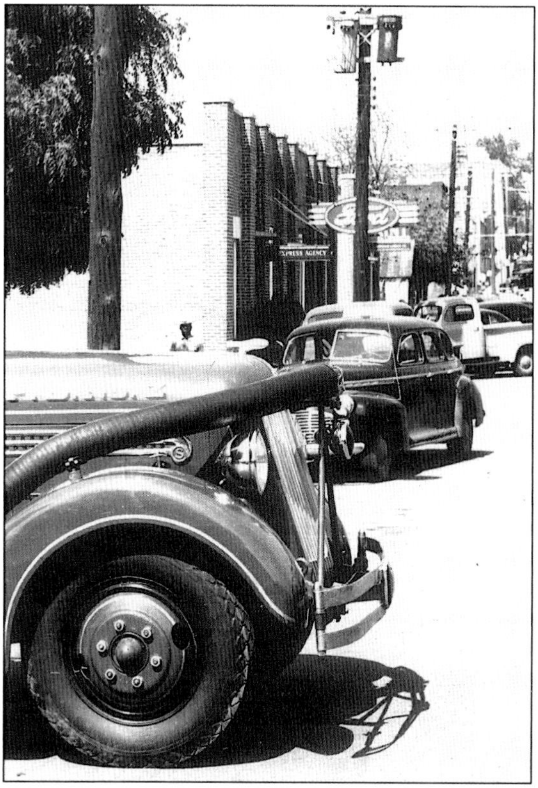

Seen on South Jackson Street are a fire truck parked on the side of the fire station, the Railway Express, and the Lolley Motor Company. (CR.)

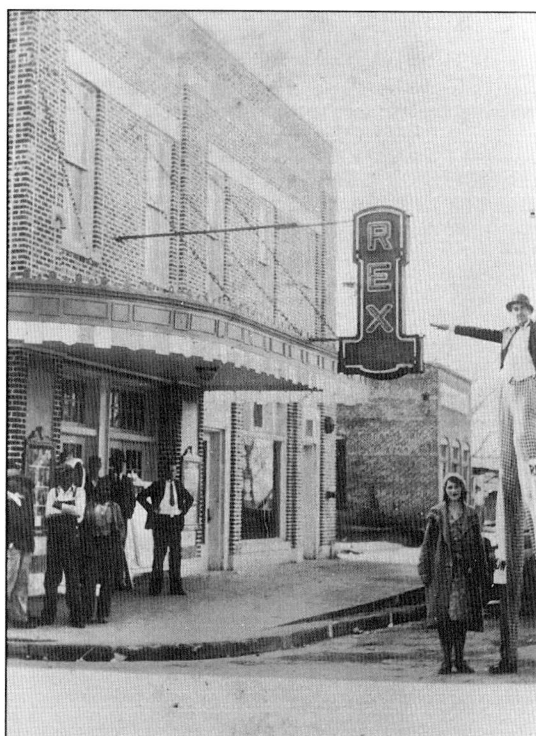

Montgomery Jewelry Inc. got its start between the Rex Theatre and the *East Mississippi Times* newspaper office. (BG.)

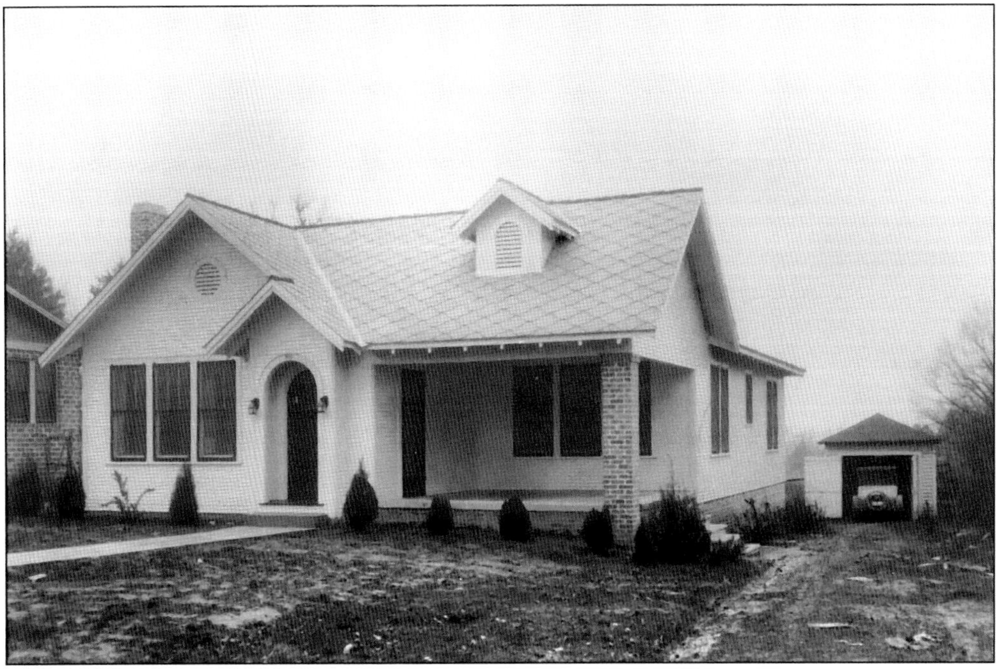

The Hartness House is pictured on College Drive in the early 1930s. (JSC.)

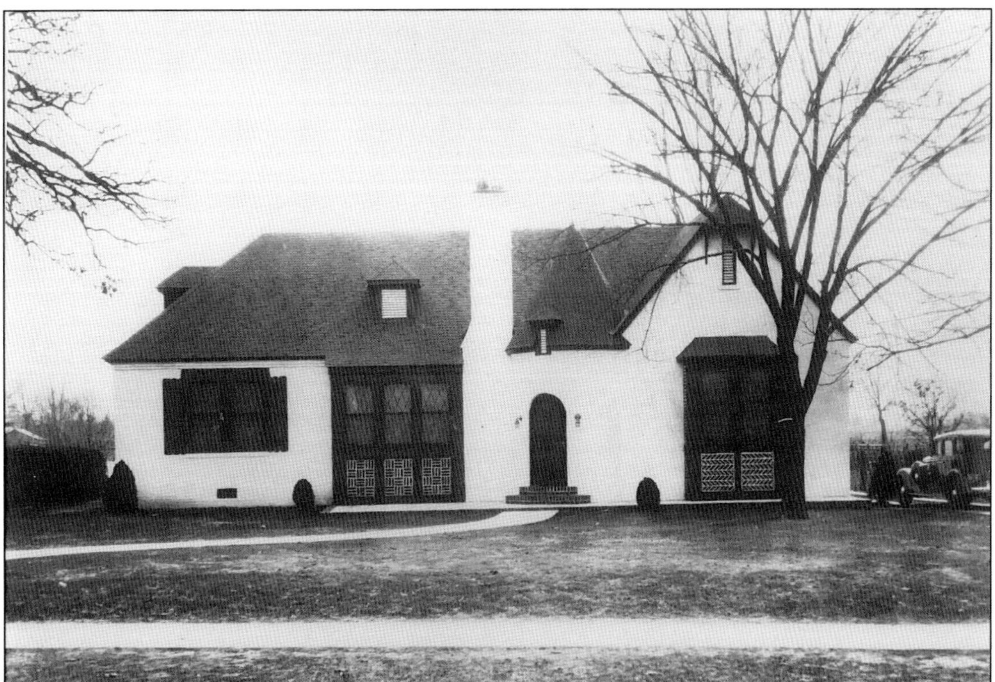

Thomas H. Johnston was the architect of the W.H. Gunn House, which was built on Greensboro Street in 1936 and pictured in the late 1930s. (JJ.)

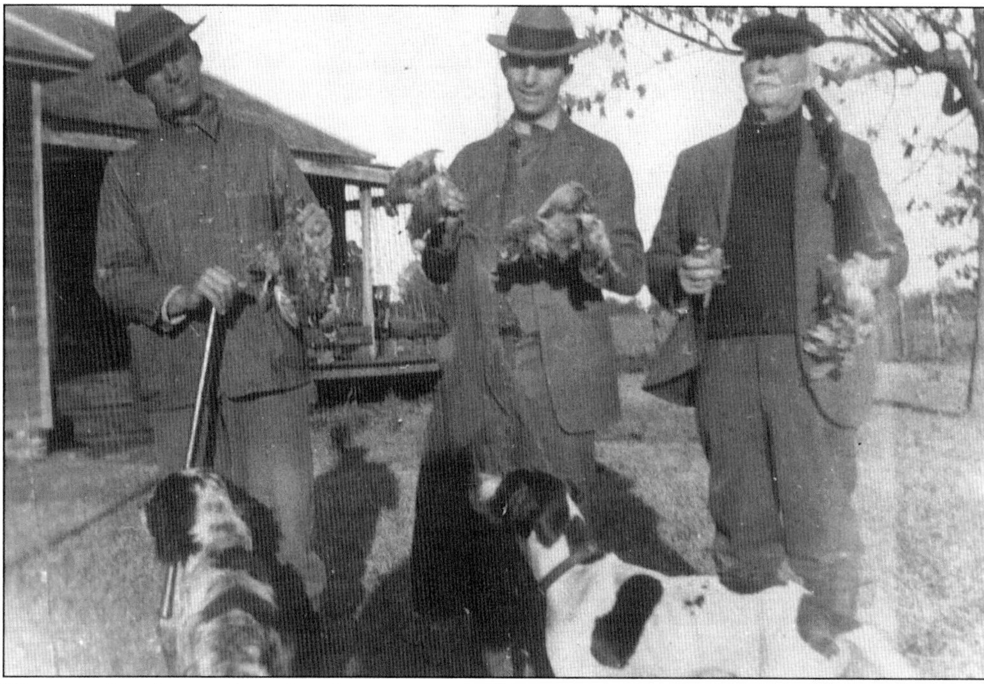

With an abundance of quail in the county, quail hunting became popular in the 1930s. (JSC.)

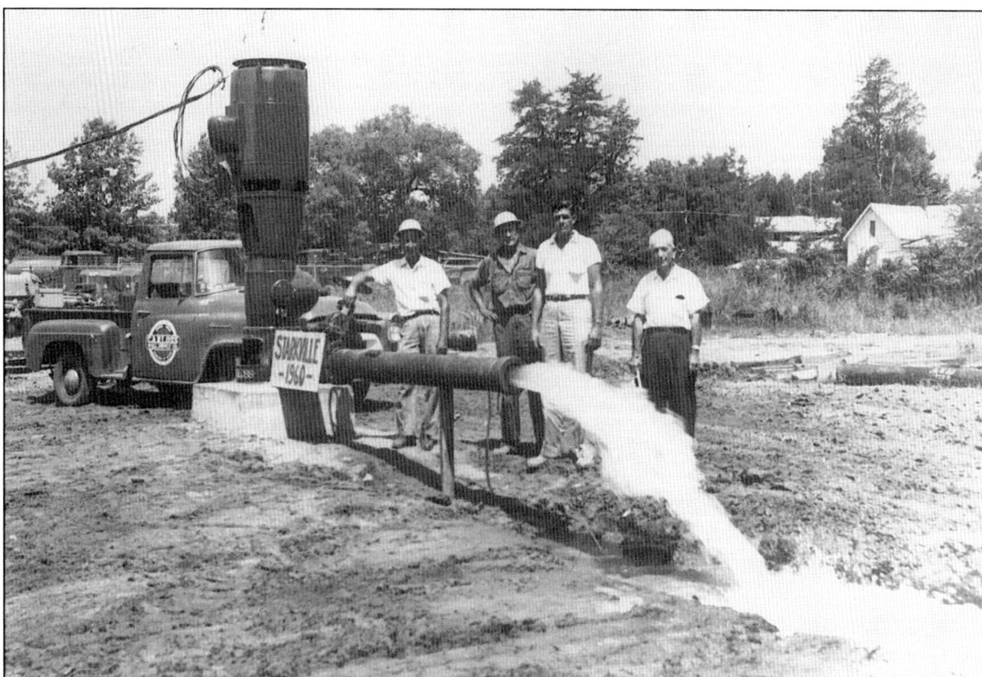

Carlos Wells workers J.P. Phillips, the water superintendent, and A.L. Goodman, the senior city engineer, install a water well on Scales Street in 1960. (BG.)

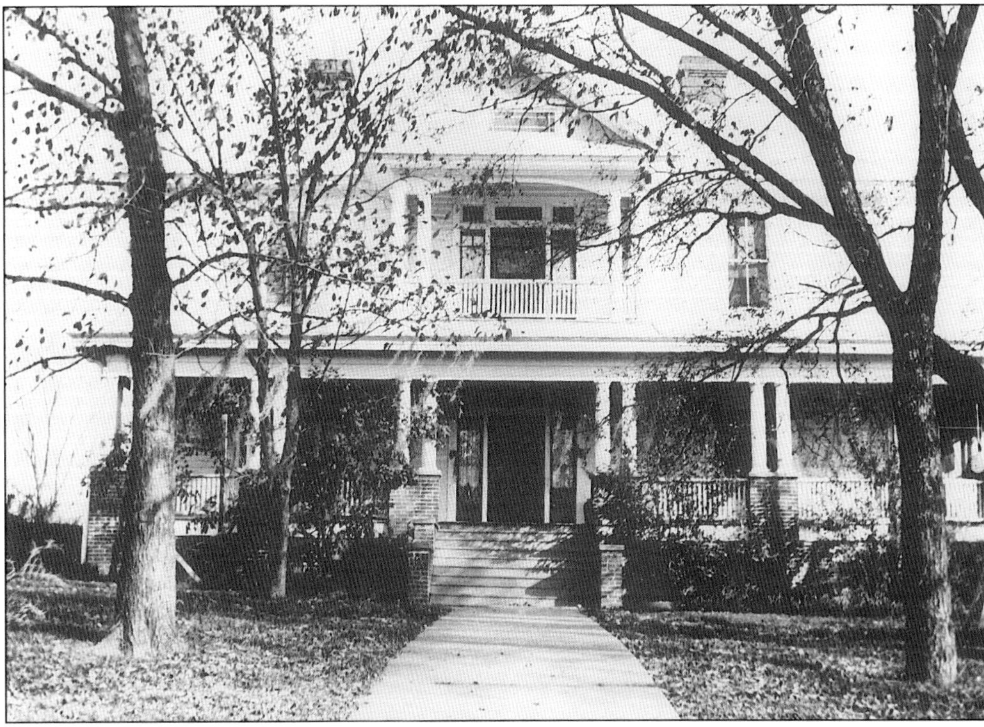
Since being built in 1912, the Sudduth House on North Jackson Street has had its porches removed. (MB.)

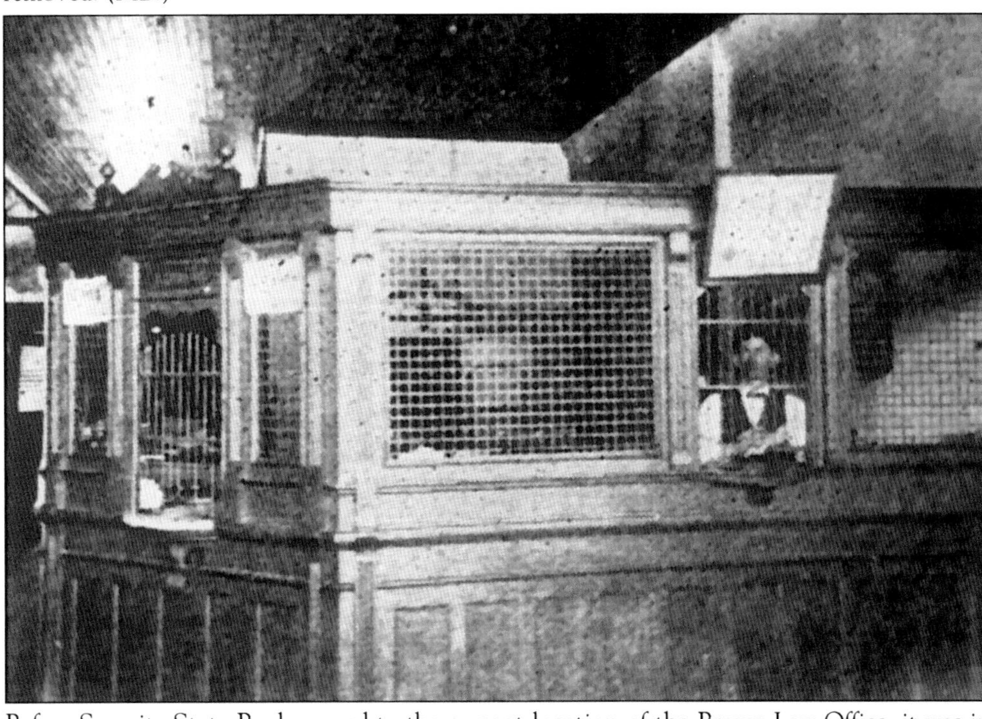
Before Security State Bank moved to the current location of the Brown Law Office, it was in the building east of the current law office. (JSC.)

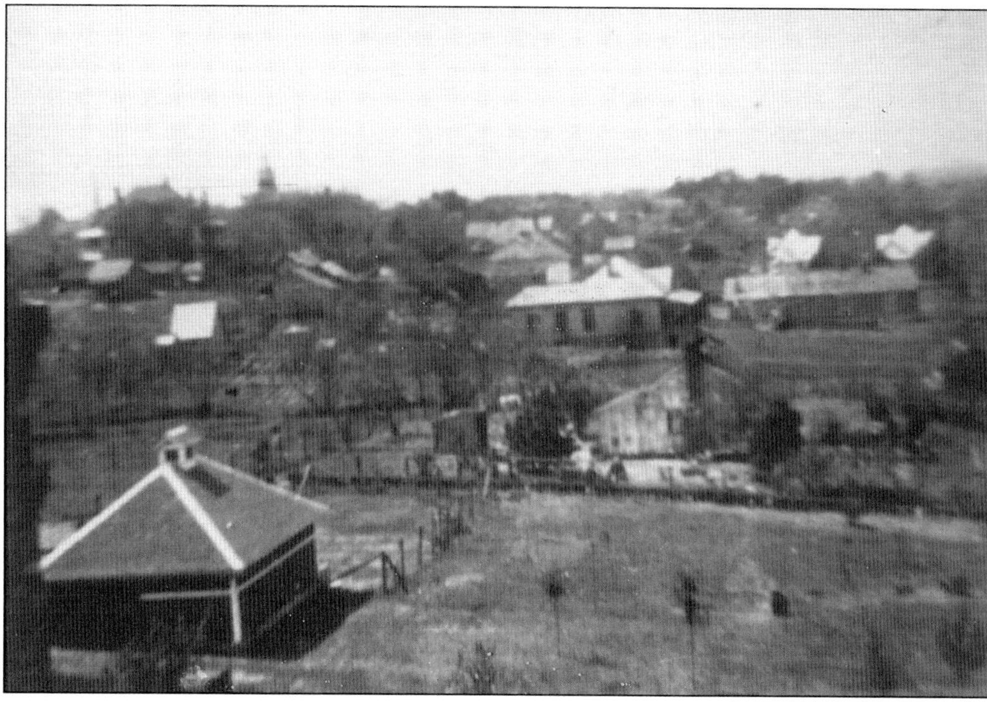

This picture was taken from the corner of Montgomery Street and Highway 82, looking towards town. (JSC.)

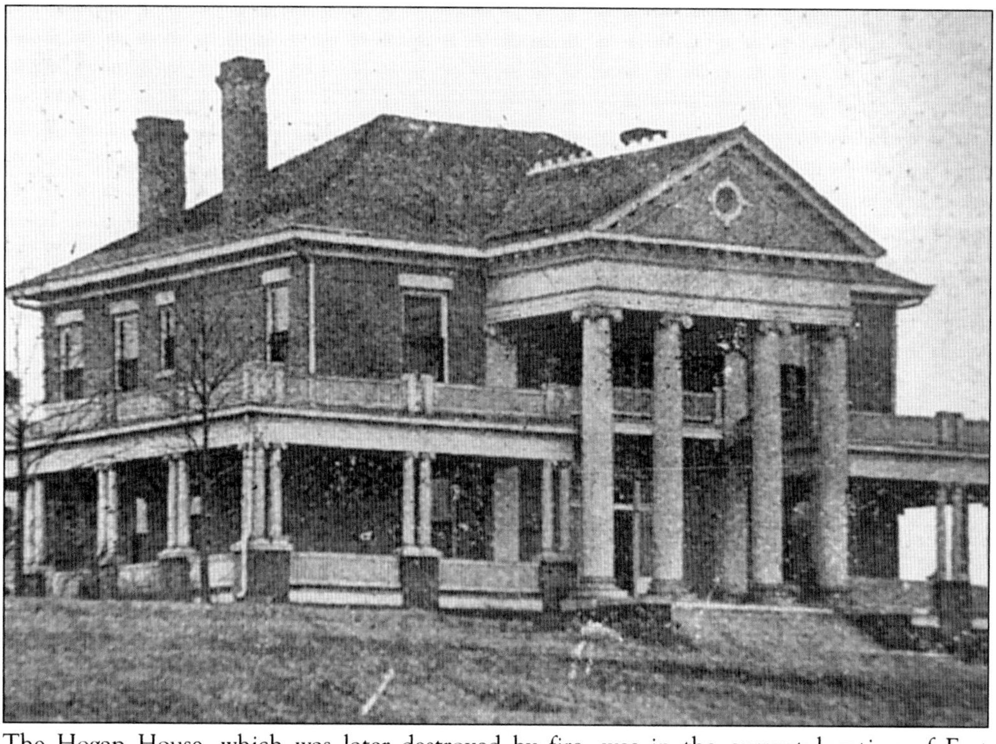

The Hogan House, which was later destroyed by fire, was in the current location of East Mississippi Lumber Company. (JSC.)

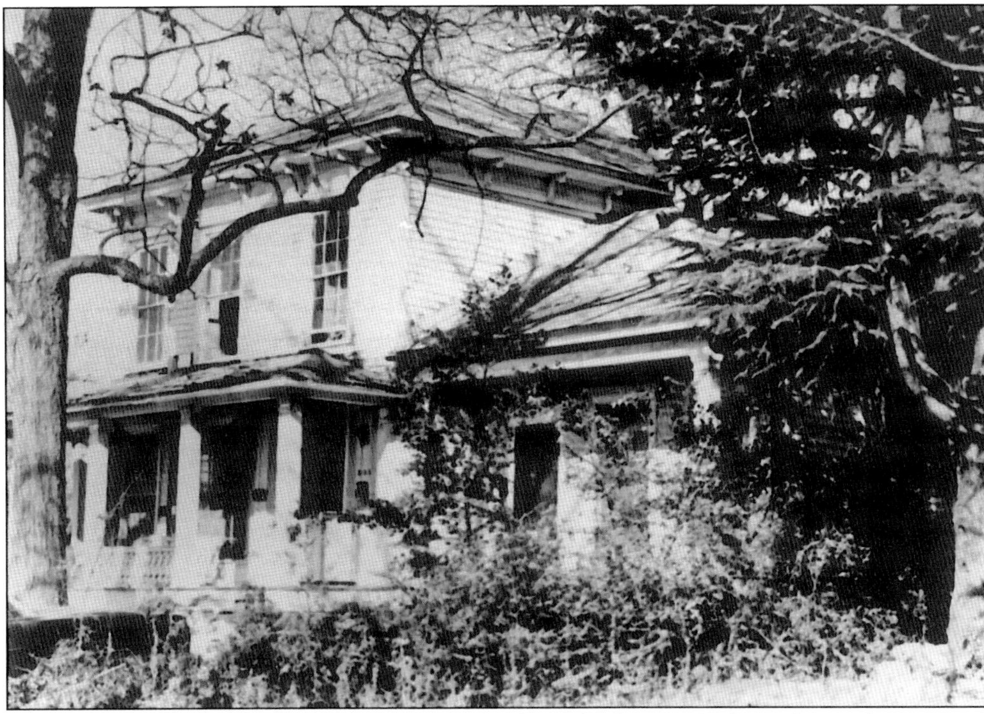

In the 1970s, Paul Sellars moved this house, which was built in 1868, from the northeast corner of Main and Jackson Streets to the Bell Schoolhouse community. (PS.)

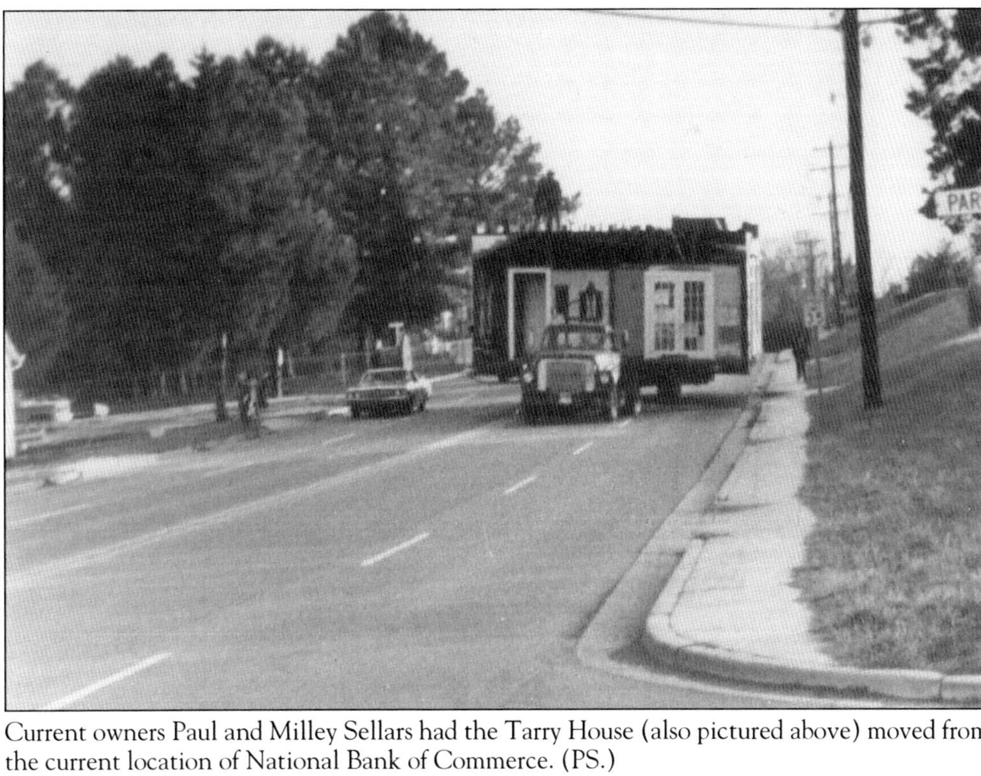

Current owners Paul and Milley Sellars had the Tarry House (also pictured above) moved from the current location of National Bank of Commerce. (PS.)

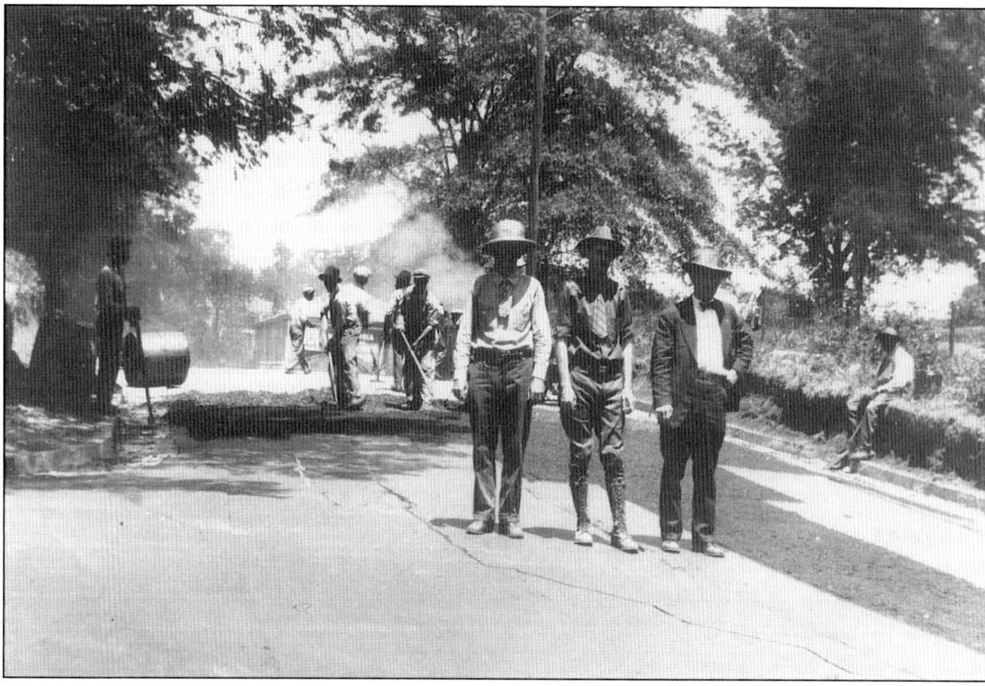

Men manually pave Lampkin Street during the late 1920s. According to Judge Carroll's *Historical Sketches of Oktibbeha County*, Starkville's first paved street was Main Street in 1923. By 1928, Starkville had paved most of its major streets at the cost of $250,000. (BG.)

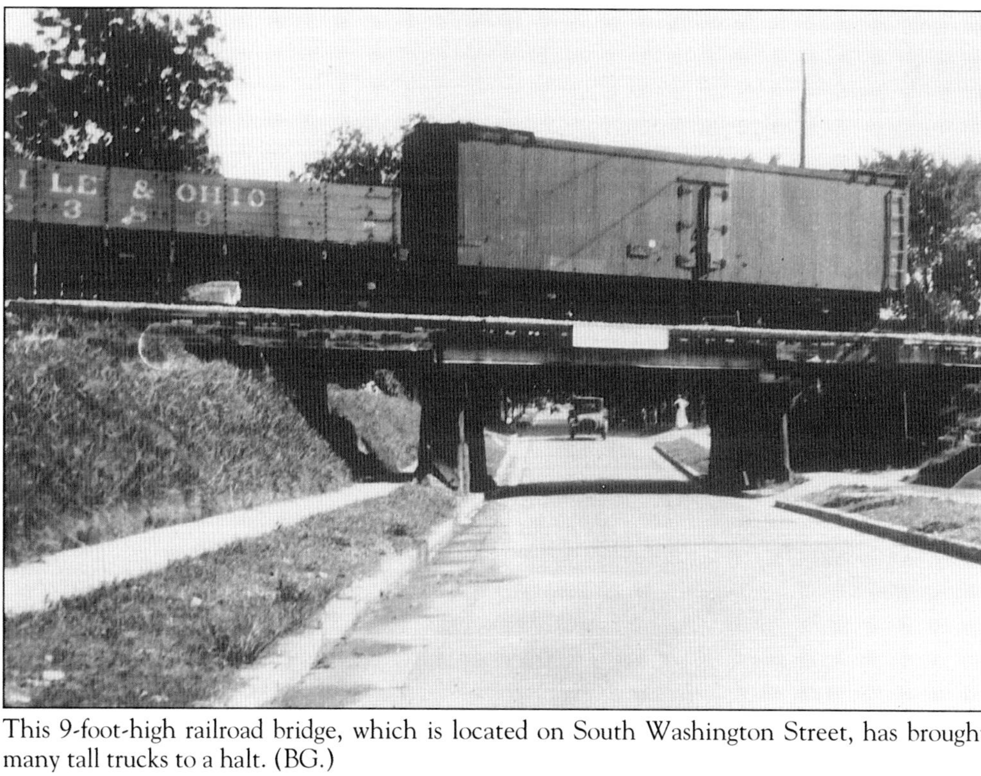

This 9-foot-high railroad bridge, which is located on South Washington Street, has brought many tall trucks to a halt. (BG.)

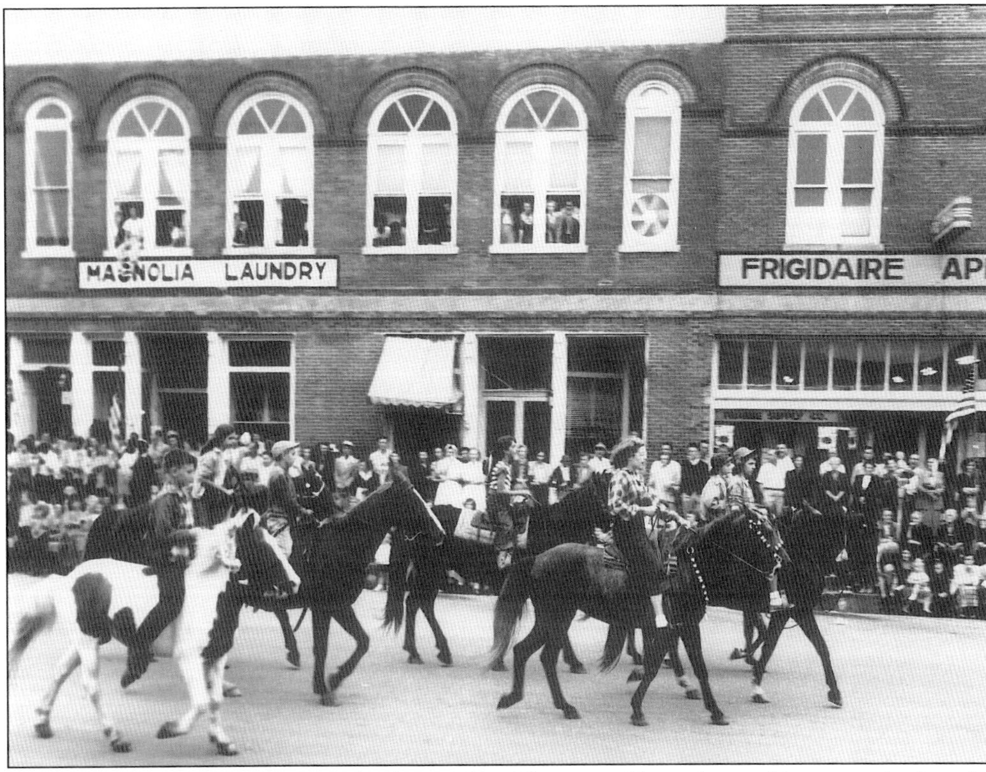

A parade marches downtown in the late 1930s. The post office is located between the laundry mat and the appliance store, which is now the Starkville Cafe. Jim Pruitt's photography studio was housed above the post office. (CR.)

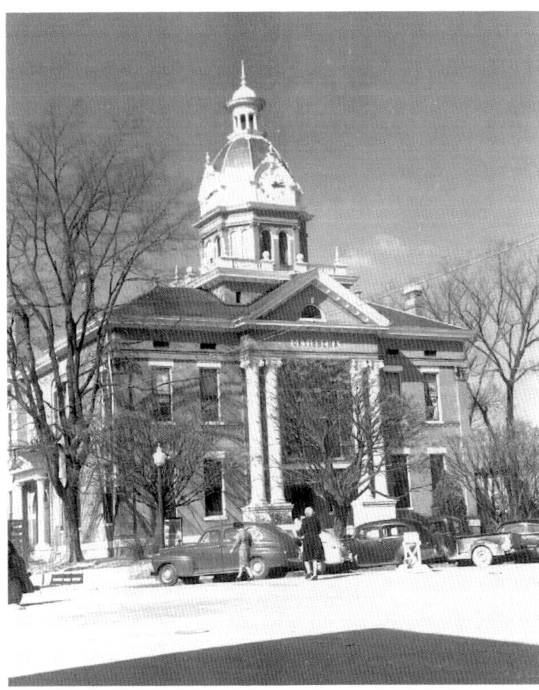

This courthouse was built in 1901 and torn down in 1961 because it was too large and expensive to keep up. (FB.)

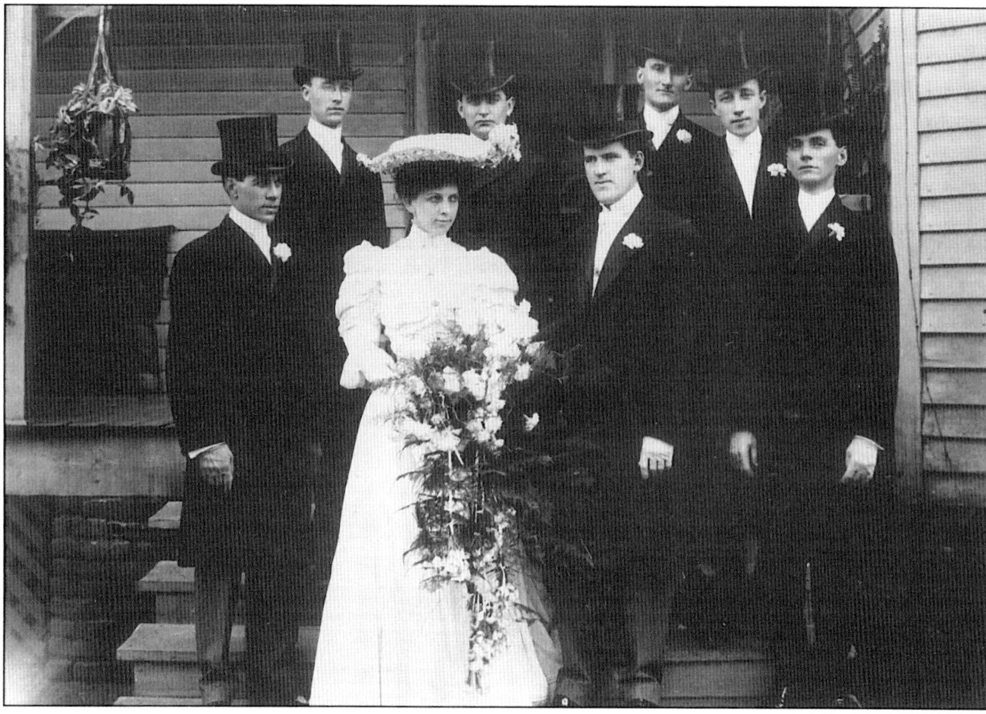

The Winchester wedding party poses on the steps of the Beattie House, which was located on Main Street during the 1900s. The groom, Mr. Winchester, served as head of A&M College's textile school. He later moved to New York to become the president of one of the country's largest textile companies. The bride, Miss Fanny Beattie, was the daughter of the town's mayor. (HB, BS.)

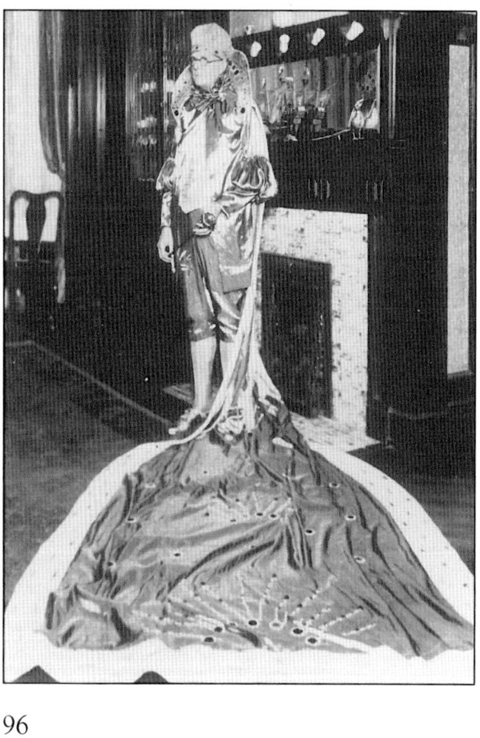

Judge Carroll's son was dressed for Mardi Gras in the Carroll's home on South Jackson Street. (OHM.)

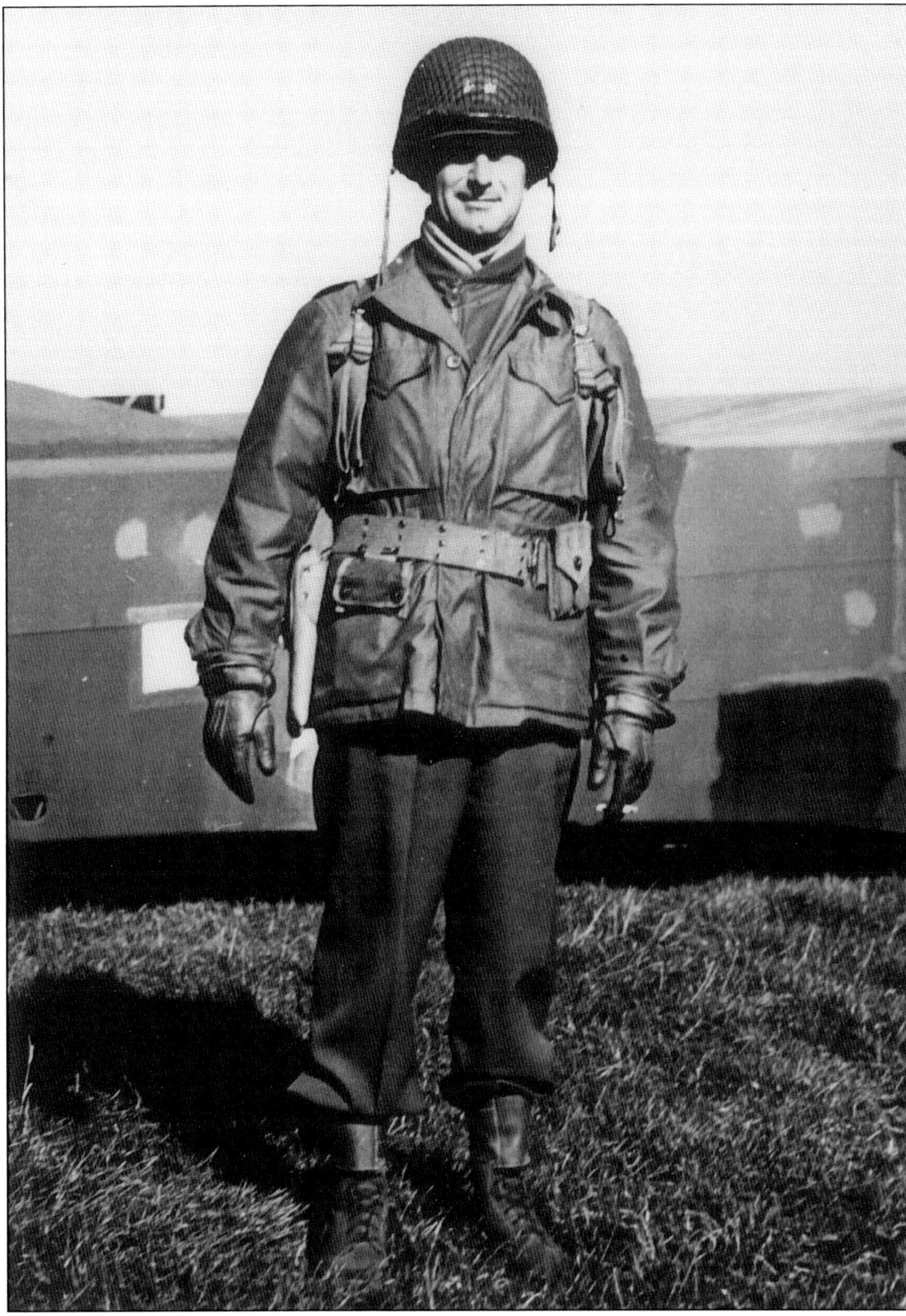

Maj. Gen. William M. Miley (12/26/1897–12/24/1997) was the last surviving division commander of WWII. Known as the "Father of the U.S. Army Parachute Troops," his 17th Airborne Division served at the Battle of the Bulge in January 1945. He and his division parachuted into Germany over the Rhine River. (MB.)

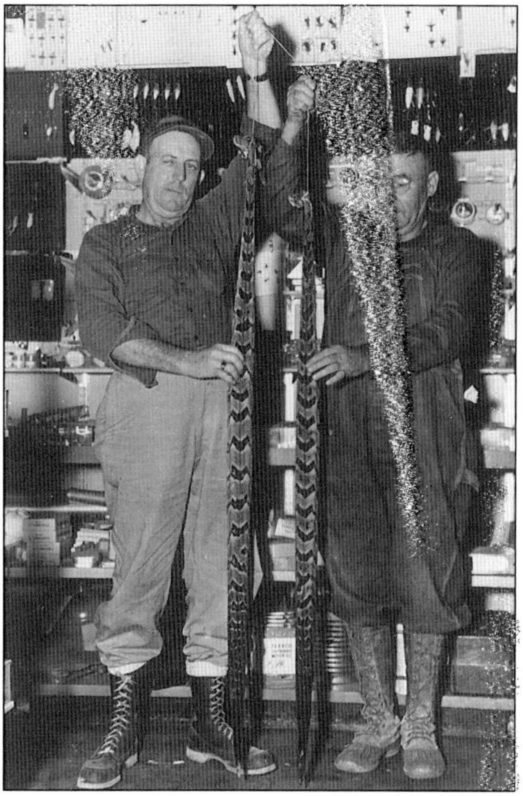

Showing off their rattlesnakes are John A. McReynolds II and Buster Blalock. (CD.)

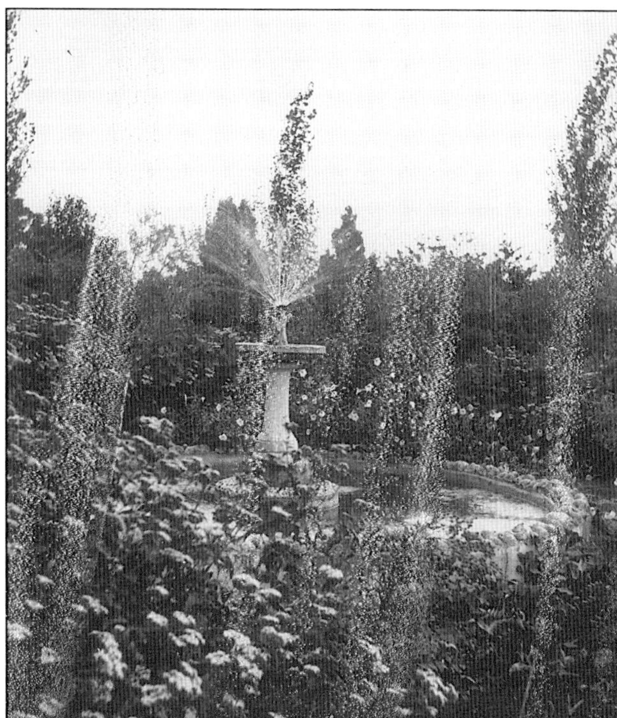

Wilburn Sudduth's mother, Miss T., had one of the most admired gardens in Starkville in the 1920s. (MB.)

Four

A&M College

The Agricultural and Mechanical College's campus modestly started with an academic building, a dormitory, a chemical laboratory, the president's home, and several barns. A&M College's first session began in October of 1880 with 350 men enrolled. Gen. Stephen D. Lee served as president until 1899. In 1932, the legislature renamed the school Mississippi State College. Today, Mississippi State University is a comprehensive land-grant institution known for excellence in teaching, research, and service.

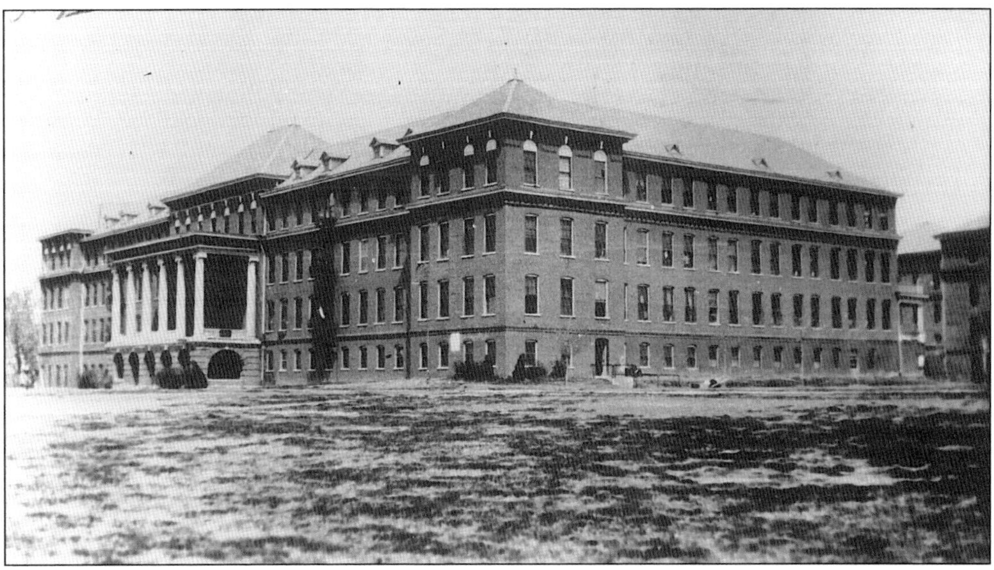

In 1880, when Old Main was built, it was the world's largest dormitory under one roof. The all-male dormitory is shown here in 1921; it later formed a square with an open courtyard. It burned in 1959. (JSC.)

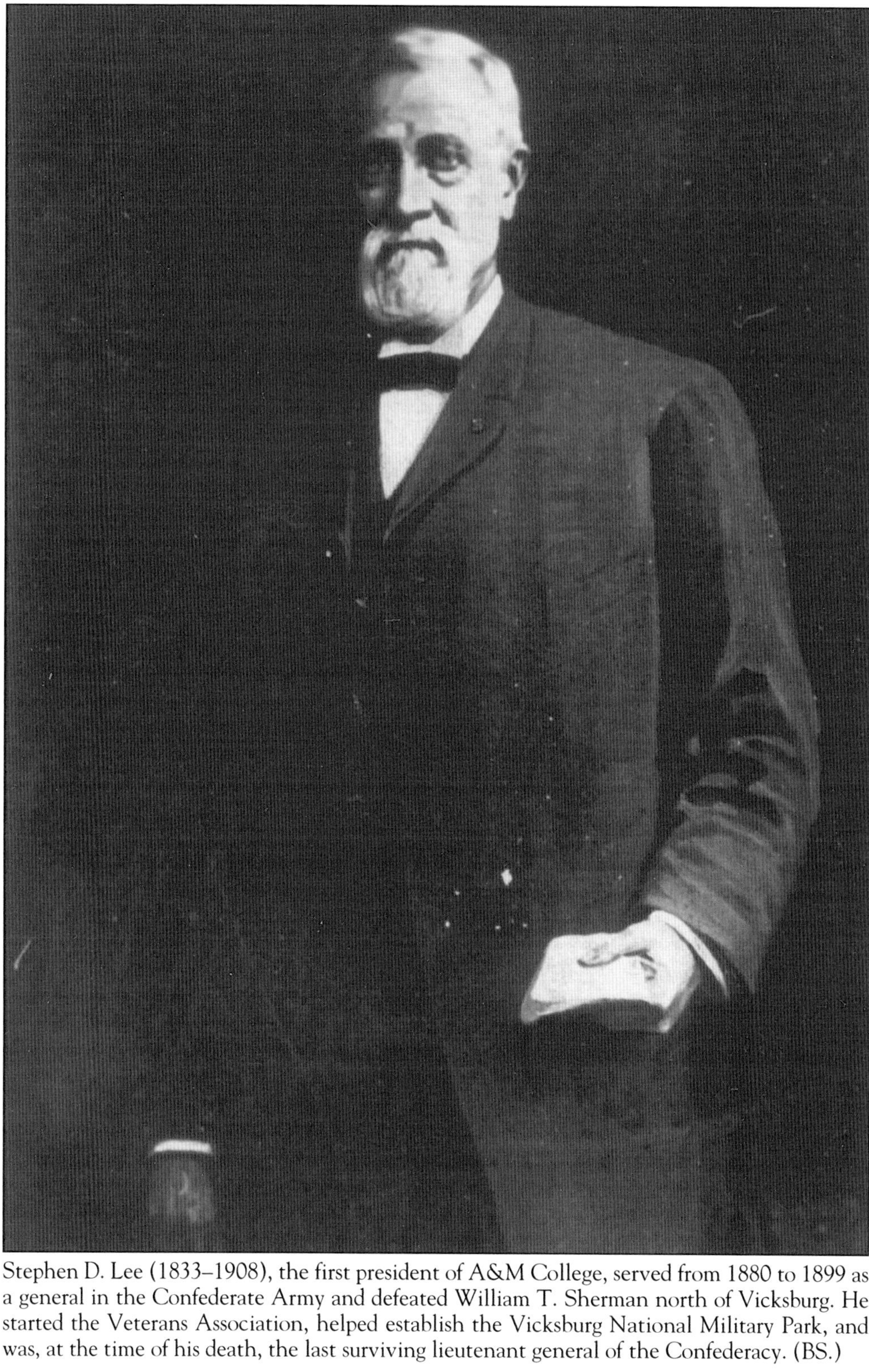

Stephen D. Lee (1833–1908), the first president of A&M College, served from 1880 to 1899 as a general in the Confederate Army and defeated William T. Sherman north of Vicksburg. He started the Veterans Association, helped establish the Vicksburg National Military Park, and was, at the time of his death, the last surviving lieutenant general of the Confederacy. (BS.)

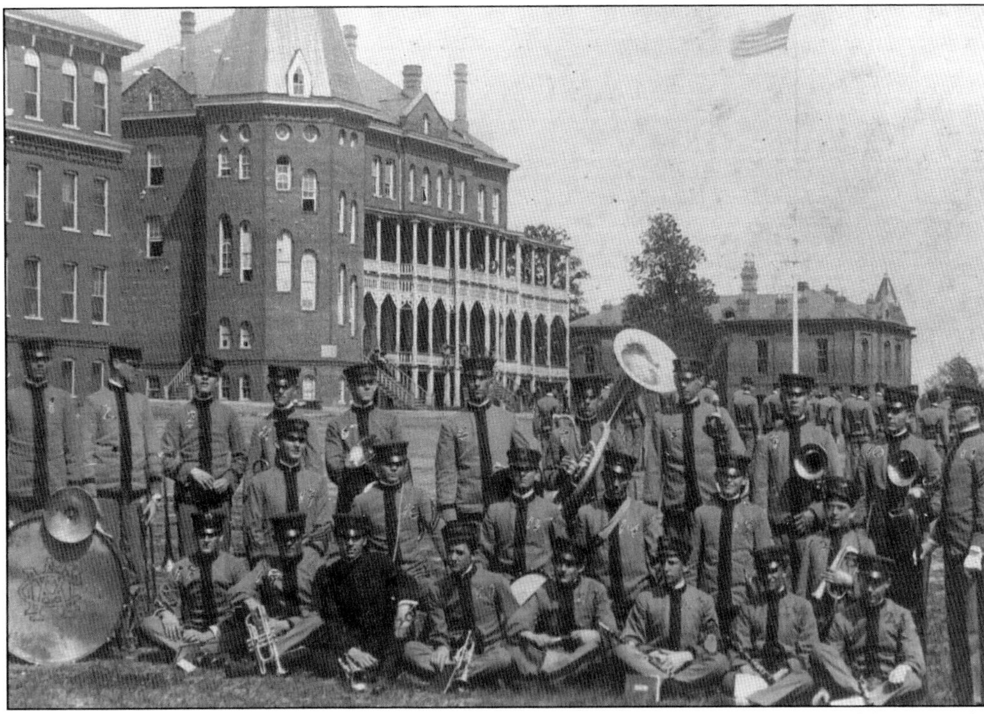

The A&M band marches in front of the first three buildings on campus—Old Main, the Administration building, and the old classroom building. (BS.)

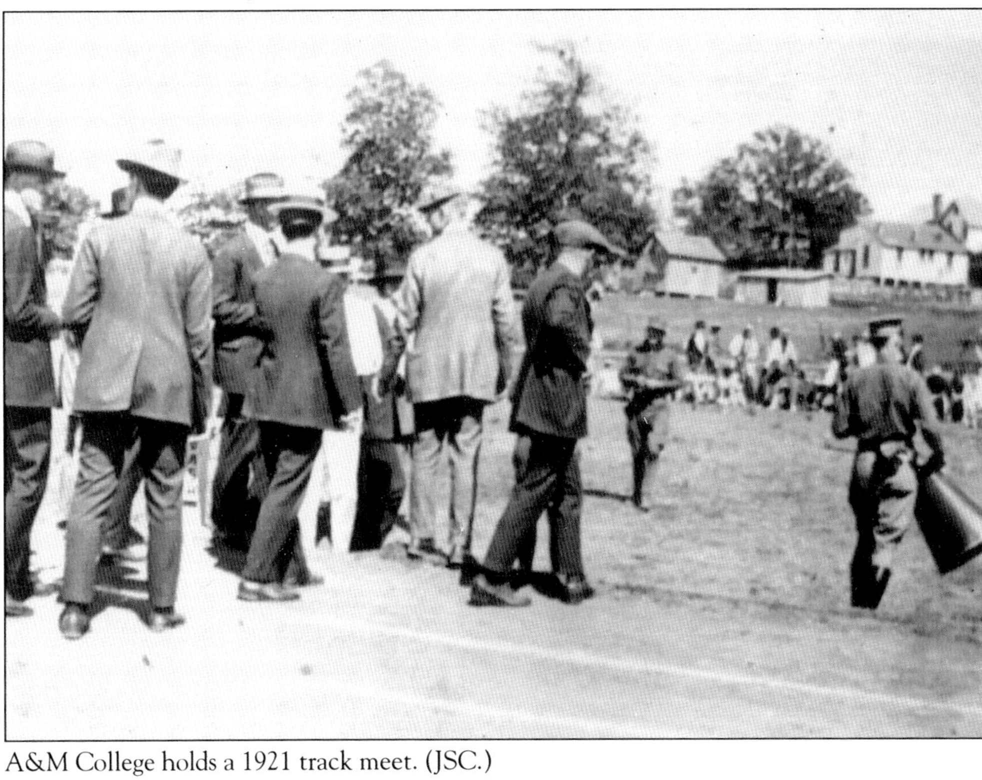

A&M College holds a 1921 track meet. (JSC.)

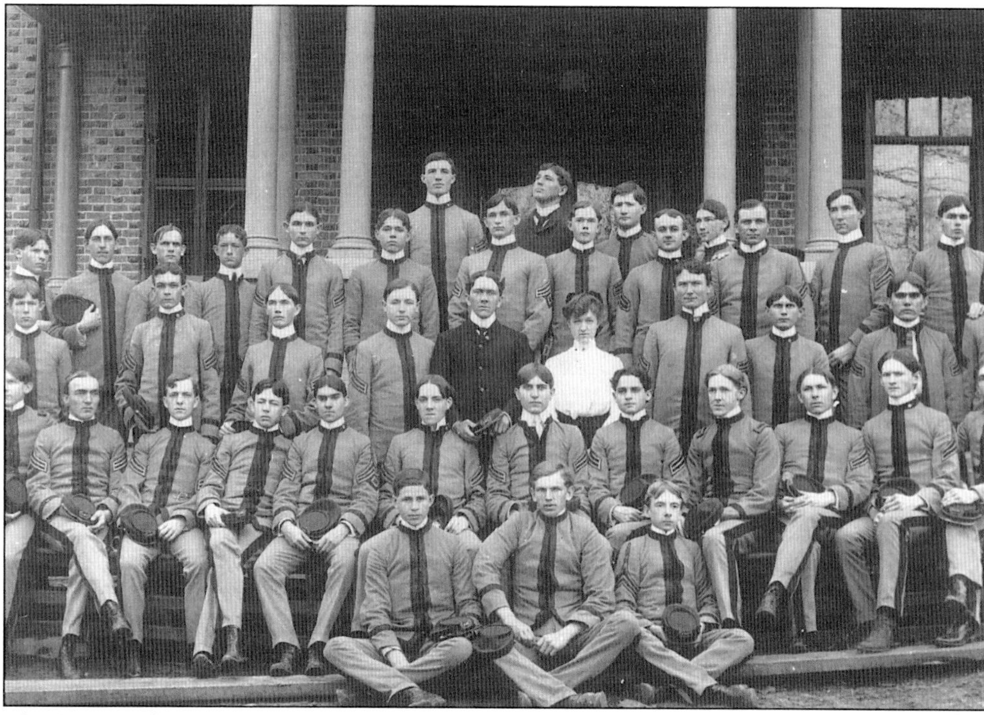
The A&M cadets were required to wear uniforms. (BS.)

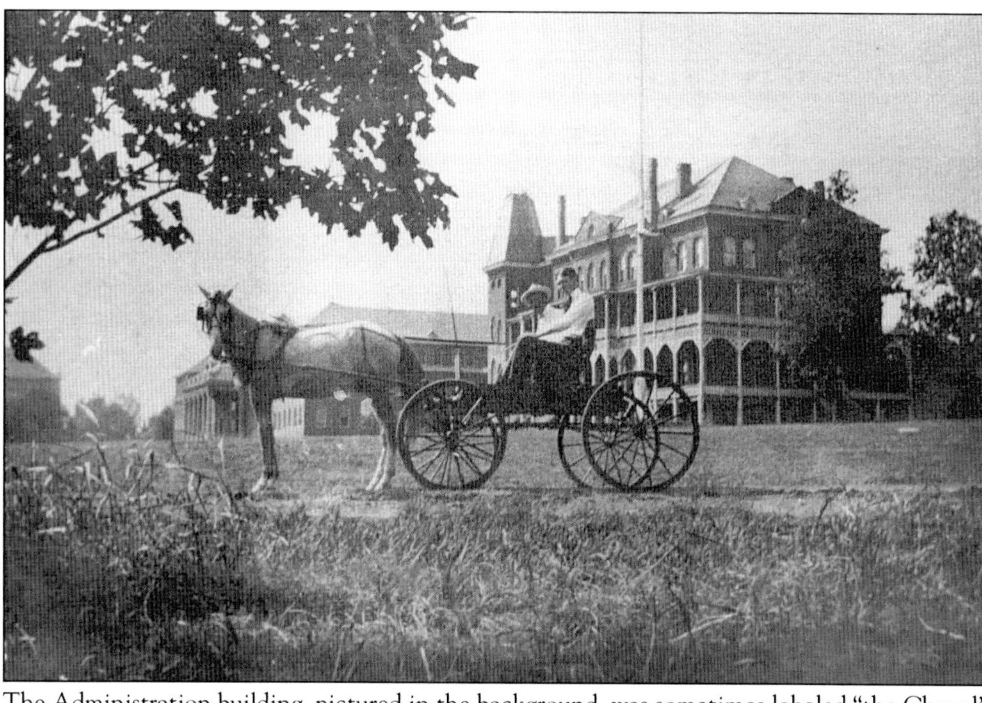
The Administration building, pictured in the background, was sometimes labeled "the Chapel" on old photographs. (BS.)

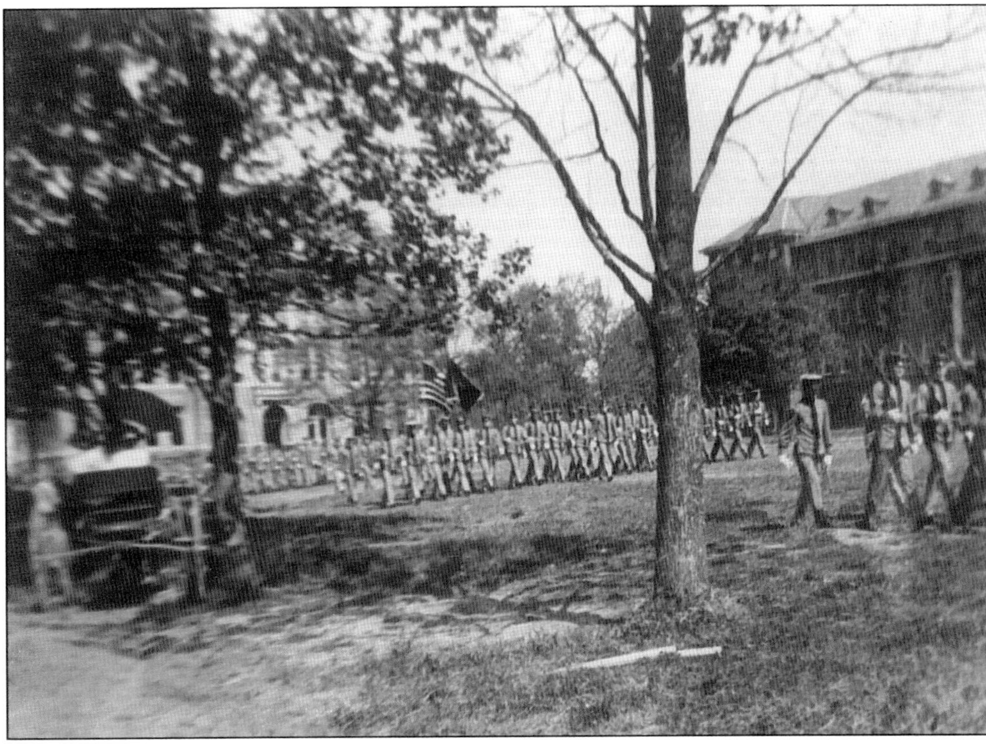

Cadets march in front of Old Main and Montgomery Hall. (JSC.)

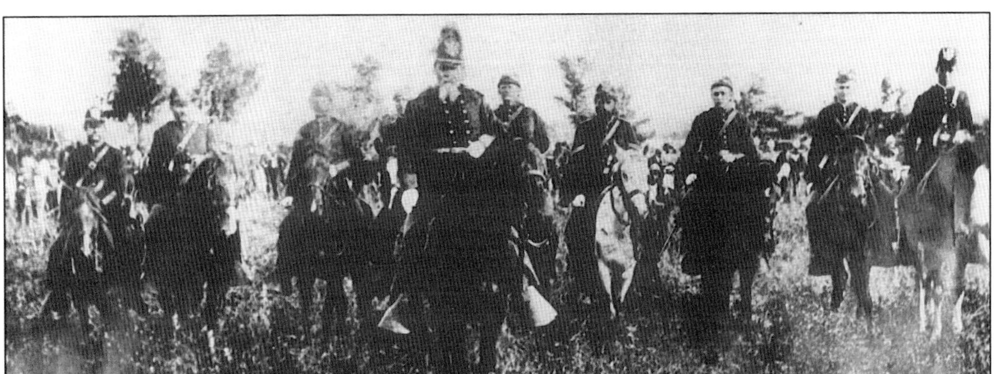

This 1800s Civil War reenactment, which was held at A&M College, drew thousands of men in attendance. Pictured are Clarence Peters, John Stiles, Bob Mitchell, "Coin" Dillie, Capt. Frank Young (in front), Will Askew, John Gray, Horance Dismukes, Bob Campbell, and Joe Partlow. (OHM.)

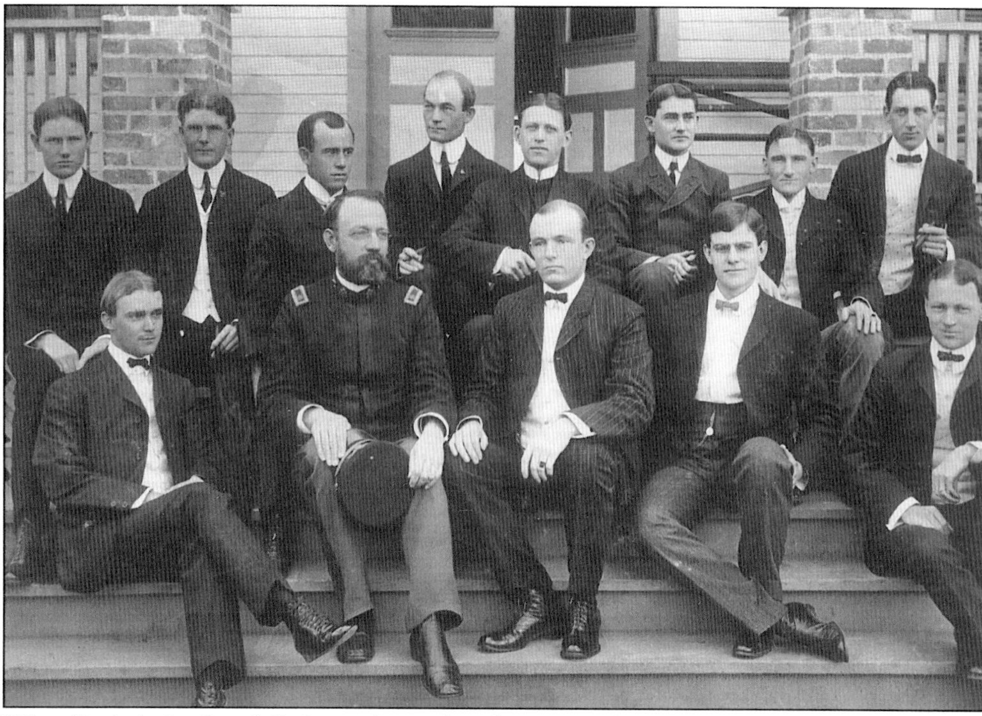

"The Bachelor's Ranch," located north of Lee Hall, housed the unmarried faculty members. (BS.)

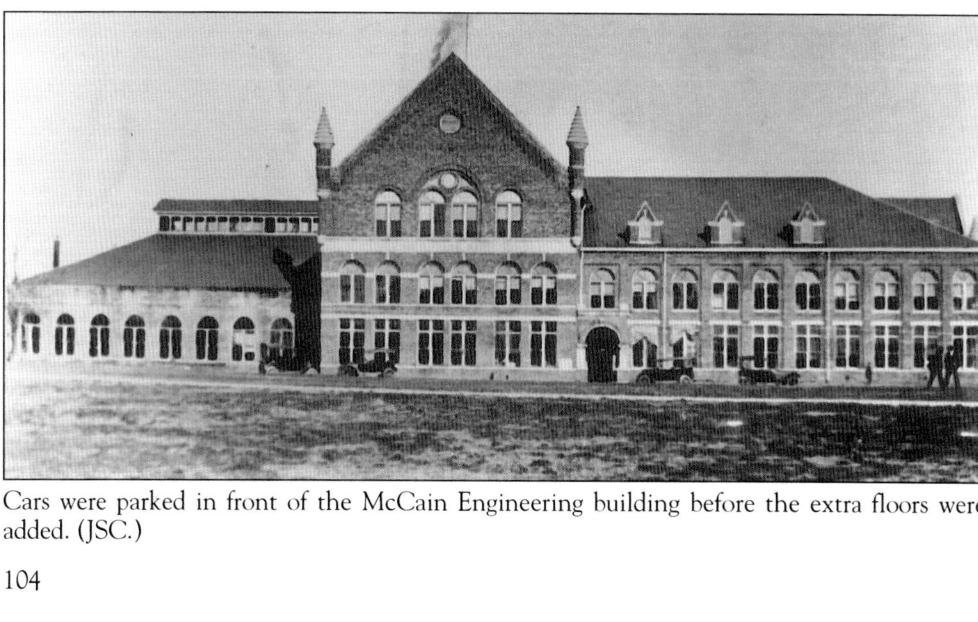

Cars were parked in front of the McCain Engineering building before the extra floors were added. (JSC.)

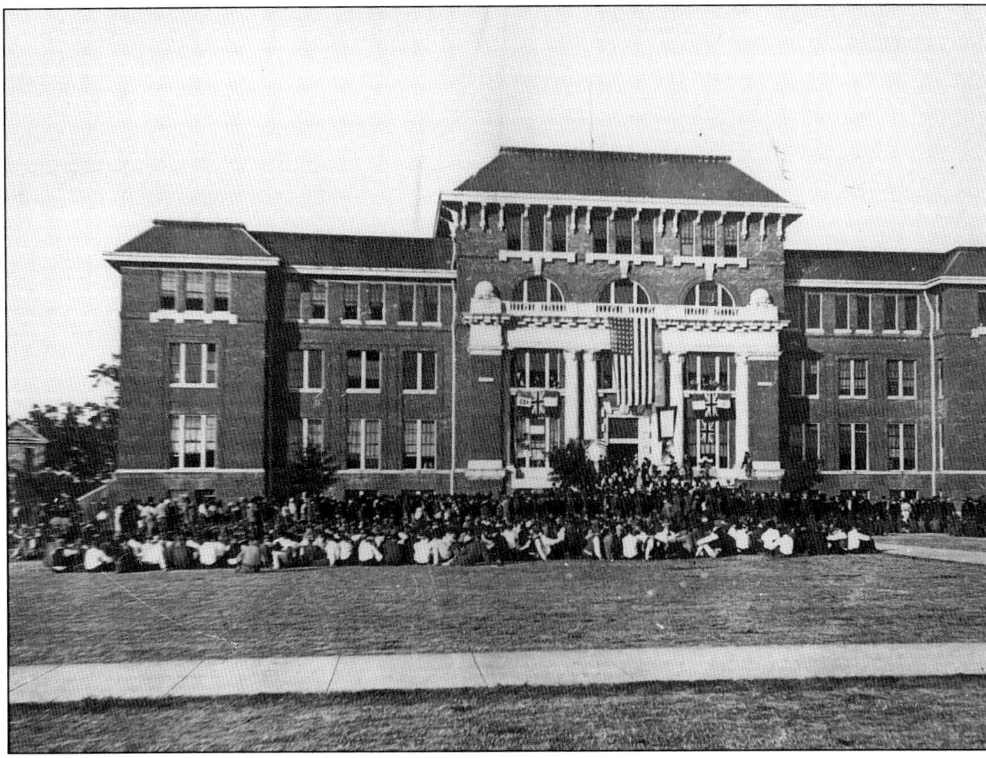

Lee Hall was photographed during WWI. (JSC.)

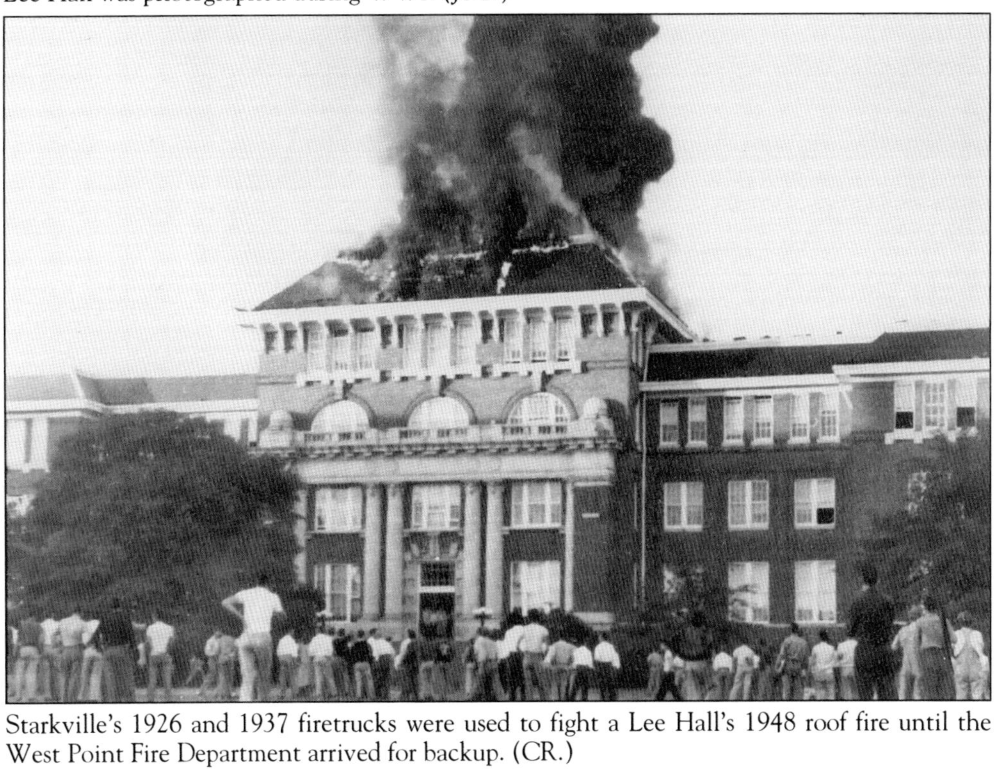

Starkville's 1926 and 1937 firetrucks were used to fight a Lee Hall's 1948 roof fire until the West Point Fire Department arrived for backup. (CR.)

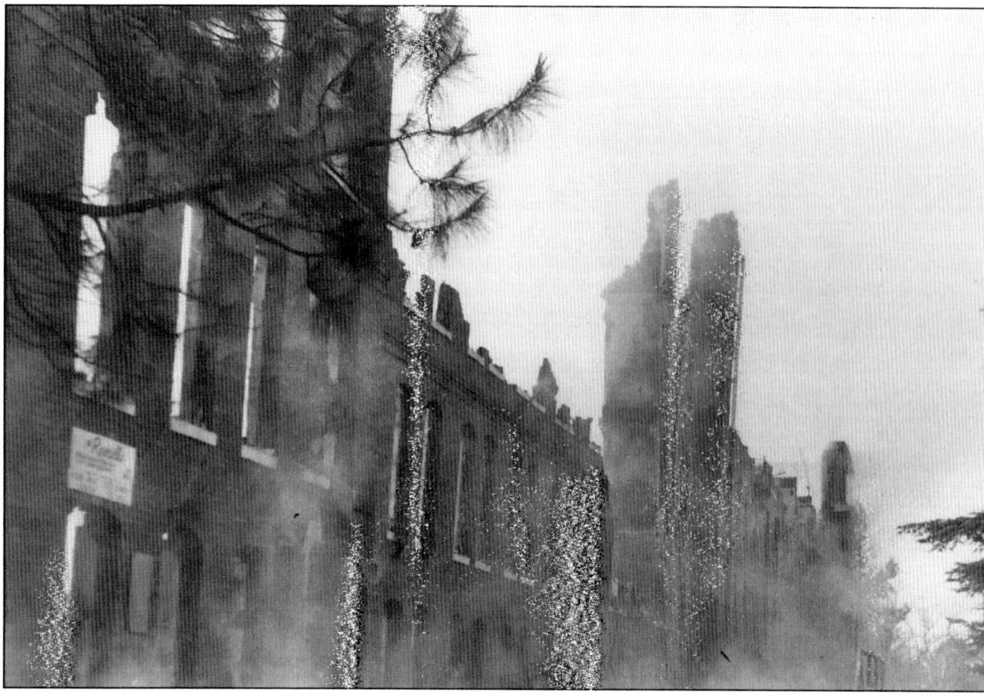

The 1959 Old Main fire suffered one fatality when a student returned to the dormitory to retrieve his radio. (CR.)

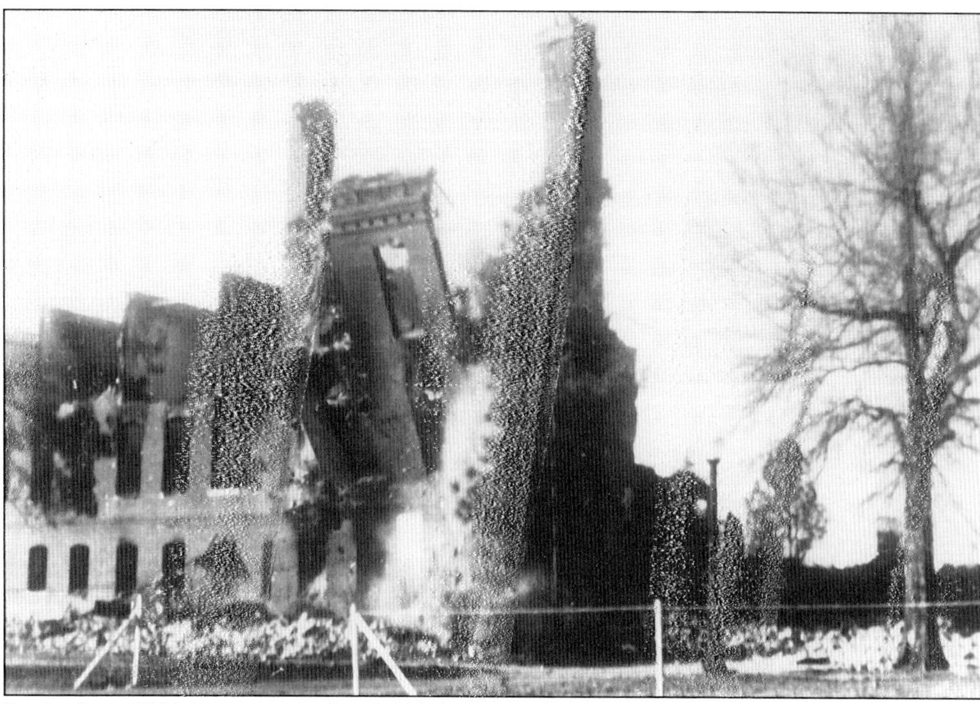

Bricks from Old Main were used to build the Chapel of Memories. (CR.)

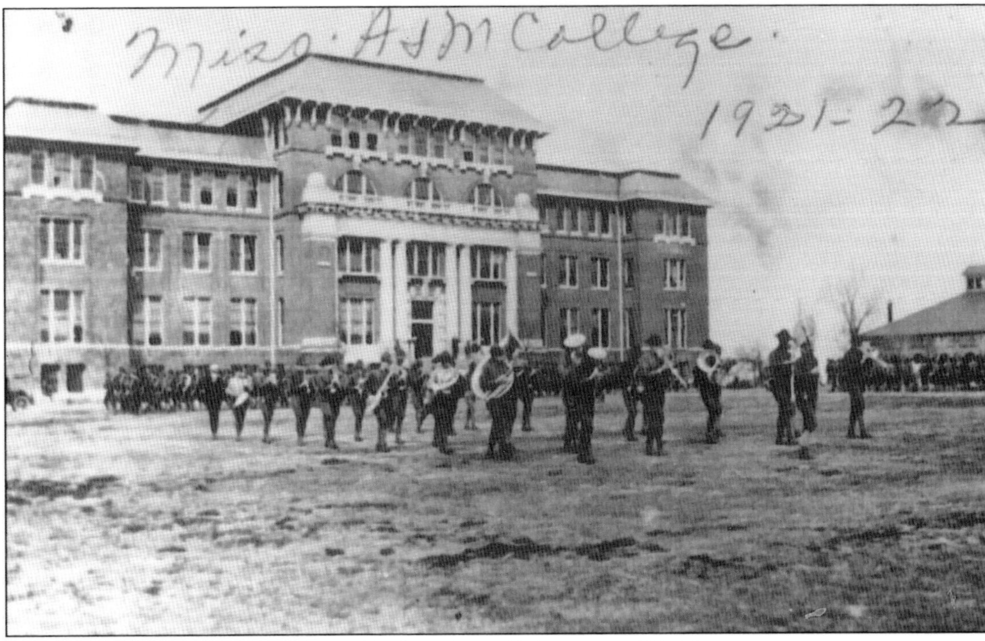

The band marches in front of Lee Hall in this 1921 picture. (JSC.)

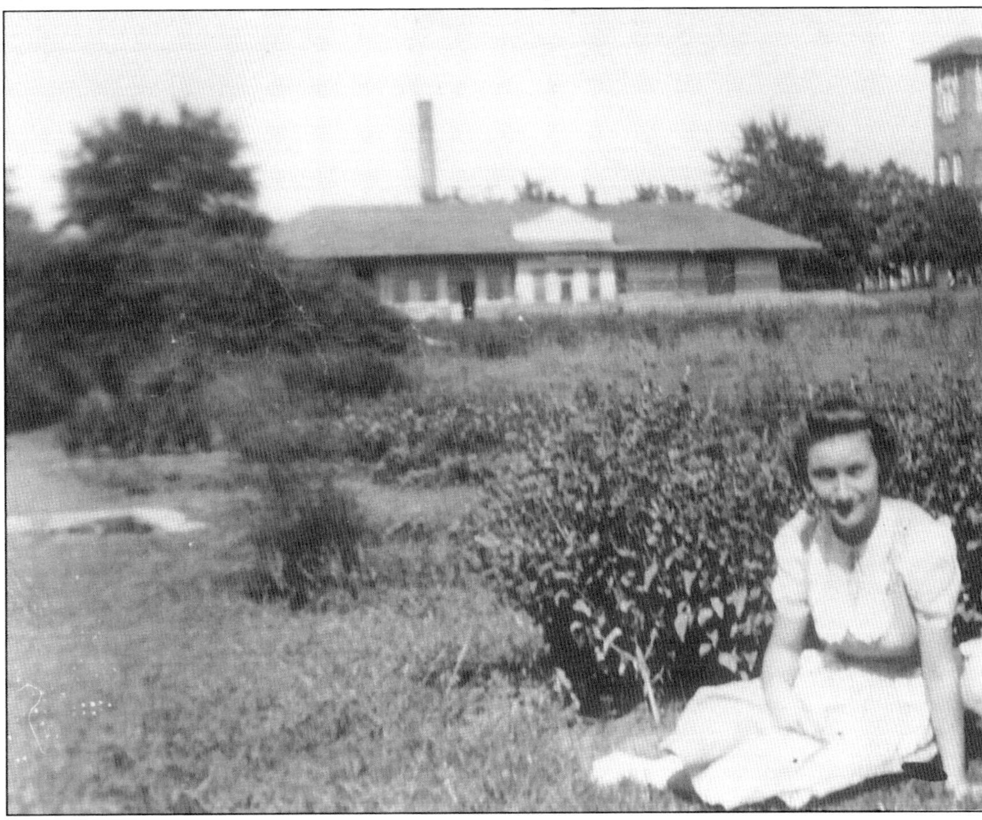

The campus's GM&O depot ran its trains during football games and carried students to and from home. (EB.)

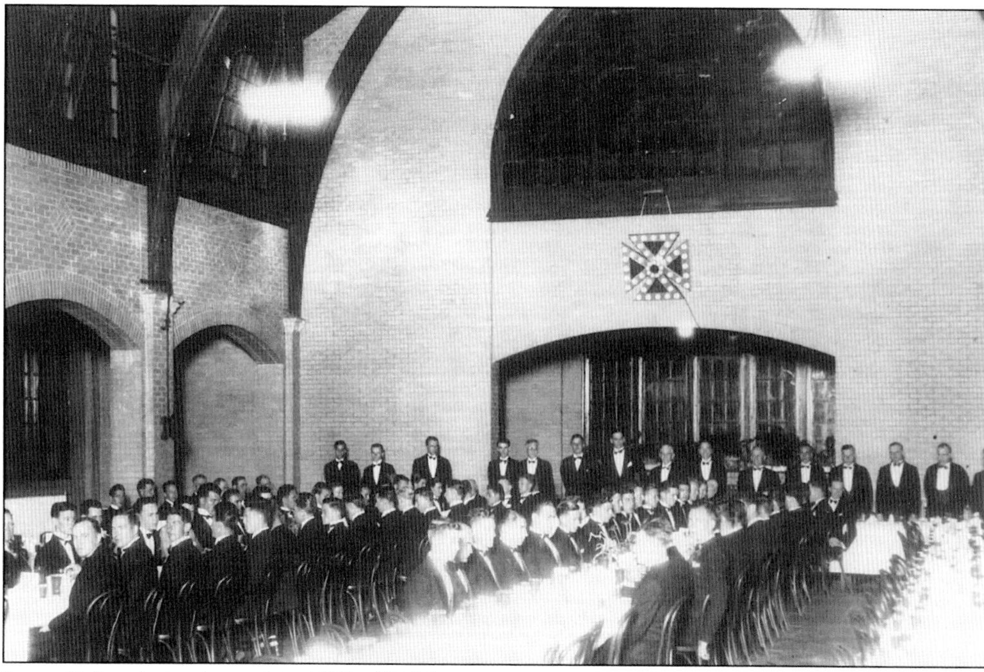

Perry Cafeteria is pictured in 1920. (JSC.)

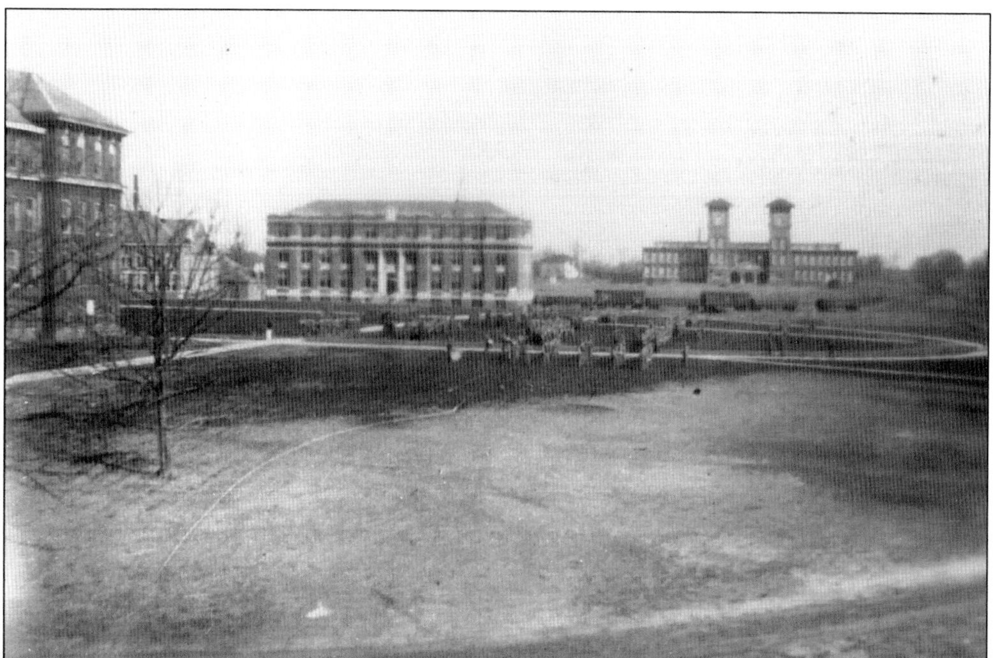

A train sits in front of the Twin Tower building, which housed the textile school. It was built in 1900, making it the campus' oldest building. (JSC.)

Taken in 1922, this photograph shows Buzz Miley (the son of Maj. Gen. Bud Miley, see p. 97), and a babysitter known as Magnolia in front of the Fire Hose House, which was near the ROTC building and steam plant. (MB.)

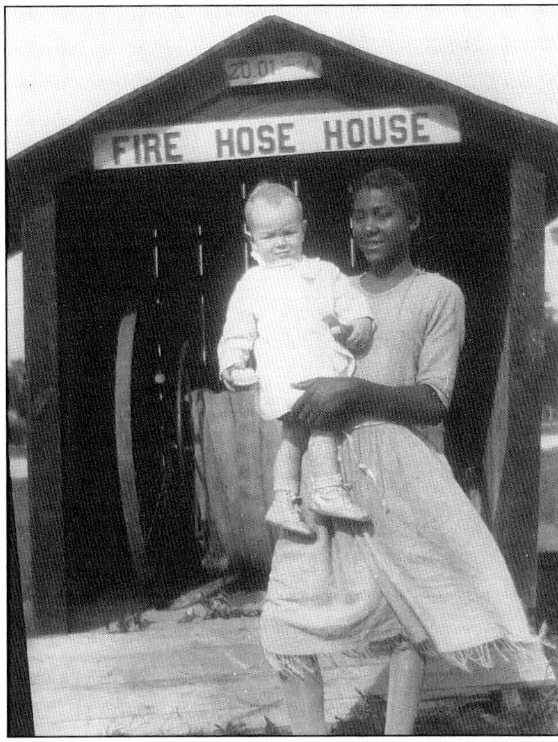

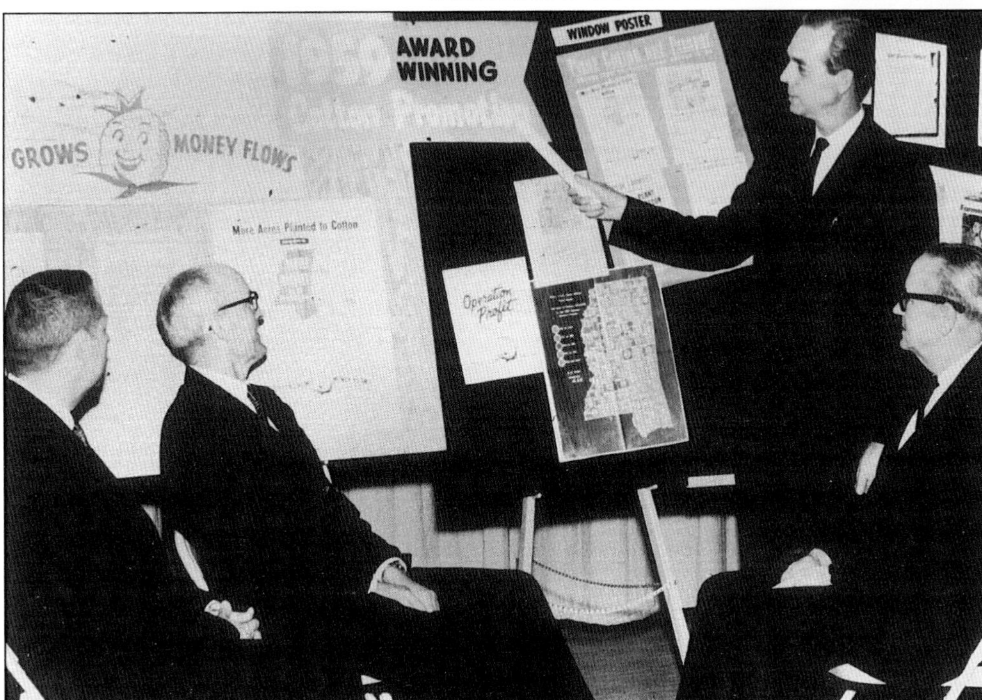

T.M. "Cotton" Waller (sitting second on the left) listens to an Extension Service presentation. In 1886, the board of trustees ordered A&M College to give six "talks" a year to farmers. These talks helped to form the Extension Service. (TMW.)

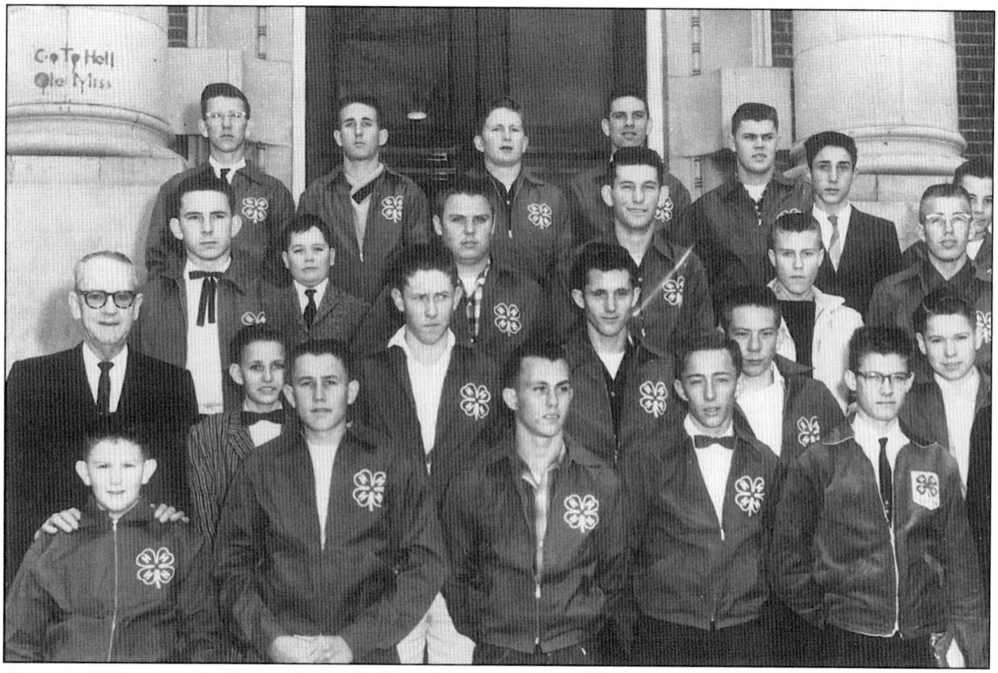

A state 4-H group is shown here before their training. The organization serves youth through agriculture education. Oktibbeha County's first 4-H contest was the "fat pig contest" held at the county fair. Notice the graffiti on the column. (TMW.)

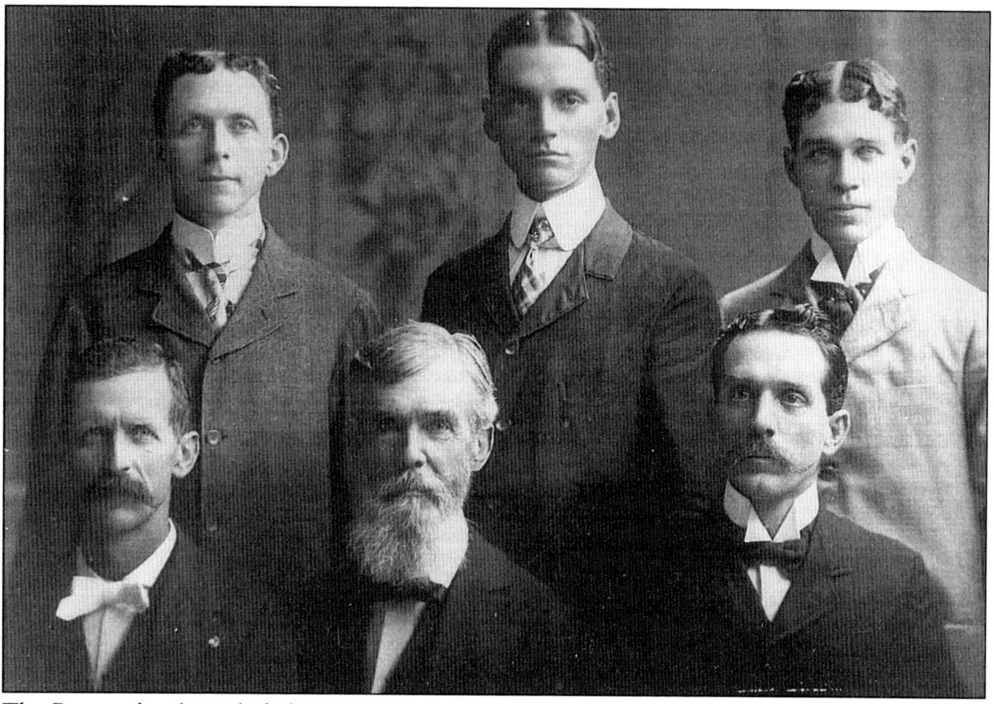

The Beattie family included Tom, John, Robert, Garnett, Henry, and Arthur. Robert was the first graduate of A&M College and the first Alumni Association president. Henry served as mayor of Starkville three times. (HB.)

Five

Transportation

Convenient access was the hallmark of every town. Travel in Oktibbeha County occurred by road, water, rail, and air.

Most of the beginning roads began as Native-American footpaths, which were later traveled by horse-drawn wagons. One of the county's most well-known roads was Robinson Road, which is the second oldest road in Mississippi. It was used to connect Columbus, Jackson, and Natchez. The first telegraph line was built along Robinson Road in 1850. The first bridge, which was built in 1832, crossed the Noxubee River in the southern part of the county on Robinson Road. The Indian Agency was near the bridge, and the Choctaw Indians were known to set up camp next to the bridge site. Stagecoaches that traveled Robinson Road and crossed the bridge during favorable weather frequently stopped at Folsom Inn, a local tavern known for its heavy drinking and nightly brawls.

Steamboats used the Tombigbee River to carry small loads of cotton to Mobile, Alabama. Supplies sent by keel boat up the unreliable river increased dramatically in cost. In the 1870s, trains made cargo and passenger travel easier and less expensive.

By 1904, the first automobiles were appearing. With the cars came better roads and more businesses. Sumpter Camp built the county's first airport in Starkville in the 1930s. With time, each method of travel grew and helped strengthen the county.

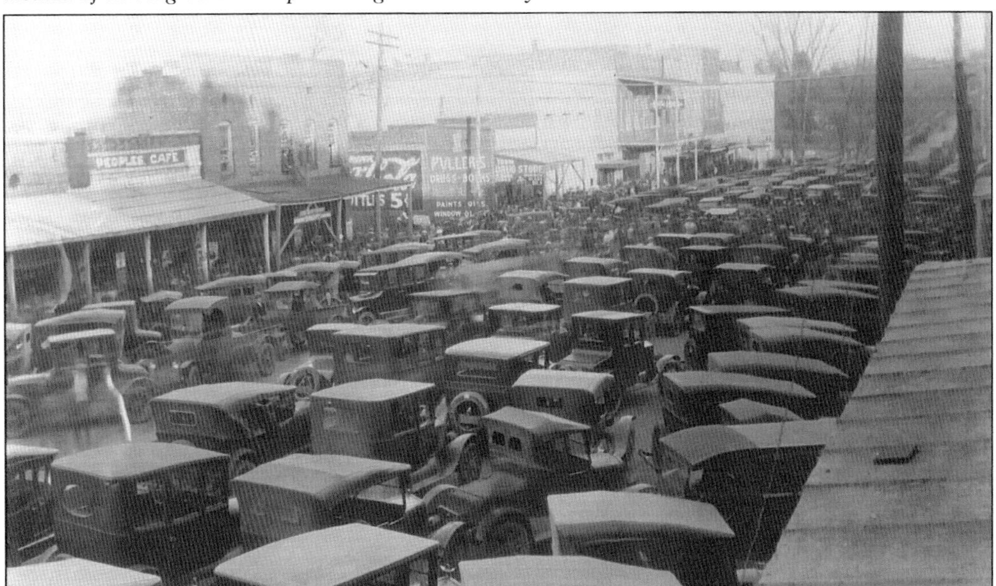

December 12, 1925, looks like a "quiet" Saturday afternoon on Starkville's Main Street. During the 1950s, the stores on Main Street stayed open until midnight on Saturday nights. Main Street was paved by 1923. (JSC.)

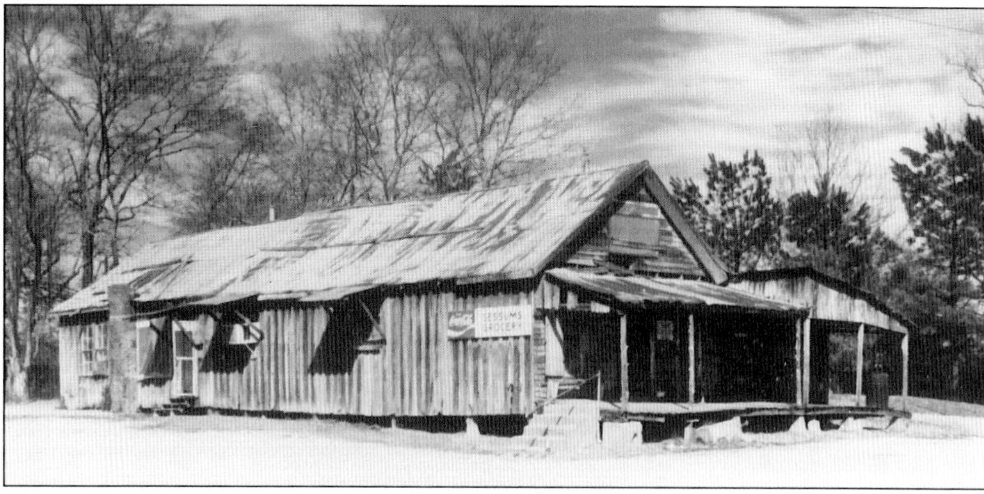

This grocery store, which was first called Sessumville, was located on the GM&O railroad. The old store also served as a post office. (MAP.)

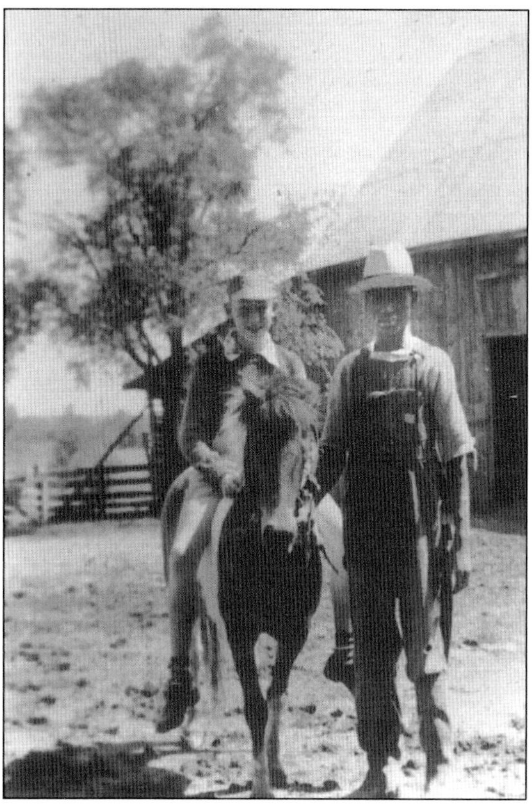

Albert Nutting is led on a horse by Bossy Watt, who was adopted and raised by William Henry Sudduth. (MB.)

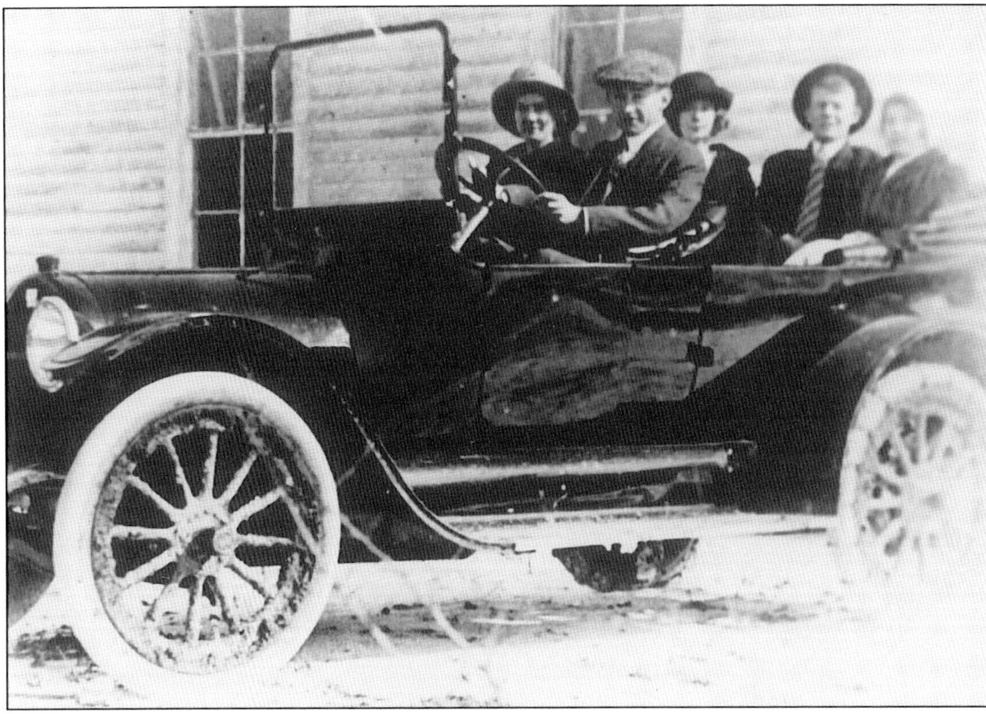

The first Buick in the county was owned by Roy and Dezree Hunt of Sturgis. Because of the poor road conditions, chains were used on the car's wheels for traction. (BH.)

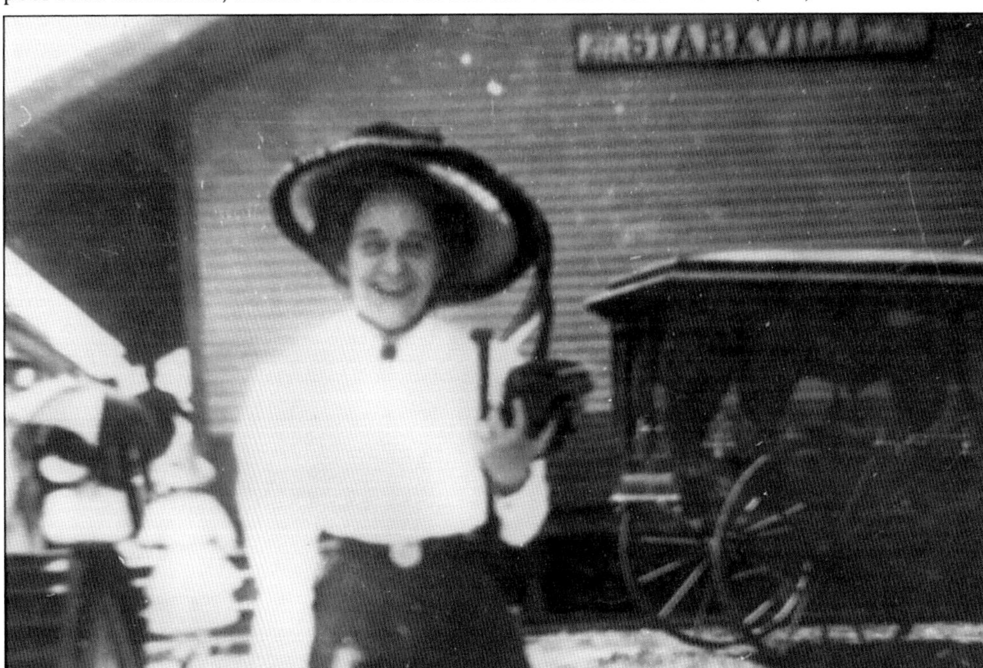

A hearse, which might have been used during the 1918 flu epidemic at A&M College that killed 40 students, waits at the GM&O depot. The Oktibbeha County Heritage Museum now occupies the depot. (JSC.)

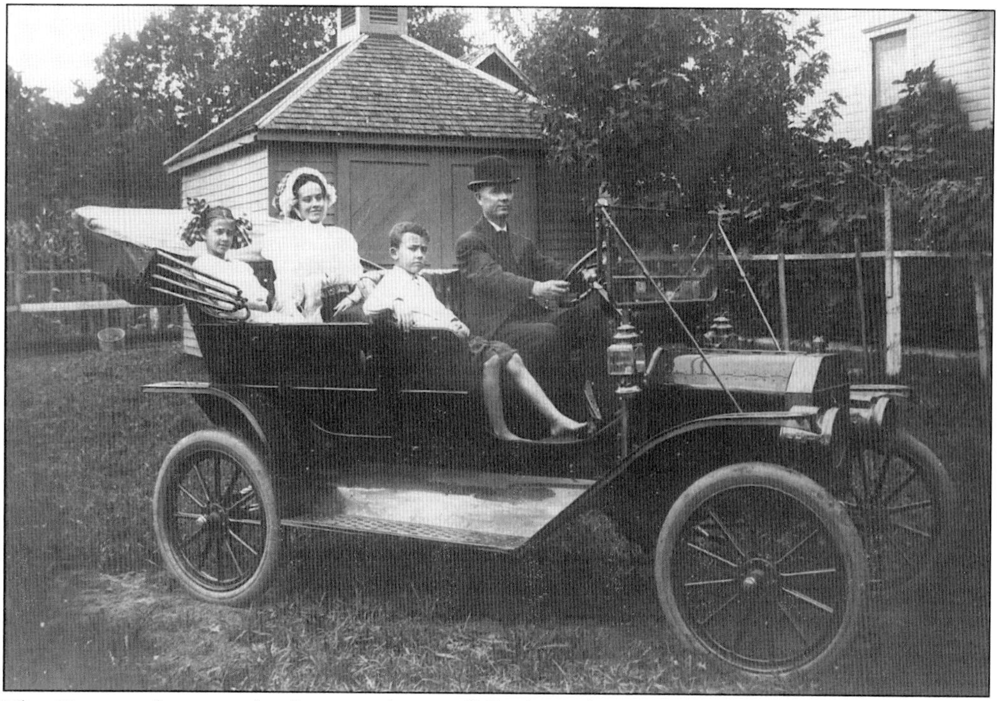

The Camps, who were the first people to sell Fords in the county, take a ride on a Sunday in 1911. The first cars in the county appeared in 1904. Four A&M College professors owned cars, including Professor Rand, who owned a kit car; Professor Scott, who owned an Oldsmobile; Professor Hand, who owned a Hanes; and Professor Burns, who owned a Maxwell. (RC.)

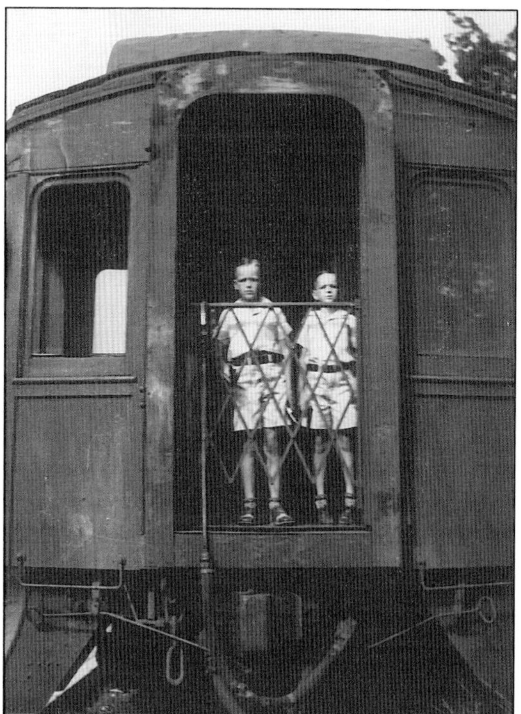

Buzz and Jack Miley (the sons of Maj. Gen. Bud Miley, see p. 97) stand on the back of a train in 1930. (MB.)

Western Auto sold Western Flyer bicycles and tricycles in 1939. A local newspaper advertisement listed a bicycle for sale for $26.95. (JSC.)

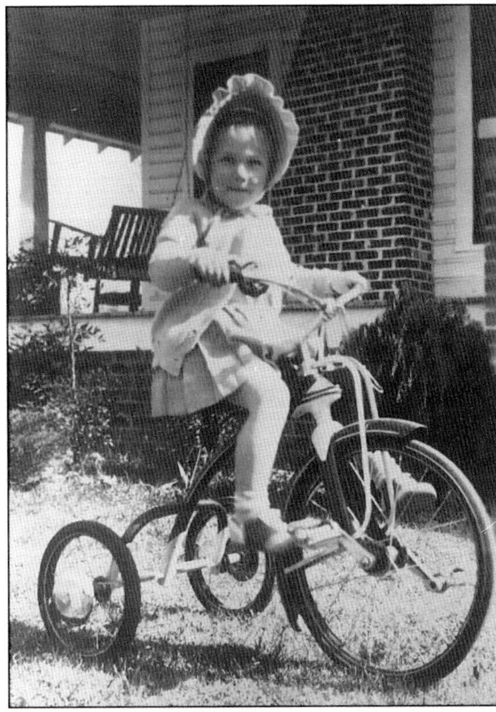

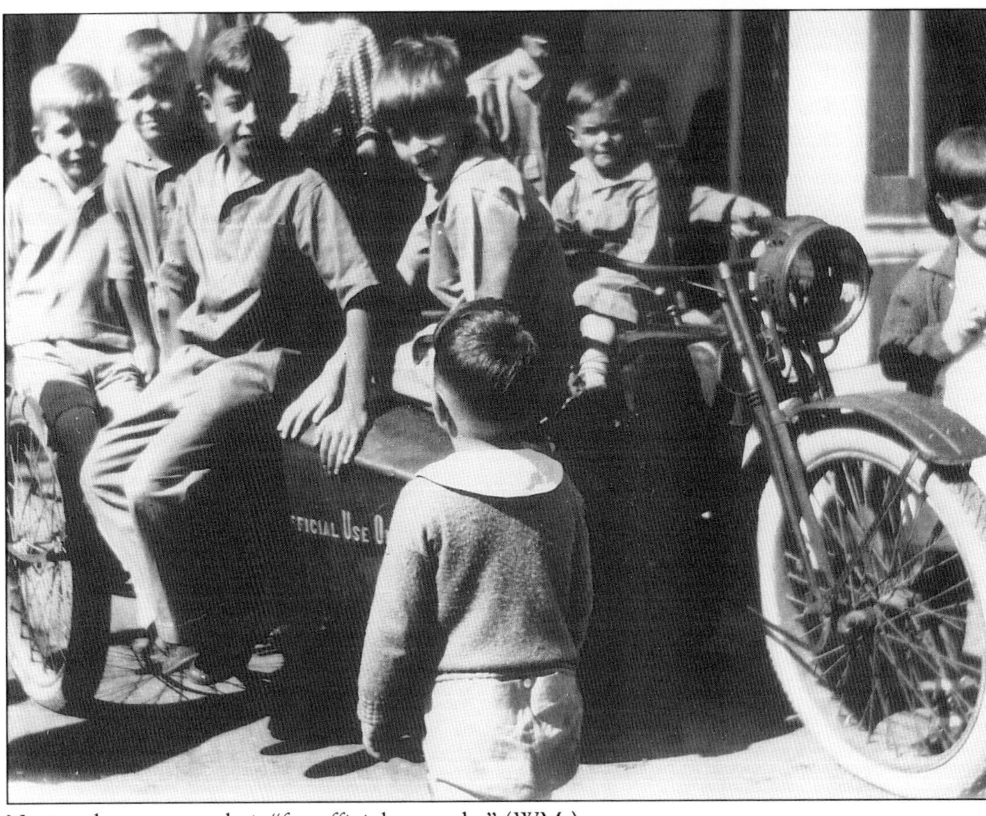

Notice the motorcycle is "for official use only." (WM.)

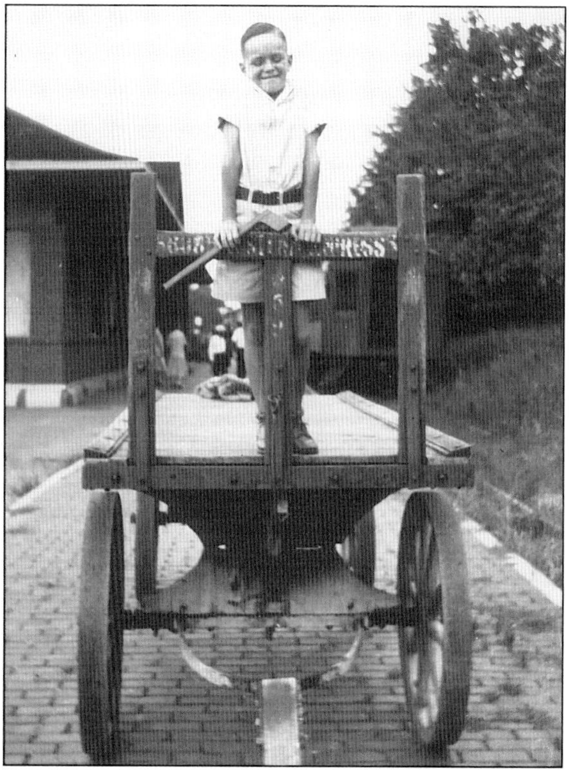

John David Miley stands in front of the Starkville Depot, which was used by the GM&O and Illinois Central Railroads. The Mobile and Ohio and the Illinois Central railroad systems ran in the county during the 1890s. Clay County passed a bond issue, which Starkville did not pass, to run a railroad from Columbus to Greenville through West Point. (MB.)

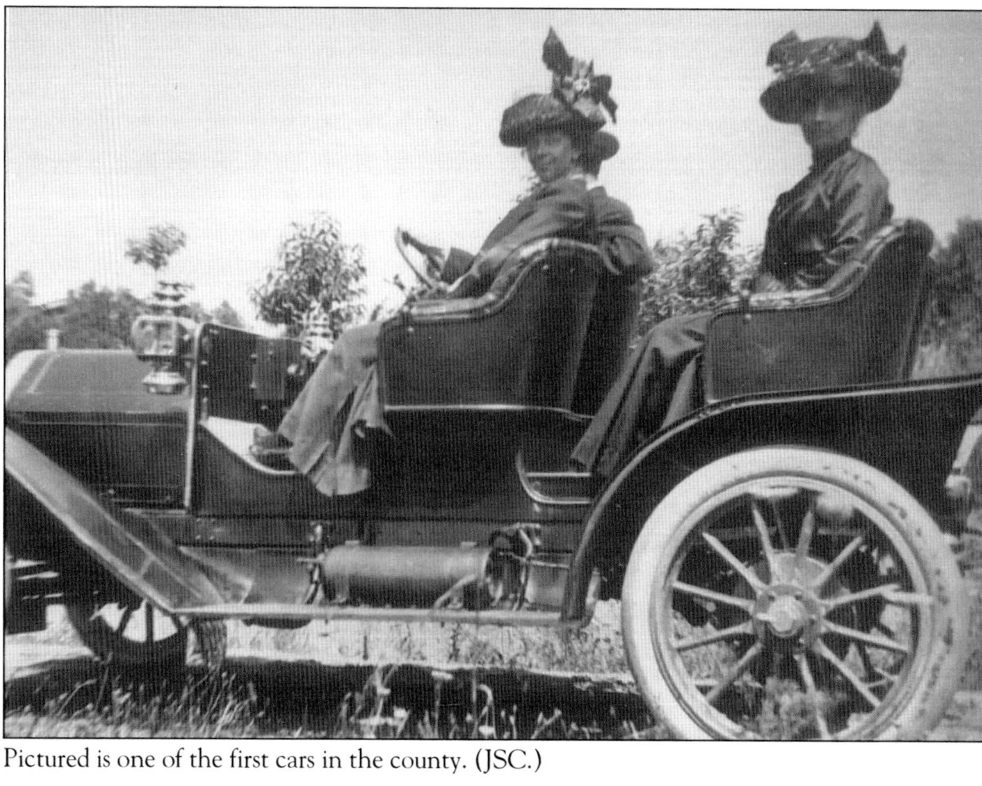

Pictured is one of the first cars in the county. (JSC.)

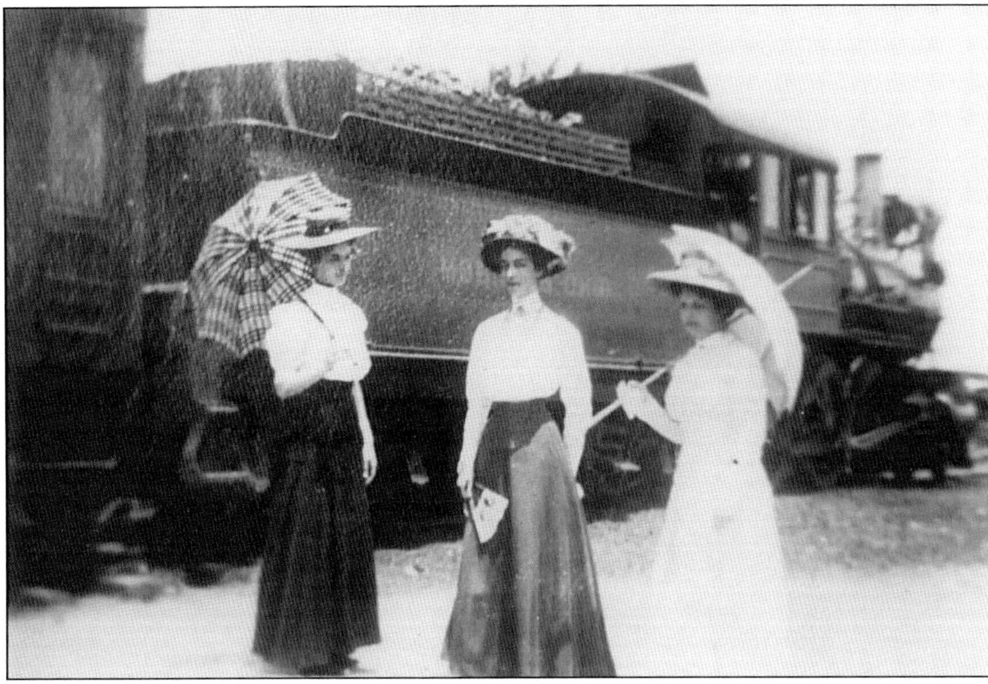

The Mobile and Ohio Railroad track ended in Starkville and ran to Artesia, which is east of the county. (JSC.)

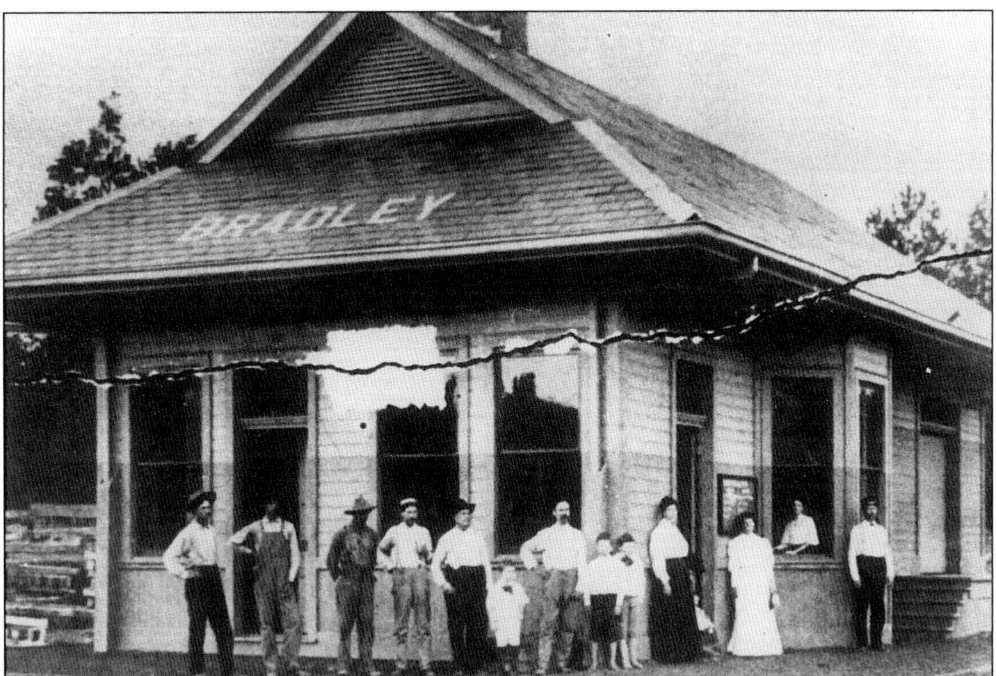

Bradley Station was located next to the Illinois Central railroad. Trains became the main means of travel during the early 1900s because of poor road conditions. (MQ.)

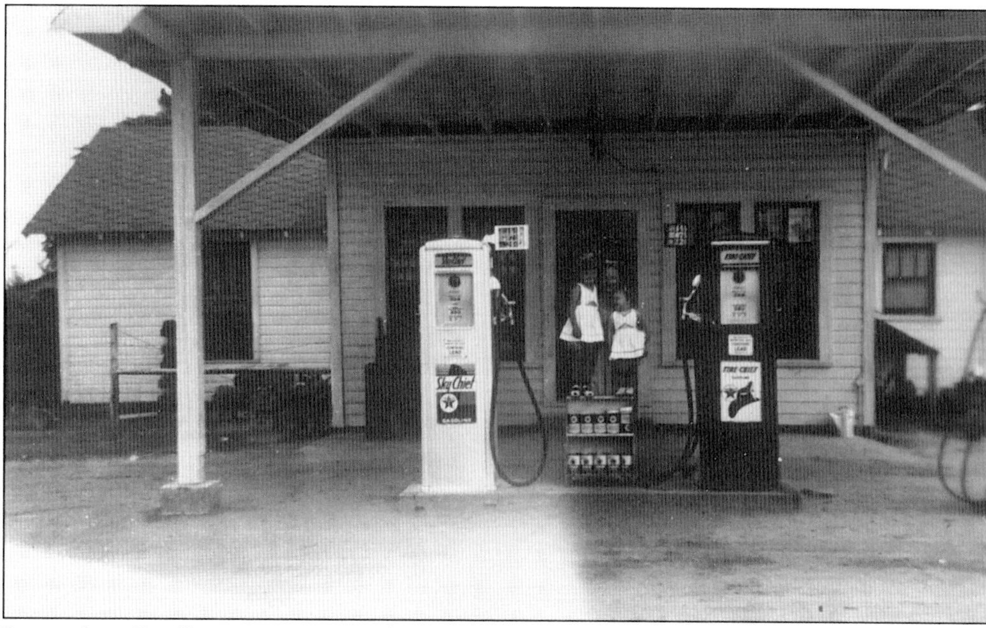

Pictured is a Bradley service station. (OHM.)

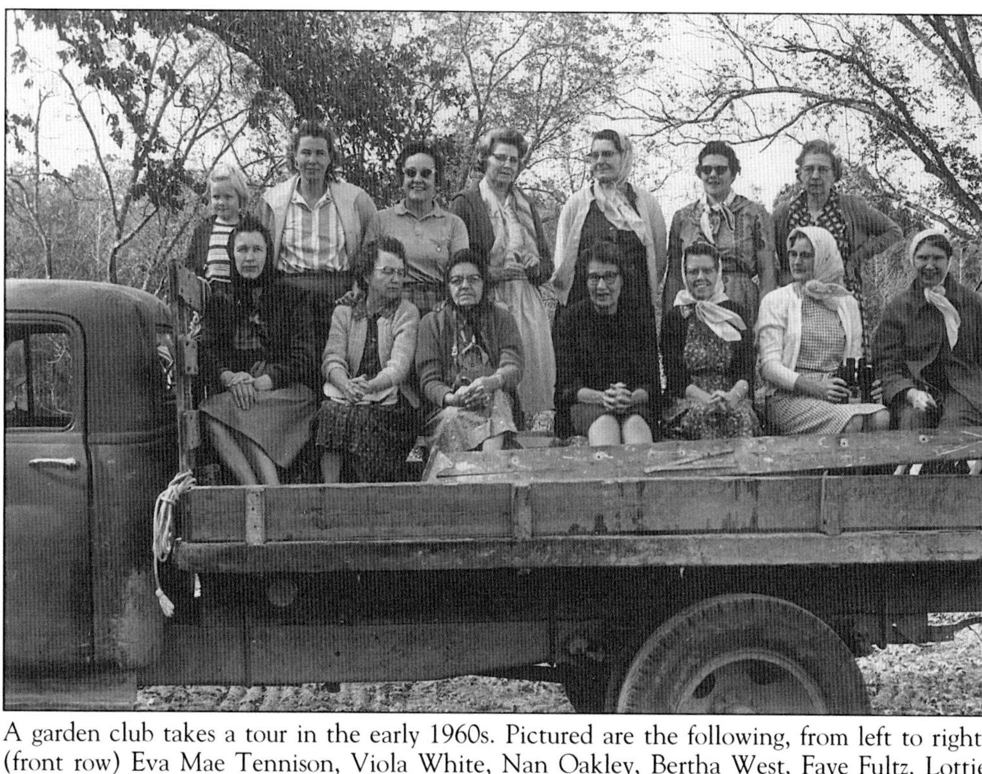

A garden club takes a tour in the early 1960s. Pictured are the following, from left to right: (front row) Eva Mae Tennison, Viola White, Nan Oakley, Bertha West, Faye Fultz, Lottie Hartness, and Marjorie Webster; (back row) Child Broyles, Julia Broyles, Mary Alice Dodson, Junnie Gentry, Julia Self, Betty Dawkins, and Mazie Reed. (FB.)

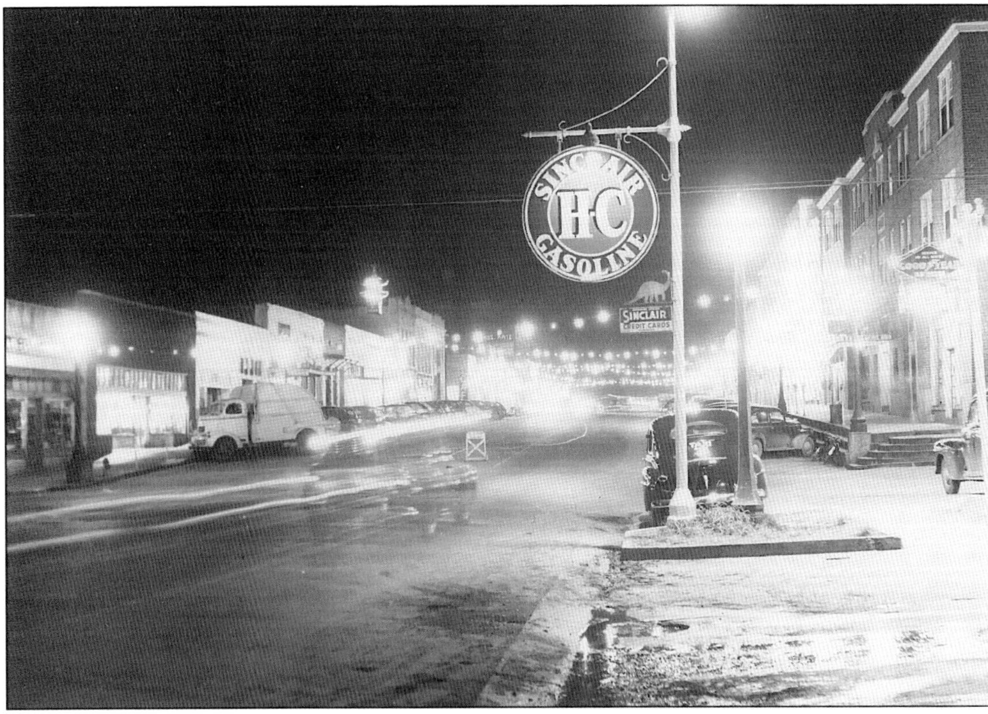

The Smith taxi, which is parked by the sign, was known for traveling back and forth to campus, seldom stopping for the traffic lights. (FB.)

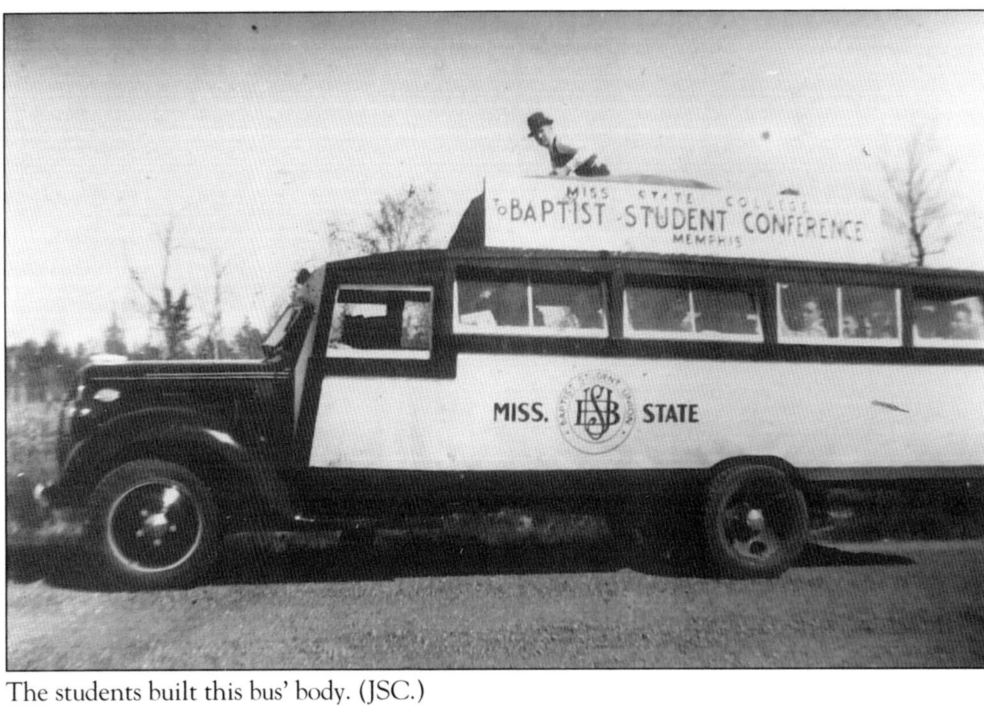

The students built this bus' body. (JSC.)

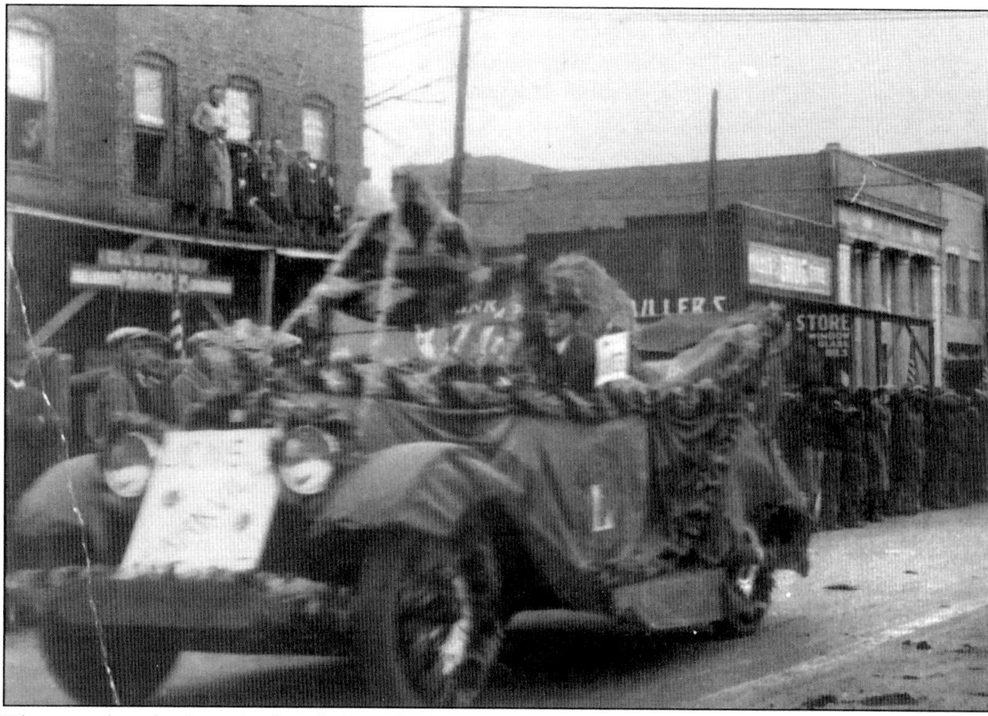

This parade, which took place before the Depression, has onlookers standing on Merchants and Farmers Bank's roof. The bank failed in the 1930s. (JSC.)

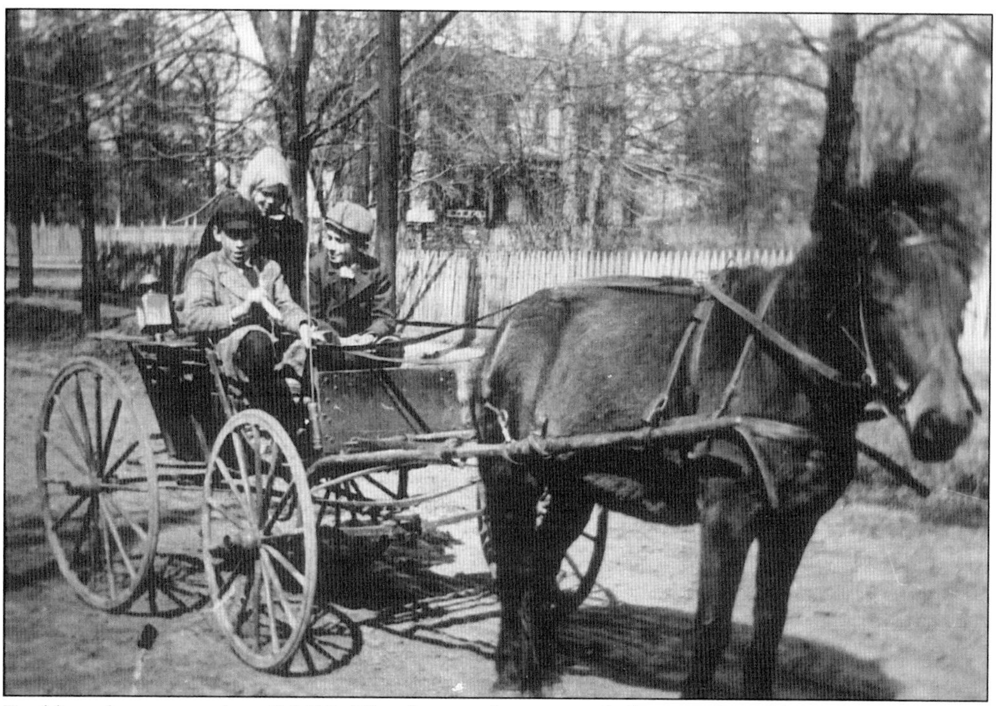

Buckboards were used until 1920. The first road was graveled in 1915, and by 1917, the county had 30 miles of road graveled. (JSC.)

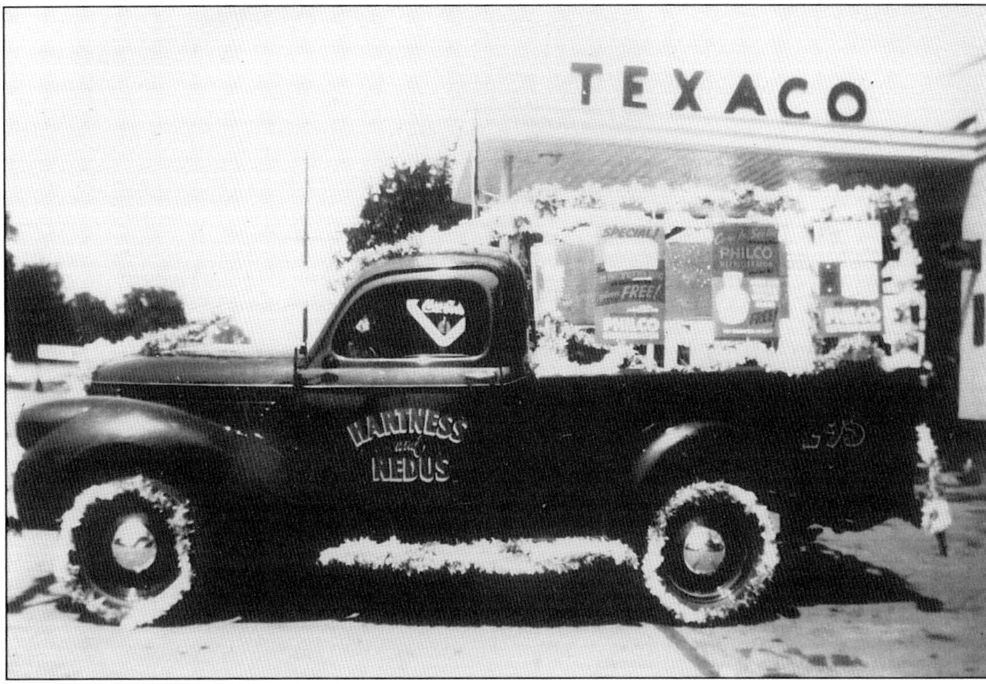

A Philco Radio is advertised on the back of this Hartness and Redus delivery truck. Grocery stores and drugstores frequently made deliveries. (JSC.)

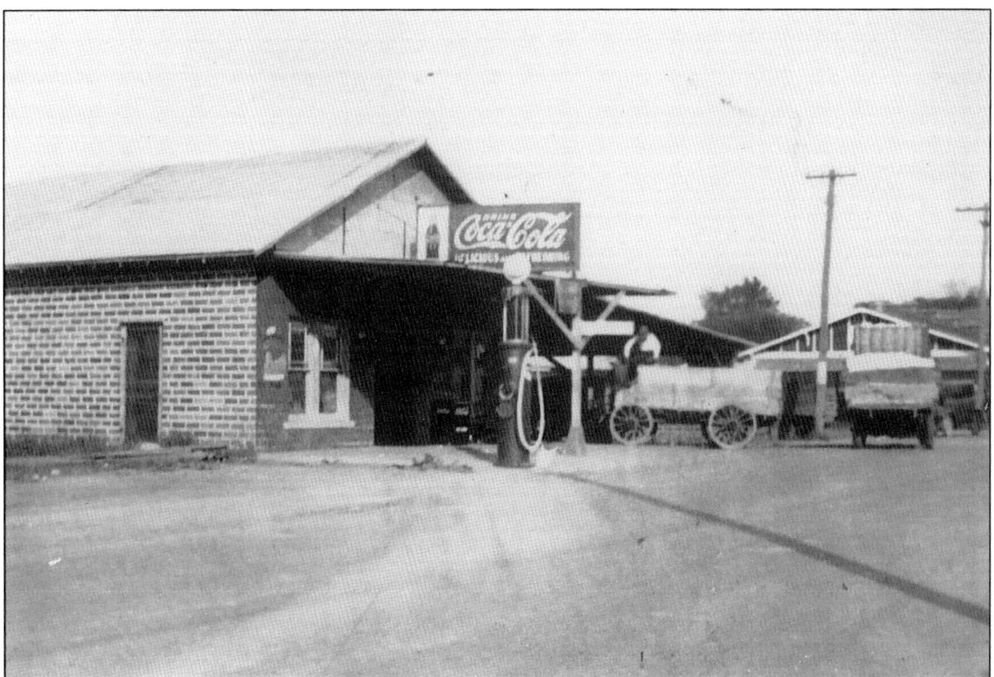

This Longview service station, which had hand gas pumps, is shown here in the 1930s. (EO.)

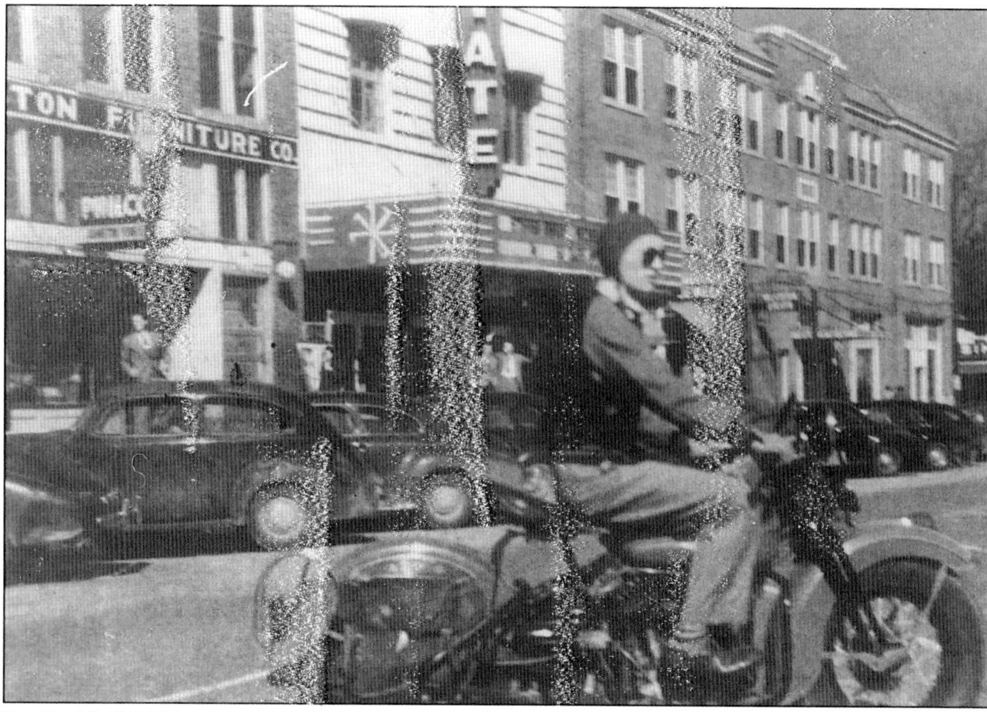

Pat Sudduth rides a motorcycle downtown with the Chester Hotel to the far right. (JM.)

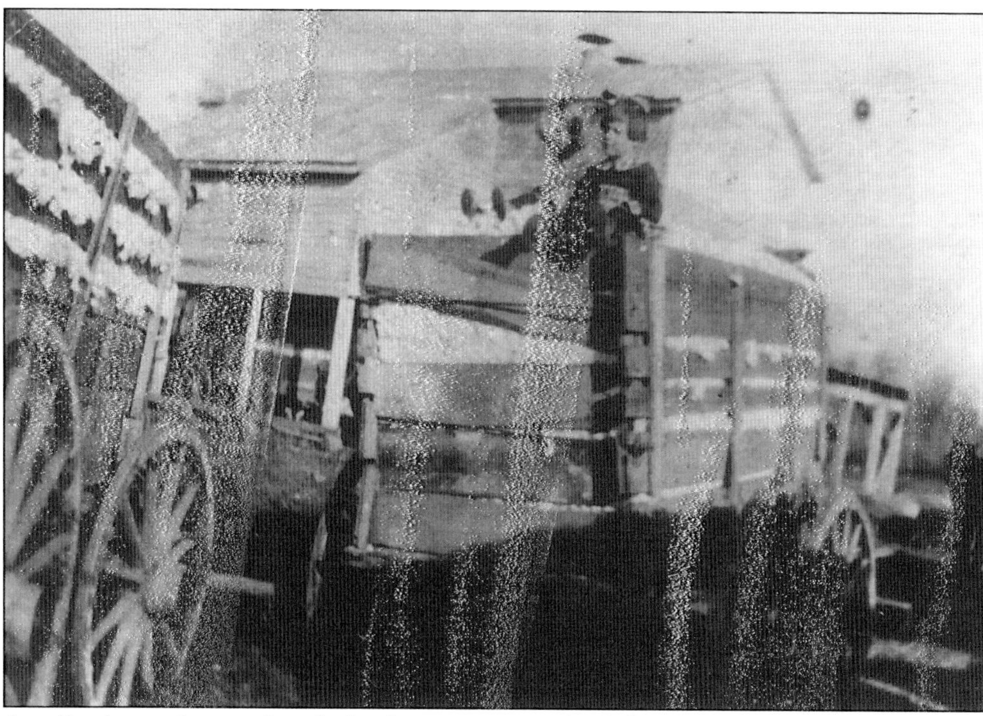
Ann Sanders and an unidentified girl sit on a wagon loaded with cotton at an electric cotton gin in Longview. (AS.)

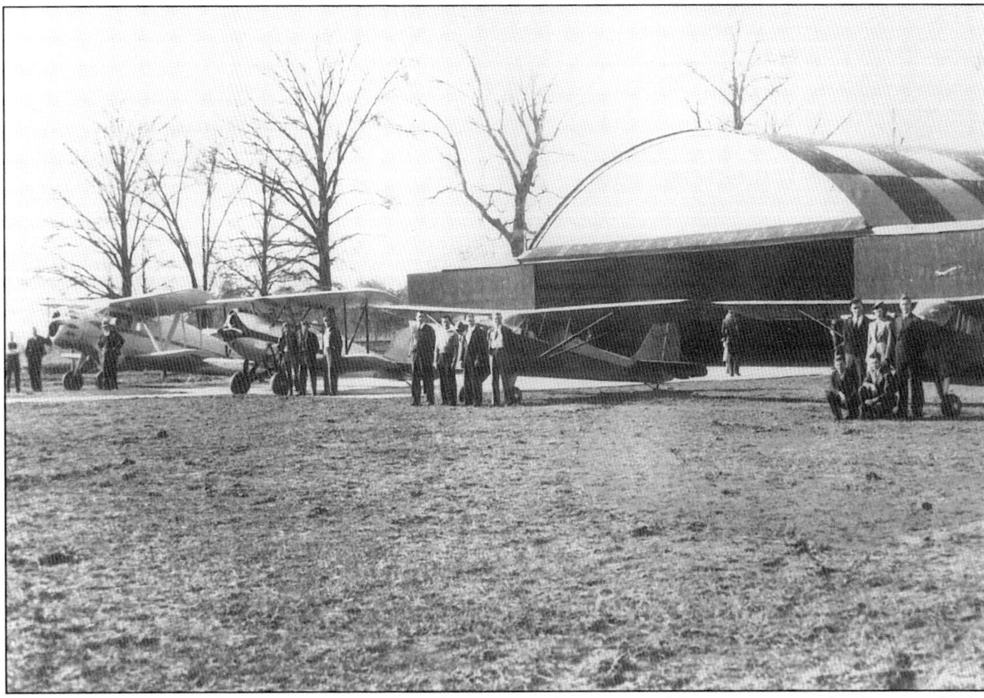

Starkville Airport, which was located in the current location of Weavexx, was built in 1932 by Sumpter Camp. The hanger held ten planes. (RC.)

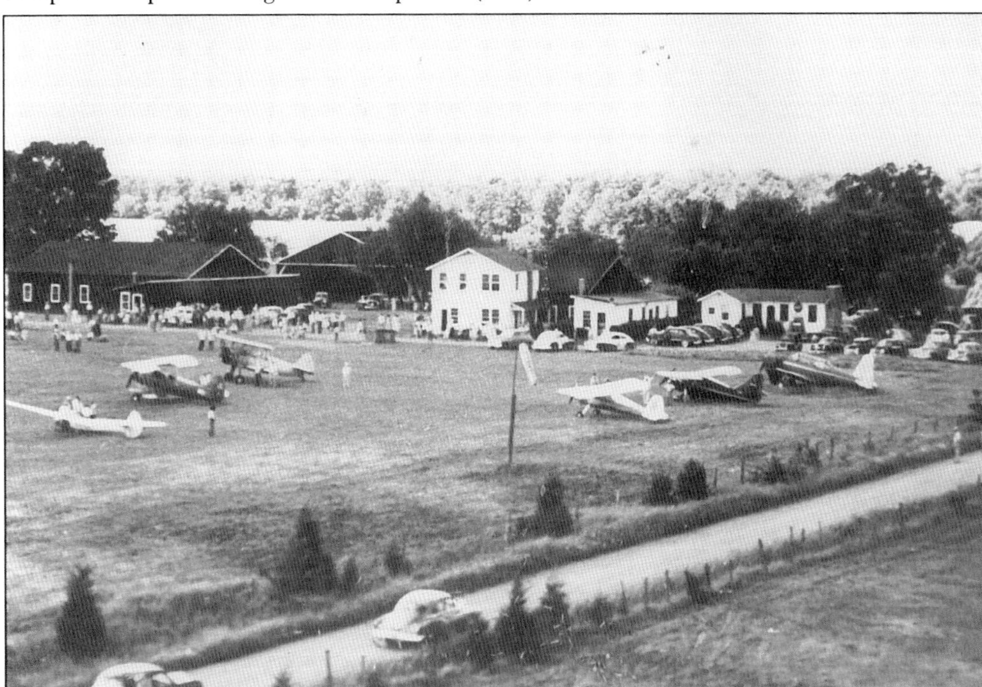

Oktibbeha Airport, which was owned by the Camps, trained 3,300 pilots in 1943. The airport had 40 planes and 30 instructors. (RC.)

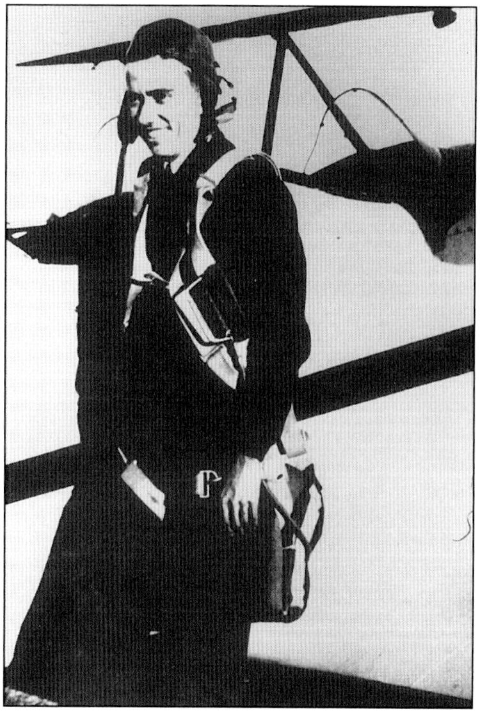

A&M College was the first southern college to have a flight training program; it was taught by Sumpter Camp in 1933. (RC.)

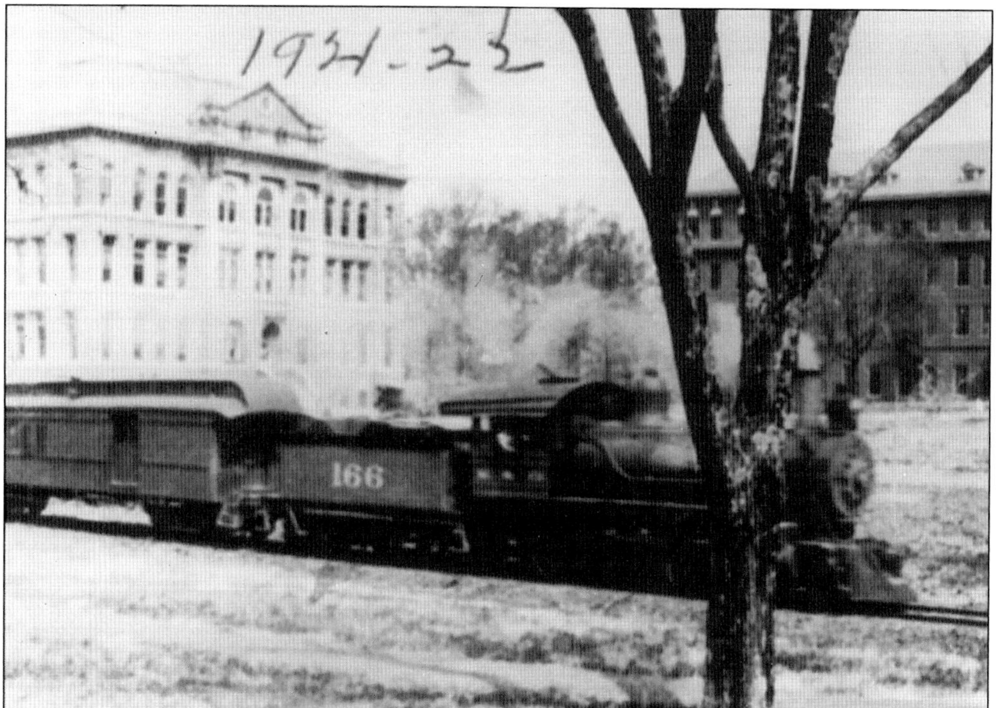

This railroad, which intersected the campus, was named after the train's engineer, A.H. "Hamp" Ellis, and was called the Hamp Line. A steam engine is shown here running in front of Montgomery Hall and Old Main. (JSC.)

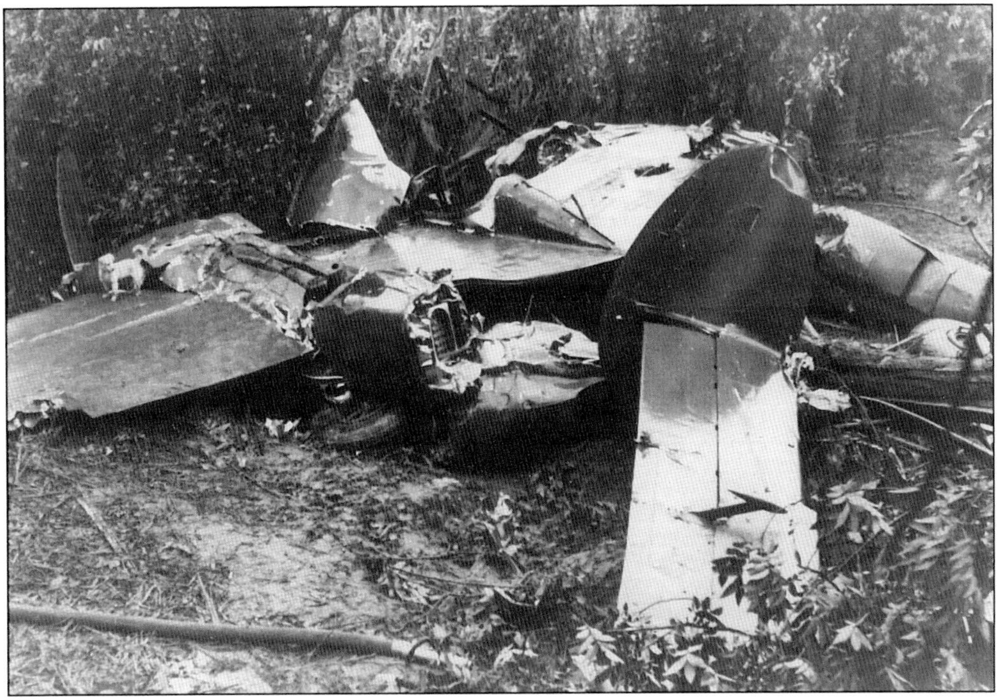

A dog perches on the wing of this P-38 Lightning, which crashed on September 23, 1951, behind the Rackley House on South Jackson Street. (CR.)

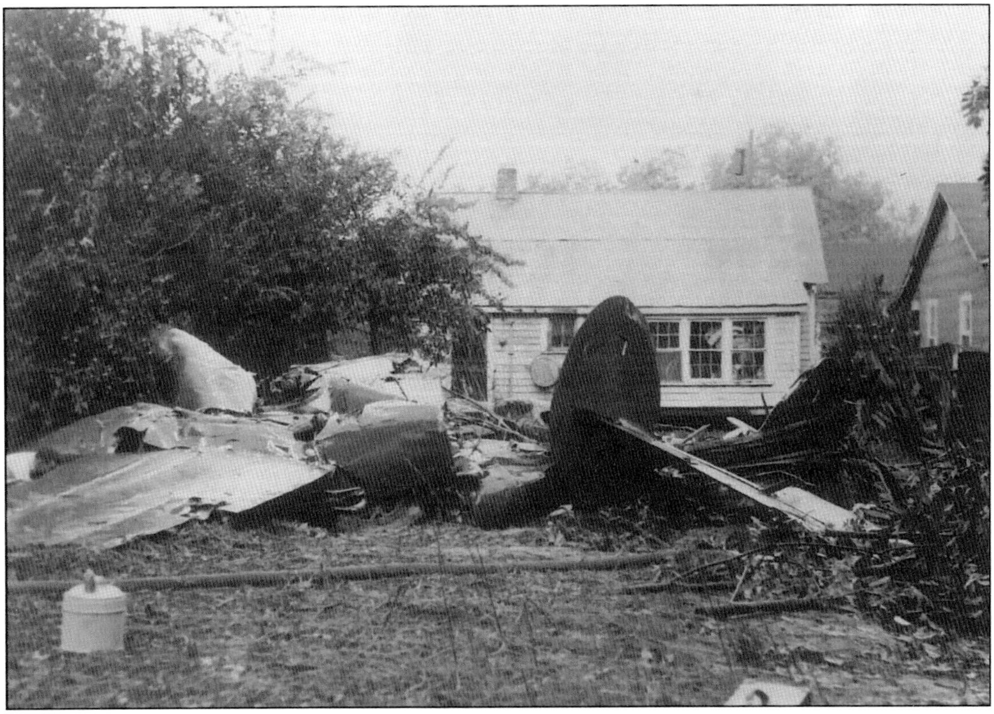

The plane missed hitting this home by 40 feet and killed the pilot, Kenneth J. Snedden. (CR.)

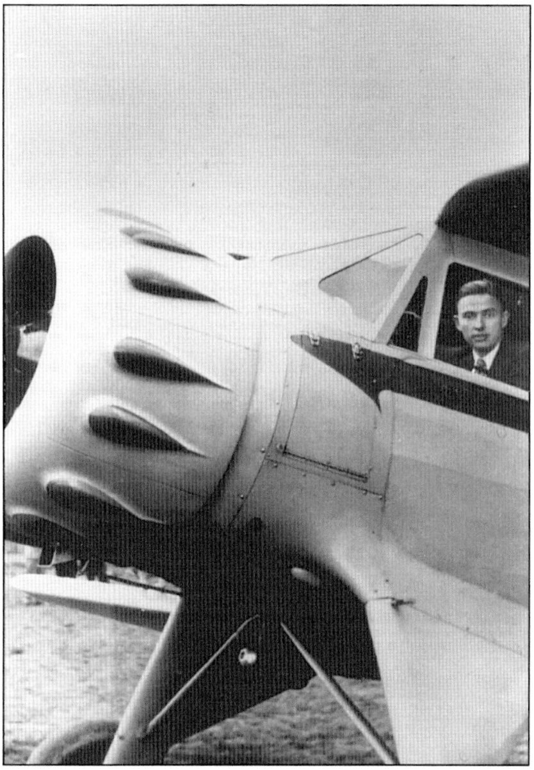

Sumpter Camp graduated from A&M College, and in 1926 he received his flying license at the Roberson School of Aviation in St. Louis from Charles "Lucky Lindy" Lindbergh. He was charged $30 per hour for his flight lessons. (RC.)

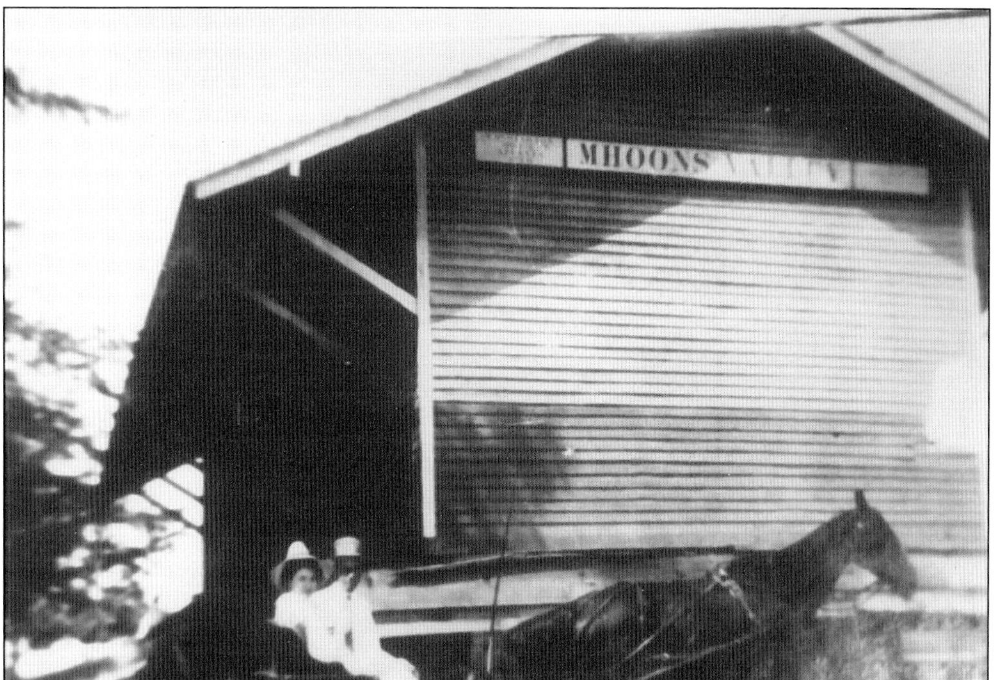

One of the flag stations on the Columbus to Greenville line was located in the northeast corner of the county. (JSC.)

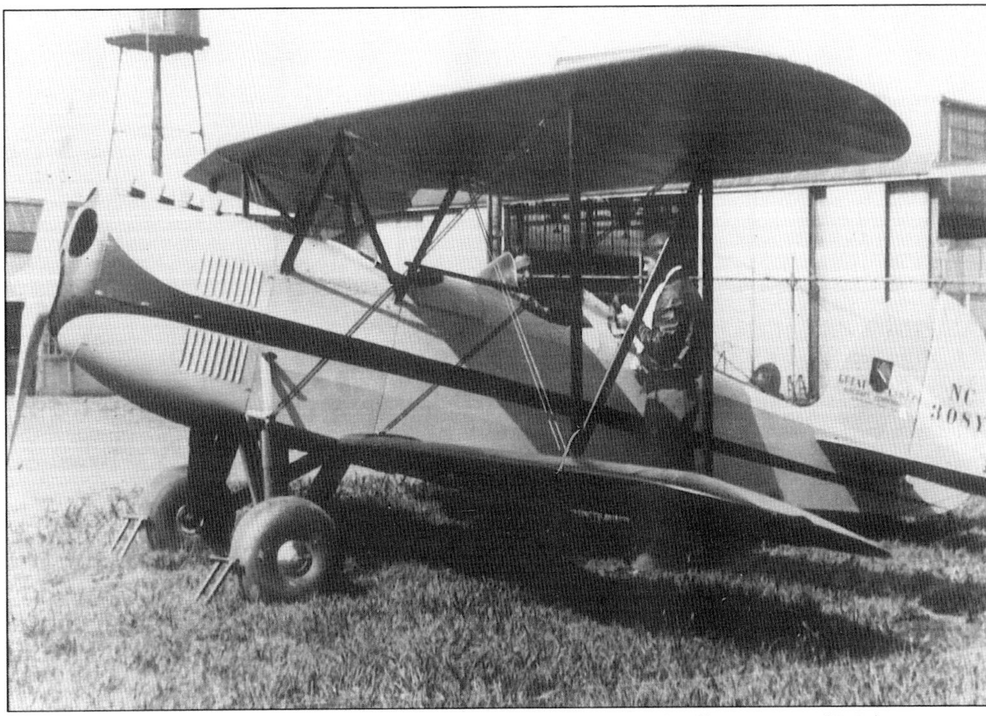

The Aeronautical Engineering building was located at the Starkville Airport. (RC.)

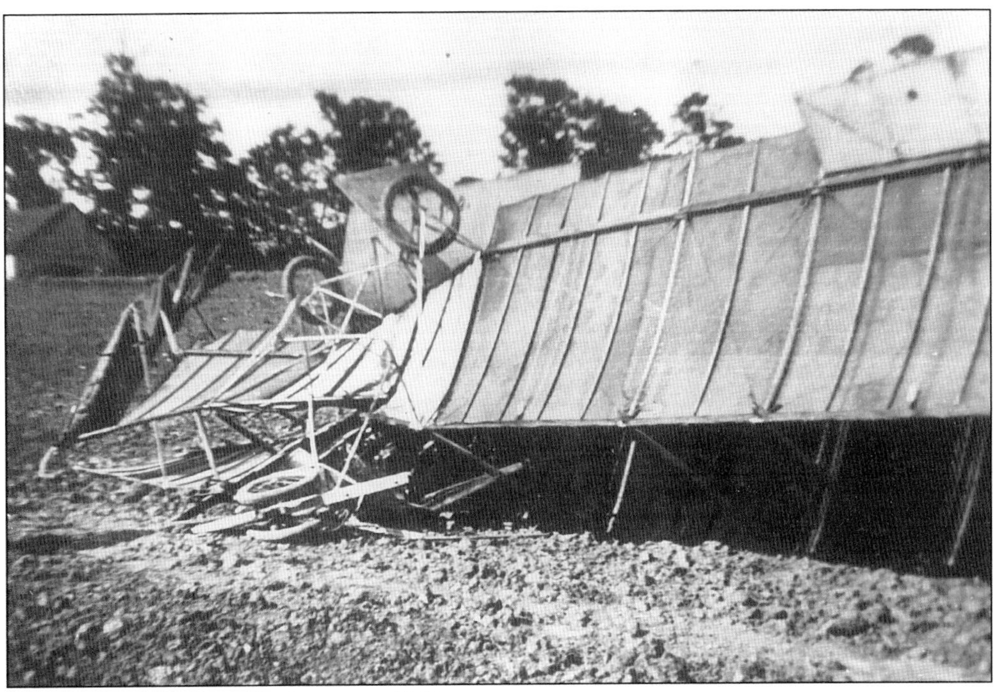

This plane crashed south of town in 1918.

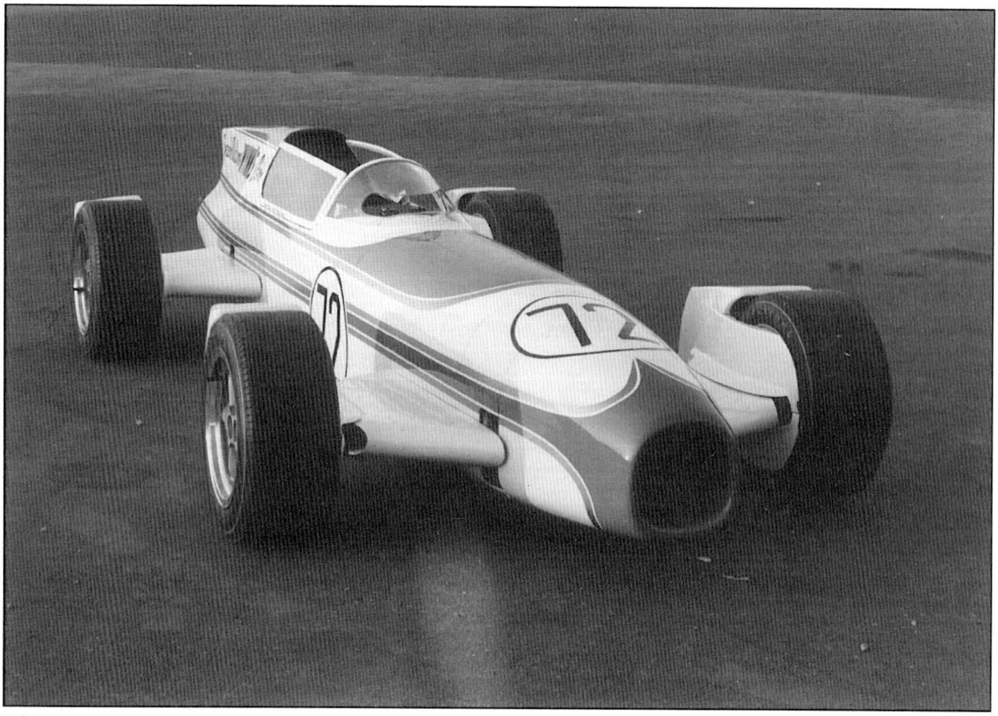

This Indy 500 turbine car was built with a helicopter engine in Glenn Bryant's basement in 1968. It was the second car to use a turbine engine at the Indy 500. (JB.)

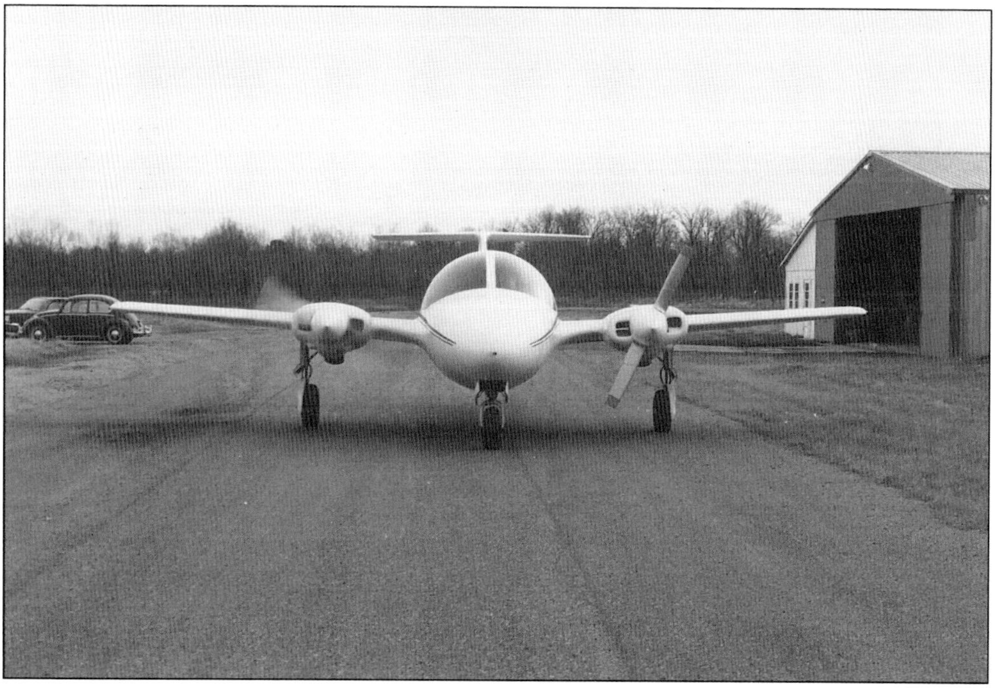

Sam Burn's BA-42 plane was built in Starkville Airport's hangar. The chief engineer was Glenn Bryant, who was a well-respected engineer at Mississippi State University. At Glenn's funeral, airplanes that he helped design flew in formation over the cemetery. (JB.)